OUT

ON AN ISLAND

The Isle of Wight's hidden LGBTQ+ history:
people, places and real-life stories

Medina Publishing

Edited by Franko Figueiredo-Stow and Caroline Diamond

Out On An Island:
The Isle of Wight's hidden LGBTQ+ history: people, places and real-life stories

First published in Great Britain in 2022 by Medina Publishing
50 High Street, Cowes, Isle of Wight, PO31 7RR, UK
www.medinapublishing.com

Edited by Franko Figueiredo-Stow and Caroline Diamond
Interviewees photographs and book design
by Jon Habens.

Printed by Imago
ISBN Hardback - 978-1-911487-64-7
ISBN eBook - 978-1-911487-65-4

All contributors' words have been included with their permission and oral history extracts are intended to be just as spoken.

CIP Data: A catalogue record for this book is available at the British Library.

Out On An Island is a National Lottery Heritage Funded Project
delivered by StoneCrabs Theatre
www.stonecrabs.co.uk
StoneCrabs is a registered charity 1115881

This book is dedicated to everyone who had the courage to share their stories with us and all those whose stories we will never know.

CONTENTS

OUR STORIES MATTER

6   Acknowledgements
9   Introduction
12   Preface
22   Interviewee Profiles
25   *Silent Love*

ISLAND ORIGINS

26   Out On An Island
54   This Is Me

LGBTQ+ PEOPLE

56   LGBTQ+ Role Models
68   Health and Wellbeing
84   Suicide
94   LGBTQ+ people in the *County Press*
101 Coming Out
138 Different is Beautiful
142 Marching with Pride
165 Going Out

POLITICS

200 Overcoming Criminalisation

210 Morality, Hypocrisy and Public
Sex on the Isle of Wight

223 Section 28

QUEER HISTORY

234 Historical LGBTQ+ People
on the Isle of Wight

236 Oscar Wilde & Lord
Alfred Douglas

238 Alfred, Lord Tennyson

239 Robert Nichols

243 Algernon Charles
Swinburne

245 Virginia Woolf

247 Ferguson's Gang

253 John Seely and Paul Paget

257 Joe Carstairs

261 Lord Louis Mountbatten

264 Keith Biddlecombe

265 Nikki Dorakis

266 Patrick Gale

267 Phaedra Kelly

270 Kenneth Kendall

271 Karl Love

272 Anna Murray

273 Tom Priestley

274 What the Future Holds

APPENDICES

282 Appendix 1: A Guide to
LGBTQ+ Terminology

286 Appendix 2: Careless Words
and Ways Forward

288 Appendix 3: How to be a
Trans Ally

292 Contributors

301 Bibliography

1. OUR STORIES MATTER

ACKNOWLEDGEMENTS

We would like to start by thanking the National Lottery Heritage Fund for grant funding which brought Out On An Island to life as an LGBTQ+ Heritage Project. Also the guidance and encouragement from the funders to pursue our idea which has enabled new business partnerships and personal friendships and helped to galvanise the Isle of Wight LGBTQ+ community. We would encourage others to work with the National Lottery Heritage Fund from the early stages of developing an idea through to submitting a funding application.

This book is the result of a great collaboration; not only has it been a collaborative effort between editors, authors and contributors, it has also been a collaboration of individuals far beyond the writing team. We are deeply grateful to everyone at StoneCrabs Theatre Company, who have supported and believed in the Out On An Island project from its very inception.

We greatly appreciate everyone who has worked directly on the oral history interviews and the detailed research involved, all those who helped us with proof-reading, copy-editing, and provided valuable feedback. We are particularly indebted to Lisa Kerley for training our volunteers in the recording of oral histories and to Mara Fraser for her skills as a transcriber; and to Clare Summerskill, Susannah Finzi and David E. Bennet for their attention to detail, questions and suggestions for the manuscript. Not forgetting our volunteers who gave us invaluable feedback and suggestions as to how the book should take shape.

We would also like to thank the museums, archives, heritage and arts organisations including the National Trust, Mark A. T. McNeill and The Classic Boat Museum in East Cowes,

Wessex Film and Sound Archives in Winchester, Rachel Tait and everyone at the Carisbrooke Castle Museum, Simon Dear at the County Records Office in Newport, Isle of Wight, Sue Godden and the Shanklin History Society, Georgia Newman, Del Seymour and Ian Whitmore at Quay Arts, Brian Hinton and Dimbola Lodge, Bishopsgate Institute and the Lesbian and Gay Newsmedia Archive (LAGNA), Anna Murray and Age UK LGBTQ+ Hate Crime project, and the London School of Economics (LSE) archives.

We knew at the start of the project that we might be dealing with a lot of hidden grief, grief that goes unacknowledged or unvalidated by social norms. Gabi Buday of Isle of Wight Counselling and Psychotherapy provided us with important guidance and counselling, particularly to those who felt emotionally triggered by the stories we collected, as well as by facing unprecedented challenges due to the Coronavirus pandemic.

Thanks go to Alan Marriott and the *Isle Of Wight County Press* who granted us permission to publish photographs from the articles relevant to our research, as well as the British Library for the Oscar Wilde images, Polly Bagnall and Charlotte Reynolds for the images of Ferguson's Gang, and all the image contributions received.

Thanks to everyone at Medina Publishing for their energy and commitment, most notably Peter Harrigan and Paul Armfield for their guidance and encouragement, Jane Hansen for her generous copy edit and proofreading and Neil McCall for stepping into our project at the very last minute.

We are indebted to Clare Summerskill and the Oral History Society Special Interest Group for all their support and guidance and to Jon Habens for the most beautiful book design.

Finally, we would like to acknowledge and recognise all our interviewees and everyone who trusted us to share their stories both as recordings and in writing. They dedicated their time and gave us fascinating, personal insights into life on the Isle of Wight and this book would not have happened without them. We hope we have done justice to the stories they were generous enough to tell, all of which are important in helping us to explain and illustrate what it is like for the LGBTQ+ community to live and work on the Island.

INTRODUCTION

Clare Summerskill

Researching and documenting the past and present lives of members of the LGBTQ+ population is, I suggest, a form of activism. LGBTQ+ folk are still fighting for equality under the law and for social and religious acceptance in this country and around the world. They belong to a marginalised community that has suffered persecution, shaming, silencing and criminalisation. Sharing stories about the experiences of LGBTQ+ people creates a number of important outcomes. It means that those who were unaware of the level of discrimination endured by a minority group in society can learn about the extent to which prejudice can, and has, impacted individual lives. It enables LGBTQ+ people, in reading about others like them, to know that they are not alone. Whether or not they are out to their friends, families or communities, they will see 'themselves' represented in such research. Being seen and hearing others narrate stories that are similar to your own leads, in turn, to feeling validated. Reading about the history of people like yourself in documentation which has previously largely neglected to mention LGBTQ+ lives, creates visibility and a sense of the historical and current significance such people bring to a society. Seeing similar lives – both in historical research and in contemporary culture – produces a feeling of a community which, in turn, can create pride. Pride has the potential to erase, or at least to mitigate, any sense of shame or mistreatment that LGBTQ+ people have suffered for being exactly who they were born to be.

This publication is consequently of great importance. It could almost be seen as two separate books: a collection of oral histories and a series of finely written and well-informed pieces about the history of LGBTQ+ people on the Isle of Wight. Fortunately for the reader, these two aspects are combined and the text moves seamlessly from one to the other, filling a much-needed gap of scholarship and providing a greatly welcomed addition to historical and contemporary documentation of the lives of LGBTQ+ people on the Island.

Furthermore, the remit of this publication is both bold and impressive, providing a vast amount of knowledge on topics including: the history of LGBTQ+-related parliamentary acts in the UK and prevalent social attitudes towards the LGBTQ+ population; biographical pieces written about LGBTQ+ individuals who had some relationship with the Isle of Wight, both famous and lesser known; comprehensive explanations of the ever-increasing terminology employed around sexual orientation and gender identity (past and present); local political and social developments pertaining to LGBTQ+ people on the Island; and, key to this particular volume, excerpts from interviews with scores of narrators speaking about their past experiences, current developments and personal aspirations for the future of LGBTQ+ people on the Isle of Wight.

We learn how several contributors to the book grew up in a community where, at best, they did not feel seen or acknowledged and, at worst, they suffered abuse for being who they were. Some explain how they moved to towns or cities on the UK mainland in order to be able to live their full authentic lives. Jared Mustafa-Holzapfel states: 'We all knew someone who'd fled the Island either because it was too much or because they feared for their lives'. But some of those whose stories we hear felt compelled to return to their home of origin, and in doing so hoped that attitudes might have changed in the intervening years. Other people moved to the Island because of their work or because of a partner, and some have lived there all their lives.

This book tells a very compelling story of how members of a marginalised group in a rural part of the UK, where social attitudes have often been described as being ten or even twenty years behind those held on the mainland, journeyed from relative invisibility within that community to holding an annual Pride march. The advent of Pride on the Island is mentioned by numerous narrators as being a hugely significant development not just for LGBTQ+ folk, but as an important indicator to heterosexual and cisgender people that they must now work on changing their own behaviour towards people with whom they live or who are in some ways different from them. The concept of Pride marches has been interpreted by some as a protest and others as a celebration but it can also be regarded as both. Pride festivals and marches in smaller, more rural communities can enhance understanding and create change by their very existence as well as provide a safe public space – at least one day a year – for members of a marginalised community who have frequently experienced some form of prejudice since their childhood. Safety is a recurring theme in this book. As Melissa explains, 'I don't know that you can be completely comfortable if you don't feel safe'.

Speaking about why LGBTQ+ people live on the Island and how they envisage the future, one narrator tells us: 'I stay to make things better, to educate and inform, to be visible and out, to be proud of my authentic self and support others in being their authentic self too'. However scrambled the multi-lettered current acronym of LGBTQQIAPP may seem, its members all belong to a community created as a consequence of our difference from those in the mainstream of society, and from the acts of discrimination that we have collectively experienced both historically and to the present day. That sense of community among the LGBTQ+ population in general and all those who have contributed to this book underpins the whole of this important publication and, alongside personal accounts of prejudice and fear, an undimming light of hope shines through on every single page.

OUR STORIES MATTER

Caroline Diamond and Franko Figueiredo-Stow

> *"I believe that telling our stories, first to ourselves and then to one another and the world, is a revolutionary act".* Janet Mock, transgender rights activist, writer of *Redefining Realness*

Out On An Island – 100 years of LGBTQ+ heritage and oral histories on the Isle of Wight – is the first project dedicated entirely to LGBTQ+ history on the Island.

The initial idea for the project was conceived from our need to connect: Caroline Diamond, project manager and freelance writer, finally came out as lesbian aged forty-six feeling lonely and isolated. Caroline wanted to meet other Isle of Wight LGBTQ+ people, but where were they? Franko Figueiredo-Stow, producer and theatre director, had recently settled on the Island with his husband and was also keen to find out if a local LGBTQ+ community existed.

It was on one of the rare LGBTQ+ nights here, in 2016, that we met. Although, from completely different backgrounds, we both had empathy for others in the LGBTQ+ community and wanted to form connections using creative projects, theatre, oral histories and the written word. On hearing many unexpected stories, some inspiring and others shocking, about a thriving gay scene in the 1990s and local newspapers naming and shaming gay men, we felt this history needed to be shared and so the seeds for an LGBTQ+ heritage project were sown.

The more we heard about life for LGBTQ+ people here, the more we thought we needed to learn about and highlight the plight of individuals who had courageously worked so hard through times when society was less accepting. This was a fascinating project to unveil and, like lifting a stone on the beach, we did not know what would wriggle out from underneath.

Representatives from the National Lottery Heritage Fund visited the Island's Classic Boat Museum in East Cowes on Friday 9 February 2018 and encouraged us to develop the project. We took their advice and continued meeting to discuss the importance of cultivating connection and change through our Island's unspoken LGBTQ+ history. We fiercely believed that *Out On An Island* would be a project that could show us that the Island can be and should be a diverse, inclusive home for all its inhabitants and visitors.

It is often said that the Island is a good decade behind the rest of the UK. It is known worldwide for its music festivals and nationally for school trips and for its high percentage of second-home owners and retirement properties. Broadsheet journalists paint the Island as a place stuck in the 1950s, there are thirty-eight heritage societies here and until a few years ago these seemed to be concerned only with preserving the stories of its land, its buildings and its aristocracy – little perspective is found on its diverse local community.[1]

By the end of 2018, StoneCrabs was ready to put a bid in to the National Lottery Heritage Fund and in March 2019 we received news that funding had been approved. StoneCrabs Theatre is a small charity with a particular interest in community work around social health, diversity and integration issues. The charity's work is overseen by a board of trustees and the company is managed by an executive director and an artistic director. They design and direct projects, work directly with all users, cast, script, project manage and deliver a range of productions and

Franko Figueiredo-Stow & Caroline Diamond *photographed by Jon Habens*

community, education and heritage projects, as well as facilitating groups in partnership with other organisations.

Out On An Island's core team and volunteers received training on oral history interview techniques before recording seventeen oral histories from LGBTQ+ people with an Isle of Wight connection. These will be archived at Carisbrooke Castle Museum's Island Voices collection and at The Wessex Film and Sound Archives in Winchester.

The team researched newspaper articles and materials from local and national archives to paint a fuller picture of what it was like to be LGBTQ+ on the

[1] Esme Ballard and John Medland. The Isle of Wight History Centre, online resource for news and links to the Island's past, from prehistory to recent times 2013. https://www.iwhistory.org.uk/heritageorganisations/ accessed 18 January 2021

Island and in the UK over the past hundred years. This was a difficult process particularly as language and terminology around being LGBTQ+ have changed and the amount of archived LGBTQ+ material available is extremely limited and sometimes ambiguous in its content.

We have uncovered some startling stories: the Island's 'gay scene', which you might expect to have grown in numbers and visibility over the years, has declined in terms of venues and socialising. The first Isle of Wight Pride in July 2017 was greeted with a mixed reception and homophobia but proved to be a huge success. Stories about the Sailing & Cruising Association and the flag used on its boats for LGBTQ+ sailors to identify each other are intriguing as they evoke memories of discreet organisations from the past.

We had not envisaged any sort of LGBTQ+ scene on the Island, probably assuming that LGBTQ+ people had migrated to Brighton and London. This can be seen portrayed in Russell T. Davies' 2021 Channel 4 series *It's A Sin*. Actually, as our interviewees revealed, some did migrate and continue to do, but many stay on the Island, in the closet or out, and others come to retire here living comfortably in rural villages.

LGBTQ+ people and allies[2] of all ages and backgrounds were cautiously keen to make their stories and contributions public. Most contributors to this publication were project volunteers who have a close connection to the Island, some have had no previous professional writing experience and we would like to recognise their commitment and patience during our editing process; biographies for each contributor are provided in an appendix. Not all of the contributors and interviewees were happy for their full names to appear in print, some prefer to use their forename only and others opted to remain anonymous, thus each contribution is credited according to those preferences.

There were people who tried to discourage us, people who refuse to recognise oral histories as an important tool to fill the gaps in history, people who, when we advertised posts looking for stories and memorabilia, told us that our research had only "a tenuous link to heritage" and that their Heritage Society was not "the place to debate about homosexuality". News on our activities received comments online such as: "Why do gay people have to march and shout it from the rooftops, straight people don't", "What is happening to the

---

[2] An 'ally' or 'straight ally' is a term used to describe heterosexual people who believe that lesbian, gay and bisexual people should experience full equality. An ally acknowledges that LGBTQ+ people face discrimination and thus are socially disadvantaged. They aim to use their position and privilege as heterosexual and cisgender individuals in a society focused on cis and heteronormativity to counter discrimination against LGBTQ+ people.

world?", "God Save Us…". The dissenting voices were outnumbered by others supporting and encouraging us, recognising the value of the project: "I feel that everybody has the right to be exactly who they are and although I am heterosexual, I thought I might be able to contribute something", "Congratulations to all of you at *Out On An Island* for an excellent event this evening. Well organised and an inspirational speaker", "What a fulfilling and constructive project, linking and mobilising the community and those involved socially, emotionally and economically, well done". Those voices have been both inspiring, and uplifting.

When we approached LGBTQ+ people to ask if they would let us record their histories, responses ranged from suspicious and reluctant to enthusiastic, one example being "trust me, you don't want to hear my story, or those of the gay people I knew. Unless you want to know about police harassment, the *County Press* outing thirty-nine gay and bisexual men and homophobic treatment from islanders ranging from verbal to full on intimidation and violence until I got away in 1995". Of those we managed to capture, one of our interviewees recalls a government instructional film that was distributed to all schools when Section 28 was introduced in 1988.[3] The film disclosed that one in ten members of the UK population are LGBTQ+. Another interviewee recalls the time when he was a town councillor in 2016 and in a town council meeting was approached by another councillor who said, "absolutely nothing against having Pride, absolutely nothing against it, but I've got to say, there are only a few of you on the Island, why do you feel the need to have a Pride?". This shows little change in the perception and visibility of LGBTQ+ people on the Island despite achieving equality in many legal landmarks; in fact, recent figures show that we form, at least, 7% of its actual population.[4]

In 2011, when StoneCrabs delivered an oral history project about Nigerians who moved to the UK because of the Biafra War, the oral historian attached to the project, Rib Davies, wrote 'History, at its simplest, is what has happened. But how do we know what has happened, through what channels do we learn about it? Who is to say which events are central and which are trivial? Whose histories are we given, and whose are we not? And of those histories we receive, from what viewpoint are they presented?'.[5] It is part of the human condition to

---

[3]Section 28 or Clause 28 was an amendment to the law in 1988 that stated that a local authority 'shall not intentionally promote homosexuality or publish material with the intention of promoting homosexuality' or 'promote the teaching in any maintained school of the acceptability of homosexuality as a pretended family relationship'. It was repealed in Scotland in 2000 and in England and Wales in 2003.
[4]Isle of Wight Council, Equality & Diversity Fact Sheet Jan 2019
[5]Tanja Pagnuco, *Biafra to England* (London: StoneCrabs Theatre Co., 2011), 7.

tell stories to each other and pass on narratives about our experiences by word of mouth. However, it is frequently the case that those who hold power and status in society determine which stories are documented and which voices are omitted or even erased from historical records.

For years, LGBTQ+ stories have been edited, censored or simply erased. Because of this our passions, fears, sadness, hardships and joys are suffocated, and history is only partially visible. Documenting the lives of any group in a community involves far more than simply presenting facts and figures relating to that population. Our story informs our culture, impacts on our health, tells us who we are, and helps shape our future. Our stories tell future generations that we lived, loved and mattered. They teach future generations the lessons of history, inspire, encourage, reassure, console, and give young people a sense of their heritage and their place in the world.

It was a lengthy process deciding how to best present all the material we have gathered. We looked for patterns, for themes, how we would frame the answers given to us at the interviews. Mostly, we wanted to present a narrative in a way that felt informative, accessible, digestible and thought-provoking.

We dedicated each chapter to a common theme found in the oral histories we collected. The chapters are made up of an article inspired by the themes and supported by extracts from the oral history interviews, personal experiences, articles and poems; stories of joy and pain, celebration and tolerance. The interviews have been transcribed in verbatim form, with colloquial language left intact.

As LGBTQ+ people, the pain we feel is sometimes that which we inflict upon ourselves, our weird imaginings, our internalised self-hatred, our own veiled homophobia borne out of years of living with hatred and violent discrimination. This is very evident in the pages that follow.

This book is a labour of dedication and love, produced collaboratively by the StoneCrabs team of associates together with many volunteers and contributors, whose dedication, passion and commitment completely surpassed our expectations, and we are grateful to them.

In our first chapter, Jared Mustafa-Holzapfel gives us a glimpse of what it was like to grow up LGBTQ+ on the Isle of Wight, an island that relies on the nostalgia of heteronormative heritage. Mustafa-Holzapfel also explains the meaning of the LGBTQ+ acronym beyond simply listing the terms, clarifying how these identities have been growing through continued activism in public awareness and acceptance in law and in social spaces.

The next chapter, 'LGBTQ+ Role Models', starts with an article by David E. Bennett where he discusses the lack of positive LGBTQ+ role models in the past and why they are important. This is echoed in the oral histories that we collected, where interviewees struggled to recall inspiring LGBTQ+ individuals and highlighted media stereotyping, and the derisive portrayal of homosexuality as a means to create comedy.

An investigative article on health by Franko Figueiredo-Stow presents the higher risk of mental health issues and the lag in dedicated, holistic healthcare for the LGBTQ+ community. Historically, homosexuality was seen as a mental health condition. Our research uncovered Island health initiatives and support services for the local LGBTQ+ community, which included sexual health and HIV prevention campaigns, the Island's Gay Switchboard and Gay Youth Network. Many of our interviewees recall those as milestones in our history.

Caroline Diamond then looks at the prevalence of suicide in the LGBTQ+ community, as borne out by our interviews, and the links to being LGBTQ+ with examples of some of those who have died of suicide on the Isle of Wight. Sadly, we find that the health needs and challenges faced by LGBTQ+ people are still not met with appropriate support. This creates a vicious circle and increased feelings of unhappiness, isolation and despair which can lead to more serious mental health issues with some people choosing to end their lives.

One of our major sources for research was the Island's printed media over the last century; newspapers such as the *Isle of Wight Observer*, *Ryde Times* and the *Isle of Wight Advertiser* which we accessed through the British National Archives. We also accessed the *Isle of Wight County Press* archives, the Island's most prominent and influential newspaper, which became a primary source of information. In the chapter 'LGBTQ+ People in the County Press', David E. Bennett provides us with a detailed analysis of all the articles published in connection with our community, how others saw us, and when and why LGBTQ+ people made the news.

Coming out is still a milestone for most LGBTQ+ people because being out is still an act of bravery, we grapple with the decision to live in or out of the closet every day. All our interviewees recall their first coming out experience. It is important that in 2021 we can safely state our LGBTQ+ identity, providing role models for future generations. We are significant in number, there are a good percentage of us living and contributing to Island life: same sex parents, retired couples, lawyers, designers, cleaners, supermarket workers, artists, council workers, health workers, chief executives, etc. Some choose to be visible and others still battle with internalised fear. In this chapter, Melissa

Gilmore provides us with a historical overview on the act of 'Coming Out of the Closet', backed up by LGBTQ+ oral history extracts and written personal accounts by Isle of Wight LGBTQ+ people.

In the chapter 'Marching with Pride', we hope to provide you with an understanding of the catalysts which made Pride an unexpected success. Our interviews recorded contrasting views. One interviewee says, "You see, I don't think Pride should still be celebrated, the actual parades, because you don't get straight people going down on floats on Union Street saying, 'we're straight, we're happy'! We've done the fifty years, we got what we wanted, so therefore we just get on with our lives". Another says "I don't know if I would have been able, if I would have felt like there was any hope of coming out on the Island without Pride. I do wonder about that. Like, because of all the negative experiences I had, I have been in every Pride parade and that was astonishing for the Island". Here, John Brownscombe writes about the story of Isle of Wight Pride. We also include written contributions from LGBTQ+ folks, family members and straight allies who felt validated and assured that the Island was finally moving towards positive humanistic values.

Another theme we highlighted was socialising; many of our interviewees reminisced about LGBTQ+-friendly Isle of Wight venues which had popular events solely dedicated to the LGBTQ+ community and allies. In the 'Going Out' chapter, Alan Figueiredo-Stow writes about the rise and fall of Isle of Wight LGBTQ+-friendly venues which played a key role in supporting our community over the past fifty years; there was a thriving gay scene on the Isle of Wight in the eighties and nineties and we learned how people knew where to go in the days before social media and mobile phones. The need for safe spaces is just as relevant today.

Predictably, very early in our research, it was clear that most of the information we had uncovered was predominantly criminal records, therefore we felt that we ought to provide a chapter that helped us contextualise LGBTQ+ history. In the chapter 'Overcoming Criminalisation', Bronwyn Hamilton-Brown and Franko Figueiredo-Stow retell LGBTQ+ history from a local perspective, backed up by real accounts, newspaper reports and other research findings. They expose main events in our queer history and demonstrate how those have impacted on the Isle of Wight LGBTQ+ community, from Nikki Dorakis setting up a local Campaign for Homosexual Equality group through to the consequences of Section 28, the ban on homosexuals in the armed forces, and more recent protests.

In 'Morality, Media Hypocrisy and Public Sex on the Isle of Wight', Mark Woolford addresses the complex issues around the act of 'cottaging' or sex in public toilets, its criminalisation, and the devastating consequences it had on the lives of many islanders who were arrested and named and shamed by the local media. Woolford questions the hypocrisy attached to such exploits: why is it still a trend and a taboo? And whilst it is still a crime for anyone regardless of their sexuality, why is it only homosexuals who get penalised? Whilst heterosexuals are rarely prosecuted for perpetrating the same act?

David E Bennett provides us with an introduction to Section 28 and how it came about in the chapter entitled 'Section 28: Politics, Intent, Spin, Impact, and Aftermath'. This chapter is inspired by oral history interview extracts and a written account from a gay Isle of Wight teacher working in a secondary school in 1988, when Section 28 was introduced. David also discusses how the Church of England opposed its repeal and the impact of growing up LGBTQ+ under an act that deliberately isolated and denied freedom of expression to young lesbian, gay and bi people. How it denied, for decades to come, the fundamental truth that homosexuals are normal people, many of whom form families and live productive lives.

You might be surprised to read one of our articles that expands on the historical LGBTQ+ figures who were born, lived and were inspired by the Isle of Wight. These are well-known figures who led queer lives, some out and proud such as Joe Carstairs and others quite hidden like Ferguson's gang. 'The Isle of Wight Hidden History' chapter begins with a contribution from Dr Clifford Williams who brought to our attention Oscar Wilde's publicity photos taken in Ryde in 1884 during a tour of his lectures entitled On Dress. Volunteers also brought our attention to, and contributed articles on, further historical queer figures, who were either born or lived on the Island. Unexpectedly, we found we had enough material to include a whole section queering the Island's history.

Queering is a tool of historical analysis. It does not mean an attempt to ascribe a specific label to a historical figure. What queering means, in the context of this book, is to embrace historical figures in their entirety, including the parts of their lives which are not so clear-cut or easy to interpret from a modern standpoint. We also realise we need to be cautious in imposing our own contemporary ideas of identity and terminology. We couldn't leave the contemporary figures out either, those are people who we feel ought to be acknowledged and praised for their work and contributions to the Island. Finally, we bring all the interviewees voices together to look at hopes and aspirations in 'What The Future Holds'.

The book doesn't need to be read in a linear manner; each chapter stands on its own. You may simply be curious and want to understand more about the extraordinary diversity of experience of being LGBTQ+ on the Isle of Wight. We hope that the book can instigate dialogue on what can be complex, sensitive topics, and provide readers with a better understanding of equality, inclusion and the value of respecting differences.

Finally, we hope this book will take you on an enjoyable and informative journey and that it will be an enlightening and a thought-provoking read.

Right > (From Left to Right)
Barry, Mick, Gavin and Robin at a day trip to a mass meeting in Hyde Park, London for the abolition of nuclear weapons, 1957. Courtesy of Robin Ford.

Here is a brief introduction to the eighteen people we interviewed for this project. Our only criteria was that they were part of the LGBTQ+ community and have an Isle of Wight connection. We are grateful to them for sharing memories and showing us aspects of the Island's LGBTQ+ history that research never could. They give a voice to a community that many believed did not exist and their oral histories are at the heart of this project. We've tried to use their own self-descriptions as much as possible.

Anonymous was born in Newport on the Isle of Wight in 1977, he identifies as a gay man and sometimes likes to use the term 'queer' as well. He left the Island to study at Southampton University, and currently resides in Brighton.

Callum was born on the Island and came out in 2017 after spending many years "hiding his true self." He went to university on the mainland and, after graduating in 2013, moved to West Sussex to work before returning to the Island. In 2019 Callum volunteered with Isle of Wight Pride, managing traders and marketing. He enjoyed getting to know what he describes as "the amazing LGBTQ+ community" and hopes to work with the committee in the future. Callum enjoys the great outdoors, exploring the Island's coastline and living out what he calls his *Mamma Mia* dreams by going on holiday to Greece and, he says, "Cher-ing" the experience with his boyfriend.

Caroline moved to the Isle of Wight in 2000. She was born in Manchester and lived all over the world due to her father's career in the Army. She has three grown-up children and came out as a lesbian in 2012.

David is a gay man who lived as a monk before moving to the Island in 1975. He owned a hotel and a flower shop and also worked on the Gay Men's Health Project in the early 1990s.

Robin is a retired teacher and was working in a school when Section 28 was introduced. He was born on the Isle of Wight in March 1942 and identifies as queer.

Jess is an Island-raised queer girl living up North. She frequently comes back to visit the island and all its beauty. She dreams of a world where people can live freely and happily as their authentic selves, and she is working to educate, advocate and raise awareness of issues that affect human rights.

Joanne identifies as a lesbian. She was born on the Isle of Wight in 1966 then lived in Ireland until she was eighteen when she returned to the Island.

Jude was born in 1948 and moved to the Isle of Wight from London in 1974. She is a lesbian who hated being a girl when she was a child.

Julian was born on the Isle of Wight and has lived most of his life here. He has come out as trans in the last few years after trying to live as a woman for most of his life. He studied music at university, planning to go into music tech, but he ended up working in opera.

Karen came to the Isle of Wight when she was six months old and spent her childhood here. She is also a big fan of Liverpool Football Club. When she was younger Karen was in the Air Cadets where she had her first conversations about her sexuality. In 1994 she came out as a lesbian and enjoyed the lively LGBT social scene on the Island and in Portsmouth during the 1990s. Karen is very sociable and has many friends, she loves living on the Island and says it is a great place to be gay. She describes herself as "ever the optimist" and says she is constantly amazed by what she uncovers on her gay adventure.

Karl L is a gay man who moved to the Island in 1992 with his partner, now husband, David to work as a Young Person's Outreach Worker for Sexual Health and on setting up the IW Gay Men's Health Project. Nowadays Karl is a County Councillor for East Cowes.

Karl S is a gay man and, although born in North Yorkshire, his family is from Portsmouth and Kent. Lately he's discovered ancestors from Chale here on the Isle of Wight. Karl went to university in London then worked as an interior architect and concept designer. In 1999 he and his partner (now husband) gave up their careers to buy and run a guest house in Brighton. The couple moved to the Island in 2007 buying a small hotel in Shanklin. In 2017 they sold the business and Karl now works as a full-time artist.

Lucy used to visit family on the Isle of Wight from 1988 and moved here permanently in 1997. She is a trans woman who was born in Birmingham.

Melissa is non-binary and lives on the Isle of Wight. They identify as queer and bisexual. Born in Scotland to an English mother and an American father, they moved to Ascot in 1992 before moving to the Island in 1998.

Michelle is a trans woman who decided to come out and transition when she was 60. Having lived and worked in several countries (USA, Ecuador, Italy and Brazil), she has now retired to the Isle of Wight. Her connection to the Island goes back many years, from family holidays in the 1940s and 50s to business consultancy in the 1990s.

Robert was born on the Isle of Wight in November 1950. He identifies as a gay man and has lived on the Island all his life. After working in shops, then in journalism, he became Secretary and later Secretary/Agent of the Isle of Wight Labour Party in his twenties, and was subsequently Chairman of Medina Housing Association. He is now Secretary of Isle of Wight Labour again and was Labour Agent in the election of 2019, and is a member of the National Association of Painters in Acrylic, trying to find time to paint in acrylic, oil, and watercolour.

Rosa is a lesbian who has lived on the Island since 2003. She has found that activities and events for lesbians here are few but the groups that do meet up are friendly and welcoming. Rosa appreciates that legislation for equality has led to improvements, but she remembers times when it was extremely difficult to be 'out and proud'.

Sydney was born in 1987 and grew up in the small village of Rookley on the Isle of Wight, before moving to the nearby town of Newport at the age of 12. She has lived on the Island most of her life, apart from a stint in Bournemouth to attend university, where she studied Fine Art. She met the love of her life while she was back on the Island finishing her Master's degree, and they were subsequently married in 2016. She is proud to be trans and identifies as a lesbian.

SILENT LOVE

Peter Woodnutt

Many a Son or Daughter, may
Well incur, a sense of shame.
Were they to express the love
That dare not speak its name!

Life is full, of ups and downs,
Don't feel we are to blame, for
You were gifted with the love,
That dare not speak its name!

Some will never, understand,
Love permeates every plain.
But remember, there IS ONE,
That dare not speak its name!

People will verbally taunt you,
Make no response, it's a game!
Resolve to, reinforce the love,
That dare not speak its name!

When, you're cruelly goaded,
The ghost of fear will remain!
But can never, stem the love,
That dare not speak its name!

Homophobia seeks its victim,
Who is beaten up, left in pain.
Brutal ignorance, of that love,
That dare not speak its name!

Stand on a Giant's shoulders,
Reach up in sunshine or rain!
Light the beacon for the love,
That dare not speak its name!

Live each day, in the moment,
Never let, your courage wane.
You can free the love you feel,
When you can speak its name

Peter Woodnutt is a gay man who was born on the Isle of Wight in 1941. His father owned Woodnutt's Menswear shop on Union Street, Ryde where Peter worked for 50 years. He came out in 1996, at the age of 55. Peter loved photography but due to an age related sight problem his main creative outlet is now poetry. Through poetry Peter seeks to reflect a positive outlook on the human condition.

OUT ON AN ISLAND

Jared Mustafa-Holzapfel

The experience of being LGBTQ+ when growing up, or as an adult reconciling or realising your sexual orientation/gender identity within wider society, is always different from heterosexual individuals. LGBTQ+ is an acronym of Lesbian, Gay, Bisexual, Transgender, and Queer with '+' standing in to embrace the evolving identities of minority sexual orientations and gender identities, such as Asexual, Non-Binary, Intersex and so forth. Over the 20th and 21st centuries these identities have been growing through continued activism in public awareness and acceptance in law and in social spaces. The Isle of Wight, as a rural community physically isolated from the rest of the United Kingdom, is often referred to as 'a community out of time'. In many ways, the Island's tourist industry relies on this nostalgia – Osborne House, Carisbrooke Castle, Amazon World and so forth primarily focus on the preservation of the past, be it architecturally or the conservation of wildlife. Large portions of the Island are also designated Areas of Outstanding Natural Beauty.[6] The Isle of Wight population has a higher percentage of individuals aged 65+ compared to the rest of England and Wales, with proportionally fewer teens.[7] The Island itself is mostly farmland or natural preserved land with a handful of small towns and villages. In many ways, it is a visually idyllic location not dissimilar to rural areas of the West Country on 'the mainland'. As is common amongst rural communities, the Isle of Wight also has a distinct Conservative affiliation. Whilst an individual's immediate family may not be Conservative, family

---

[6]Pepper Creative, 'Safeguarding the Future of the Island's Finest Landscapes,' accessed July 10, 2020, https://www.wightaonb.org.uk/.

[7]JSNA – Demographics and Population, 'JSNA – Demographics and Population – Census 2011', accessed July 10, 2020, https://www.iow.gov.uk/Council/transparency/Our-Community1/JSNA-Demographics-and-population/Census-2011.

members and others within their village will be. When you add the 'village mentality' of everyone knows everyone else (and their business), it can be very claustrophobic. What does such an environment mean for any individual who is different from the average white heterosexual person within the community? The interviews and stories recorded here from other LGBTQ+ individuals provide first-hand accounts of this phenomenon.

For clarity I want to take a moment to explain what LGBTQ+ means, beyond simply listing the terms. These identities are split between sexualities: a lesbian individual is a woman who is attracted to other women, a gay man is attracted to other men, whilst bisexual individuals are men or women who are attracted to either men or women. And by gender identities: a transgender (or trans) individual is someone who identifies as a different gender to what they were assigned at birth, i.e. a transwoman is a woman who was assigned male at birth, and a transman is a man who was assigned female at birth. Note, a transgender individual is not inherently heterosexual – you can be a transwoman and a lesbian, for example.

Not all trans individuals will undergo what is colloquially known as a 'full medical transition' but the process can include: hormone replacement therapy (HRT); secondary sex characteristics surgery such as double mastectomy (the removal of breast tissue) for men or conversely, breast augmentation; facial surgery, for example to smoothen the jaw bone, voice feminisation surgery which involves the removal of the Adam's Apple for women; and gender confirmation surgery or 'bottom surgery' as it is called within the trans community. The latter surgery is sensationalised by the media as 'the surgery' and refers to the surgical adjustment of genitalia to match the individual's gender identity. Not all trans individuals will undergo all of these procedures, including gender confirmation surgery. It is very common, for example, for men to have a hysterectomy – removal of ovaries and womb – but not to have either the high risk metoidioplasty or phalloplasty gender confirmation surgeries. Whilst the vaginoplasty is also high-risk, it is more common for women to have this surgery due to superior results and personal preferences. Technically, gender confirmation surgery as a category includes the 'secondary sex characteristics' surgeries I have previously mentioned, although the nature of these procedures and how they differ has been so frequently confused by media sensationalism that they are frequently discussed as if they were entirely different things.

Non-binary individuals, like trans individuals, do not fully identify with the gender assigned at birth but can identify as neither male nor female, whilst some non-binary individuals identify as mostly female some days and mostly male on others. Non-binary individuals can still identify as trans and some undergo some of the medical treatments trans individuals do. Someone who identifies as Queer can fit into any of these LGBT categories but may find that the identity that best fits them otherwise is too restrictive. An Asexual individual is someone who is not sexually attracted to any gender but may still be romantically attracted to someone. Aromantic is effectively the opposite of Asexual; they experience sexual attraction but not romantic attraction. These identities are not absolutes, romantic capacity varying widely between individuals while others identify as 'gray-ace' or 'demi-sexual', being only attracted very selectively to individuals, often those with whom they have formed a serious romantic relationship. These identities are not exhaustive – hence the '+' in the acronym – but all of the interviews and stories within this collection will be referring to these identities and it is important for the reader to have an understanding of what they mean.

These identities are not inherently 'hidden' in their differences. Some LGB individuals are able to keep their otherness hidden, i.e. a lesbian couple might not hold hands when walking down the street when a heterosexual couple might. Opposite-sex bisexual couples are most often perceived to be heterosexual, reducing the harrassment they experience but at the cost of robbing them of their identity and making it more difficult for them to identify with other bisexual people. Bias about lesbians only being butch/masculine and gay men only being feminine creates a space for feminine lesbians and masculine gay men to not be 'outed' as LGB on the street. These individuals are referred to within the LGBTQ+ community as 'straight passing'. Many LGB individuals do not have this privilege as their natural femininity as a male, for example, is visible and can attract harassment, verbal or physical, from family, peers, and the wider community. Trans and non-binary individuals, especially during early stages of transition, rarely benefit from 'passing' and so are often more in danger from abuse. As a trans and queer individual growing up on the Isle of Wight I experienced this first hand. Whether bullied at school or shouted at in the street, I did not feel safe. The only stories of trans individuals were either those who went overseas for surgery and never came back, those who were spoken of as if deceased (but they'd actually just left the Island to live their lives authentically), or those who were freaks of nature and the butts of the jokes thrown around by adults and children alike.

As a youth I chose to flaunt my, at the time, 'lesbian' identity as an act of defiance. Yes, I was queer. Yes, I also considered myself to be a freak of nature but I was alive, I existed and whilst I was terrified of potential physical abuse,

I wanted the community to know that they themselves were not 'perfect'. With hindsight I was very fortunate that physical abuse was minimal, but verbal abuse was very regular. People I knew were physically abused, their homes bricked or spray painted. We all knew someone who'd fled the Island either because it was too much or because they feared for their lives. The worst hurts came from parents of my friends who tried to stop them interacting with me in case I corrupted their children. From family members who pretended I didn't exist, just like they'd written out the other LGBTQ+ relatives I didn't know existed until years later. I transitioned away from the Island and to this day some wider family either do not know I exist, or if they do, I am not welcome among them.

In many ways the Isle of Wight I know could be described as a place where differences were not welcome, where you must never speak of them. They cannot be acknowledged because keeping up the appearance of civility was more important than acceptance. I do know, however, that this is not the only experience of LGBTQ+ individuals here. Visiting now, LGBTQ+ couples can be seen on the streets of towns, holding hands in public, not in defiance or out of fear, but comfortably because they can. There is even an annual Pride event now. With any change there is struggle, and the journey has not ended for the Isle of Wight just as it has not ended for the United Kingdom at large. The stories told in this collection from other LGBTQ+ individuals memorialise these struggles and their triumphs, big or small. I hope readers of these accounts do so with an open mind, because these narratives are those of real individuals. Whilst the community at large is fighting for social acceptance and legal protection, LGBTQ+ rights are taking a more public stage each decade. Know that we have always been here; you most likely have a few of us in your family tree, whether you know it or not. We are not scary, but many of us were or are scared and hoping for a better future for the next generation.

Robin

I identify myself as queer and I was born in 1942. I am an Islander, born and bred sort of thing, and I do like history and I do like records of the past and I felt that I come from a period when being gay was not easy to put it mildly – it was certainly not easy for me – and I wanted, as it were, to have my statement there, if you see what I mean? A type of validity of my queerness really.

I think I was aware only when I was about fourteen. I mean people did grow up more slowly then, you know, there's no doubt about it. But I realised that I fancied the boys in my class usually and I wasn't interested in the girls but at the same time I felt that I had to say, you know, express an interest in girls because, you know, not to do so, of course, was an exclusion thing. But all the time there were two or three boys I really fancied. So I came across this word homosexual which believe it or not I had not heard of before, at least I certainly didn't know what it meant and I suddenly thought, "I'm homosexual", and I felt very pleased funnily enough. I can remember this quite clearly. I felt very pleased because I supposed I'd nailed it but I'm afraid I found it all very difficult to live with after that first exhilaration. It must have been about 1955 or 6, yes, 1955 or 6. I must have, oh gosh, yes, it was one of those terrible scandals. I don't know if you know about the Montagu scandal do you? Well, Lord Montagu from Beaulieu, not the current one. Something blew up that [he] was exposed as a homosexual and it was a terrible scandal, you know, a Lord, my goodness! And I think I must have looked it up. Something like that. But the trouble is my first exposure, you see, was totally negative because the man was in jail for homosexual offences. I can remember sitting on a bus with my parents when this was going on and I remember being aware of it and some drunk kid down below on the bottom deck told me, "Oh, Lord Montagu, how many boys have you been through?". So the whole bus shivered in shame.

I wasn't getting a girlfriend, I think that's how it started pointing out. I was very, very friendly with a boy actually, I mean, I think that he must have been gay too but, of course, it was the great unmentionable. I'd rather not give his surname, his name was Richard and, I don't know, there was something about him but nothing ever expressed itself sexually at all. I went to an all-boys, I was one of those who failed the eleven-plus, the dreaded eleven-plus, and I went to a secondary modern school which was all boys. That wasn't too bad in a way because there wasn't any competition much to get girls but then I went on to the grammar school and there was co-educational and I think you were expected, you know, there were parties and all that sort of thing which I avoided because I knew that they would be strictly hetero and I would stick out like, and, of course, throughout my life, my own life, I made horrible attempts to pretend I was straight, kissing girls and that and not liking it and that sort of thing. But then there was this terrible sense of sadness and of the image. If you ever saw anything on television that was vaguely arty, for instance, ballet, people who were watching it would say, "here come the nancy boys", you know, that sort of thing. Every image was negative.

Sydney

I am a trans lesbian woman from the Isle of Wight. I grew up in a more rural part of the Island in Rookley. I had a quite mixed childhood in many ways I think. I had a very nice childhood at home. My parents did very well by me. I lived with my extended family, with my grandmother, my grandfather and my aunt and my parents in quite a big house and it was very nice. It was a sort of idyllic English country childhood; there was lots of going for dog walks and playing in the woods and picking mushrooms and all that sort of good stuff and the contrast was with things at school. I had a very bad time at school throughout pretty much my entire school career; I was bullied and teased and taunted and various things going on. I think I was perceived as being, funnily enough, being quite effeminate and that was, certainly back in those days, I think these days it has improved a little bit now, but back in those days school tended to be homophobic. I mean, when I say it was homophobic, transphobic wasn't even on the radar because trans people weren't even on the radar! I grew up and had that kind of thing going on.

I didn't have any kind of real thoughts about gender identity and so on until puberty hit. So I was one of those people who, I suppose, when I was a child I was just a child and didn't have any sense of anything, sexuality or gender, anything. When I started going through puberty I started getting very depressed for some reason that I couldn't quite put my finger on. It was sort of childhood signs and things looking back, nothing was noticed at the time really. I think my mother said she wondered was I gay? What was going on and that sort of thing but at the age, I think I must have been about thirteen or fourteen, I had encountered the idea of changing gender and things in science fiction books, fantasy books and things like that, I was a very voracious reader, quite introverted as a child.

So I thought it was wonderful, but I thought it was fantasy, a made-up thing like being a superhero or something like that! I thought, "I'd love to be able to fly or be able to turn invisible, and I would love to be able to change gender, that sounds cool, but I can't do that". Then I obviously at some point, despite the lack of education and things going on, of course this was the era of Section 28 and there weren't any trans people on telly and all of that, I discovered I think that it was real, that people did change, that you could become … a boy could become a girl and a girl could become a boy eventually and that was quite a revelation to me and that began a long, very long, dance of me trying to allow myself that, denying it, repressing it, and so on and so forth.

I had this very instinctive idea that this wasn't something that I could openly talk to people, even my parents or anyone, about. I didn't have any friends in real life that I could talk to about it, I didn't feel comfortable with even my best friends, kind of bringing this up. The environment was so hostile towards any kind of … but I think my parents would have been alright but it was just one of those things. I turned to the internet and things like that for some kind of support or understanding of what was going on and unfortunately that wasn't a great idea because the information available online back in those days was quite bad for trans people. I got myself into all sorts of … down all sorts of rabbit holes … there was a lot of stuff that was obsessed with ideas of who was really trans and who wasn't and I managed to sort of convince myself that I was just faking it somehow. It's very strange looking back but I managed to convince myself that. I am completely going off on a tangent.

I got physically assaulted on several occasions. Insults hurled at me in the street, I got spat at and things and all sorts of crap. None of it felt like it could be … that I could go to the police.

Those kind of negative experiences kind of pushed me very much back into the … it seemed for a while maybe, looking back, I was going through, ramping up a process which would eventually have led to me working everything out and coming to terms with everything in my early twenties, mid twenties, but that kind of experience pushed me back, right back into the internal closet as it were. I did that kind of thing which is quite common, overcompensating in a way, so I took up masculine hobbies and started wearing a beard.

I know I must have had several conversations with my mother during my teenage years. I have very, kind of sometimes, very vague memories. I had a lot of dissociation before I started transitioning and taking hormones and things – feeling dreamlike and robotic and things like that, it was common, so a lot of memories … a terrible thing is that I am recording my oral history but

Sydney

a lot of memories seem quite vague. My mum definitely recalled me having several conversations about asking her what did she think, in a vague way, did she think I was gay? What was up with me? As it were. It was all kind of very … like I said, I had all these ideas, this information available on the internet. I was trying to look up rational explanations for why people are gay, why people are trans, all this sort of stuff and I came across this sort of idea that trans people are sort of 'super gay', that you are straight and then if you are a little bit feminised, you become bisexual. If you are a bit more feminised you become gay and then if you are a bit more feminised you become transgender and obviously a side effect of that would be that all 'real trans women' would be attracted to me sexually which I'm not! So that kind of made me think, "Oh God, I must be just some weirdo". And I actually tried to date men for a while and sort of went though all … I sometimes joke that I've been every letter of the LGBT, certainly before you get to the I. I am everything LGBTQ! Or have been at some point in my life, tried to be, or thought I was, or gone through that – nothing kind of made sense until I eventually gave myself a kick up the arse.

So over the next year I started having conversations with my wife, I had conversations with people, with support people online and stuff. So I was laying the groundwork and I eventually got around to shaving my beard off which was a big thing because I had had this beard for ten years and it was like a big trademark. I had it braided, it was quite long, when my friends first saw me without it they all gasped. Some people had never seen my face underneath it. In fact, my wife had never seen me without it which was quite … really liberating. Well, it was scary at first because a) I used to work up for it because I had this idea that one of two things was going to happen when I shaved this beard off, right? I am either going to look in the mirror at my clean-shaven face and one of two things is going to happen; I am going to either know that I am trans and that I need to transition and that's huge or I am going to know that I've made a huge mistake and I will have lost my beard and I will be really sad. Well, I kept the braid. I cut the braid off and kept it and I have still got it.

I was thinking that I could clip it back on if I needed to! [Laughs] But I didn't as it turned out. I looked into the mirror and I knew, I saw my face under it for the first time in years and years. I was also really worried that I had got really old and stuff but actually it kept my skin quite nice. So yeah, that specifically and then after that it was just transition rushed and within a couple of months of that I was out and legally changing my name and starting the medical process and everything.

One of my biggest regrets is …I mean, I remember when we were getting married joking about, "we should really be extraordinary and I should wear a dress and you should wear a suit". Yeah…as a joke. One of my biggest regrets in life is getting married as a man especially because the friend who died who was my wife's sort of best person, best man – we both had best men essentially, he was her best friend, so any kind of renewal or anything would be very emotional … anyway.

So, obviously, in the years of thinking about transitioning and then I had built up in my head the idea that transitioning would be very, very, very hard socially and that, obviously given my experiences on the other stuff beforehand, I was sort of prepared to lose most of my friends and you just don't know, even people who seem decent maybe, you don't really know, maybe they've got some negative opinions but actually it turned out that for whatever reason, obviously things have not got completely better on the Island by a long stretch but it turned out that actually everyone was great. People have been ignorant in the sense of not quite knowing what to do or what to say and people slipped up especially in the first few months, people would slip up and get my name wrong and pronouns wrong and things like that which is pretty normal, they've known me for years and years, however many years as someone else. But everyone sort of put the effort in. It went really well. My family were great with it; my wife loves it. I feel so much happier now even though I have hard days with it still.

Robert

I was born on the Island in Freshwater Bay in 1950. I identify as a gay man and had a fairly conventional family, I had two parents, one brother, grandparents living with us for much of the time and I went to a Church of England primary school and thereafter to a secondary modern school and after that to a grammar school. Excitement wasn't really the overriding feature of the place but, you know, it was a pleasant enough upbringing in its way.

At primary school, I think I always knew that there was something that was not usual in that I knew other boys were interested in girls even at that age and I was always blissfully uninterested in girls and unfortunately interested in them [boys] which didn't get me very far in those days. Well, I was just drawn more to boys than girls physically, as it were, and even just looking at them. I wasn't interested in looking at girls, I was a young misogynist, I suppose, in a way. On the football field and the showers and all that, you know, I knew where I wanted to look. At the school, you know, there was a playing field and I observed more than I played. I was a better observer than a football player, they used to put me in goal which I thought cruel. But, I mean, you didn't do anything at that age, of course, but I was aware that one had to be careful. I don't know how I was aware of that but I was. I was about ten, I suppose. I was pretty well aware of what I was by that point although I wouldn't have applied a word to it. Secondary school, yes, that was a bit more exciting in that there was a fair amount of adolescent fumbling going on there which one had to pretend not to enjoy as much as one did basically! Because, there were games, you know, so you would have one lad grabbing somebody else's bits and pieces and, of course, one was supposed to back away in disgust and horror which I usually managed to pretend to do.

Lucy

I always knew, I was, you know, I was wrong, I was transgender so. Well I knew I was different when I was about four years old. I remember playing with a friend of mine's mum's shoes and with his sister's toys and sort of thinking, "oh, yeah, I like this, I prefer this to mine", what I have to do, you know. What clothes I have to wear and what toys I have to play with. It was my friend's mum's shoes. High heels, I think those were a pair of red high heels. I used to trot around the garden in [them]. But at the time, being only four years old, it was just accepted, you know, it was just something, you know, just playing dress-up. It was always a bit more to me. It always felt right to me.

I used to like wearing tights, that was the main thing I used to like wearing but when they all used to go out or I used to feign. I used to say I was sick or something and I used to be able to know that as soon as everybody went out I used to raid my mum's wardrobe and dress up. Just, no, I'd just sit there. I was just in me bedroom, I didn't dare venture out of me bedroom just in case. It was just a typical boy's bedroom. I always knew it was different, I always knew it was wrong and I always had this thought that my parents wouldn't love me if I did these things. It was always a real, real, a real big secret.

I hated school. I really, really detested school. I was mummy's boy, I wanted to be at home. I wanted to be at home with my mum all the time … I think it is mainly just because I was so shy. I was so shy … I used to write me own notes. I used to write me own sick notes. So that was funny. Teachers must have known that I had written them myself but especially when … I didn't mind football and I didn't mind cricket but when it came to rugby and athletics and things like that I hated it. So I did try and get out of it.

Yeah, privately I wanted to be a girl. It only really started to get a problem in my late teens...yeah, yeah, and then I … in my late teens it started. I started to struggle with it. Before it was just in the background and I could hide it but it was in my teens when I started to get, late teens, when I started to get depressed. I just used to get depressed. Apart from the dressing up, that was it. I was living at home still, I was still living at home. Yeah. I left school, left school at sixteen. I joined the Post Office doing a YTS (youth training scheme). That was quite … I quite enjoyed my … I liked that because they treated you, you were being treated more grown up. They treated you as a grown up. You did two years on-the-job training and you also went to college as well. So college, I actually loved it. Yes, because they actually treated you as adults and treated you a lot different. I just found it more interesting. Yes. I did do quite well at it, I got a couple of distinctions in the two subjects I did, so I did so much better at college than I did at school. There were a couple of girls I quite fancied but again, being so shy I never took it any further.

Uh, the thing that made me depressed is because I couldn't be feeling like that, that's … having a relationship, it did bother me but the main thing was the fact that I couldn't express myself as being female. That was the worst thing. I had to keep it buried all the time. It feels like it is pushing me down, defeating me. I spent twenty-seven years in the Post Office. I just trundled along, you know. Pretty much until I was in my early forties at least, I just didn't do anything. I just suppressed absolutely everything. No, it was pretty much usually one-on-one, a one-on-one experience.

We came to the Island in 1997. Because we had family down here, they used to have a restaurant in Newport and we just started coming down on holidays and just fell in love with the Island so we decided to move down. There was less and less in Birmingham for us. It just felt very different, just so much nicer than Birmingham so we decided to relocate. I was 27. I don't think there was anything over here. I just used to pop up to London a couple of times because it was all still a secret, it was still a secret from me mum. Well that's it, there was the massive high of going up to London and then coming back was just a massive low, you know, realising that I can't be this person I was when I was up in London.

Joanne

I was born in Cowes in 1966. There was me, I've got an older brother who's eighteen months older than me and then there's eight years between me and Luke and ten years between me and Kieran. So three boys and me. I think I was more, I was like one of the boys really! [Laughs] And Mum and Dad obviously. I had a lovely childhood, we grew up in Ireland, it was hard for my mum, my dad was a bit of a drinker, he um, typical Irishman. He wasn't a bad man, he wasn't, but he um, you know, typical, the drink. So Mum brought the four of us up but, do you know what? We, yeah, we had a good family, it was good, yeah, all three even to this day, very close. Um, like, parents have gone but we're still 100% there for each other. [School was] Irish Catholic. Nuns. Horrible they were to us most of 'em. Very mean. But do you know what? We just got on with it, you just, that's the way it was. Do you know what, I had my best friend Anne, and we just, there was no issues, do you know what I mean? Never, they sort of, you did as you were told and it was as simple as that. So, yeah, no issues, it was fine. Absolutely fine.

Me and my best mate Anne, and it was just the two of us really. There were sort of vaguely other people around but it was just, we were best mates and we went everywhere together, we went roller skating, yeah, it was us. There wasn't really anyone else, quite selfish really I suppose.

The negatives would be the, the nuns, being hit. I was always in trouble for talking. I called it helping but it was, I was always getting whacked. Terrible really. I never learnt either! [Laughs] But, um, it wasn't, it was a positive time for me, I never, like as far as being gay it didn't enter my head at school, I just went to school and there was never any issues. Yeah, it was fine.

Did people talk at school about being gay? Not, no way! No, God Almighty! Not in an Irish Catholic school! It was unheard of and even if you'd thought it you wouldn't have mentioned it. God, no! It just was unheard of in Ireland too, you just wouldn't have talked about it. Our sex education, I remember, was about a sanitary towel, that was it. There was no, but then how could they because they were nuns? You know, not like you'd say the Magdalene sisters, they weren't like that, but they were very strict and no, you'd never have mentioned the G word. … Oh my God you'd have been hung, drawn and quartered, like, cos, like, we moved here in 1984, I was eighteen, didn't want to come, my girlfriend Joan stayed in Ireland. Obviously we were devastated. I could have stayed in Ireland because I was eighteen but I was very close to my family and my mum begged me to come.

Jude

I'm a lesbian. I was born in London, I grew up in Bermondsey which is south-east London. I was convinced that I was a boy and in this day and age I probably would have been shot full of hormones and I dread to think. But I did hate being a girl and when I got my period, which I wasn't quite eleven, I was absolutely horrified because up until then I lived believing, not thinking or wishing, but believing that one day they would notice that I'm a boy. So, I then grew up and I was fine being a girl really. Yeah. And I found that being a girl actually offered you quite a lot of control back in the 60s.

So I grew up, got pregnant at sixteen which was a shock-horror to the whole world because that was 1964, was whooshed off into a Catholic hostel for unmarried mothers which on the gate had a plaque saying, 'Saint Joan's Hostel for Young Ladies', which I thought was quite ironic, especially as the house next door had a hostel for young men! I did wonder if they had got someone pregnant so they had got put in there. So yeah, I had my baby. At some point, well 1974, I was part of running a squatting group in London in Battersea, or Clapham, and we'd become quite respectable and the council handed us property. Initially they didn't, we'd homed a couple, a young couple in a six month property and one day they came bouncing round to me saying, "June! June! We found a perfect squat for you!" And it was on the Isle of Wight. [Laughs] So, it was in Carisbrooke. So the next day I think, after I'd finished work we, or maybe I took the day off work, I can't remember, and got in my car. I had someone living in, a male, living in my house at the time because I didn't drive then, so he drove us down, over the ferry, off to Carisbrooke, down a little lane and found this magical fairy-tale house, a cottage, right on a stream going through the garden, a ford right outside the door. It was like, I was like every, or the majority of city girls, that you grew up with this dream of a cottage in the country and roses around the door and, you know, having your children running free in the fields!

I had been to the Island but that was in '67, so then seven years on, 1974, we arrived, looked at this cottage, all the windows were smashed out, floorboards had been pulled up, we had to literally hack the brambles, it was like something out of a fairy story. Hacked the brambles to get through, looked in, fell in love with the place, went, "Right, OK", turned back, went back to London and I must have had the day off because I had to get back, we had to get back to London in time to collect the kids. So, by then I'd got two children. I put my notice into my job and three weeks later we moved to the Isle of Wight. Thinking back, we could have got here and found that the place had been knocked down, that it was inhabited, anything. So that was fine and I then started shortly after that, I started my nursing training. The people that I had mixed with in London and then when I was down here, it felt and maybe this is my interpretation of what it was, it felt almost, in London definitely, it felt almost compulsory to be bisexual. So I took that label on, you know, it was like, so that was, well I guess I had taken that label on in London but I'd never done anything about it. I just ogled at a few people. [Laughs] So '74, lived in that cottage for about a year.

Karl L

David and I moved to the Isle of Wight in 1992 after I'd finished college, teacher training college, at Ilkley. I was offered a job on the Isle of Wight because of some of the specialist work I had been doing during my training at Isle of Wight College. So I came here essentially as a young person's outreach worker for sexual health and HIV prevention. Yes, we were here for about six years, seven years I think it was, and we moved off the Island again in late 1998 and that was because essentially the work which I had been doing had come to an end in its funding and, whilst they offered me a job at the very last minute to do with something else, I had actually found a job elsewhere then. So then I went off to work in Kent for about ten years, or twelve years I think it was, where I became the Kent Drugs and Alcohol Education Advisor for young people for the whole of the county.

I came here with my partner, David. This year we have just celebrated 30 years together which has been a really good year for us. We had been together about two years when we first moved here, we didn't have two pennies to rub together, we didn't even know what house we were moving to. We were found a property on the Island by a most fantastic colleague, Kay Marriott, who was then working in sexual health because my money to pay for my job was funded out of sexual health and HIV money or the 'AIDS budget' as it was then described.

It was quite a substantive budget but I was going to need to do HIV prevention work on the streets late at night in Ryde and a little bit in Newport and so that project was a two-year project and then progressed from that to becoming one of the very first outreach workers for gay men's health work, as it was described then, specifically for gay men because of course women weren't counted in the equation were they at those times? It was thought not to be a high risk for women in those early days because it was very early, so I became an outreach worker who was working, if you like, as part of a sexual health team trying to prevent the spread of HIV and AIDS amongst the LGBT community on the Island. Apart from LGBT didn't exist as an acronym. But even before that I was very involved with the community here, the gay social life, which was quite fascinating really.

So my experiences were both professional and within the community. I was here to provide a service and I had this huge advisory committee to protect me as a gay man and my partner on the Island in what was then a very difficult, you know, it was thought that there might be some, if you like, risk to me because of the work I was doing, because people were being attacked, assaulted and so on in those days, and because of my sexual identity on a small island. But I have to say that we enjoyed every minute of being here and we very, very rarely came across any discrimination directly against me or David, who's my partner, and we lived very, very happily here and the only reason for moving off the Island was that the funding changed and I am very grateful for that funding changing because it was as a result of them starting to introduce medications that actually helped people survive and continue and live a full life as they are doing now.

Anonymous

I do, I suppose I am a gay man because I do, I am a man who likes men, but I think 'queer' is more political and a lot of the time I do feel political about it, there's a lot of aspects of the gay community that I don't kind of, I don't know, I don't sort of feel I click with and then some aspects of the gay community I do click with and then some aspects of the queer community I don't click with and some aspects of the queer community I do click with [Laughs]. So I suppose, I don't know, I find that the term 'gay' has a lot of heavy connotations but I suppose I am a gay man.

I grew up in East Cowes, I went to school, in East Cowes for the first part and then in West Cowes for the second part. School was very, um, I grew up in the 80s, it was very kind of full of bullies and it was quite hard and being gay was quite difficult back then and this was even before I came out or even that I knew I was gay and the term 'gay' was thrown around a lot as being very negative, it was a very negative thing to be, to be gay was very negative. So, it was very difficult, I think if I was in my twenties in the 80s it would have been awful because of the AIDS crisis but it was very difficult back then to be gay. But growing up at school I think a lot of the other kids saw me and picked up that I was gay and they used to say things and things like that. So, it was quite difficult back then.

Karen

I came to the Isle of Wight when I was six months old with my Dad and my real mum. He got a job at Fields in Sandown. So I basically grew up on the Island. In the 70s I was always on the beach, had lots of friends, my family life wasn't great. Yeah, I just had a normal upbringing, really, me and my baby brother.

I always remember having crushes on girls wherever I went. At school, wanting to be with friends, I can remember particularly being ten and thinking that Olivia Newton-John in Grease was quite hot. It was just always… and I really liked Charlie's Angels as well but I didn't think anything of it, it was just I liked them, I thought they were, well, they were crushes, I was attracted to them but I didn't think anything beyond they were just a crush because you grew up in a straight world and you had to have boyfriends. So, it was just a crush and I liked them.

Melissa

My experiences on the Isle of Wight growing up as a queer person. We moved here when I was eight from Ascot. I grew up in Ascot and then in London, not London, sorry, in Scotland before that. So I kind of realised that I was not straight as a teenager so it was around fifteen or sixteen and actually the catalyst for that was I was with a friend at the bus station in Newport and I saw someone from the back and I turned to my friend and I was like, "oh, they're really hot", and then they turned around and it's a woman and so my friend was like, "Oh my God! You're gay!" I was like, "no, I'm not, I'm not!" And that continued for a long time but that was kind of a catalyst in my brain that made me think, "am I? Am I?" Because I did realise I still found men attractive, "am I?" And I kind of figured out that, yeah, yeah, that was me, I was attracted to not just men, I was attracted to women and other genders as well.

My friendship group at the time were kind of a group of people who, we all kind of later in life started coming out over time until, I think, the minority in our group were straight cisgender people and that's not uncommon to the queer experience from kind of other friends and people I've talked to. We were quite into a type of music like emo and scene and rock music that meant that that wasn't something that was unheard of and that wasn't something that I really worried that they wouldn't accept.

Karl S

I was born in the North East of England. We came to the Island thirteen years ago. We had a business in Brighton and the idea was we were going to sell up and move to France. We went over to France and we saw a property we liked, we fell in love with it and when we got back to England and told people that's what we were going to do various elderly relatives said, "well, if you go off to France that's probably the last time we'll see you, so think about it, do you need to go?" And we said, "well, OK, we'll stay", and then it was a case of trying to find somewhere to move to. We wanted to move out of Brighton, well, we'd already moved out of Brighton actually, we were in Seaford. We looked around and we knew we wanted to be in the south and we knew we wanted to be by the sea so we looked in Cornwall and Devon and places like that and then we saw in a magazine a picture of a house on the Isle of Wight and we thought, "well that looks very much like the place we were going to buy in France, let's go and have a look at it". We saw it and we said, "right! Let's do that, it's kind of going across the water but it is not actually going abroad as such, it is still the UK". It was a small hotel/guest house in Shanklin and so we bought that. It does prove that you should do your research before you make a big move. If we had done the research we may not have come here but that's why we came here, that's how we came here. The business that we bought wasn't what we thought we were buying and then when we came over here, we didn't really like it. We didn't know anybody. I'd never been to the Island before and we'd come from Brighton, we'd come from Kemptown in Brighton which is very gay, before that we'd been in London – very gay – and we'd done the clubs and the pubs and we'd been to Ibiza and Mikanos and Miami and all that sort of thing. We'd done the gay life, we'd bought the T-shirt and we knew that we were coming somewhere that wasn't particularly gay and we knew there weren't any bars or clubs or anything like that. However, we were quite surprised that there was nothing and there was no way really, apart from going through things like Gaydar or something, there was no way really of meeting other gay people. People were quite unfriendly, there was quite a bit of homophobia really. And as I say, the business that we bought, which was a lot of work, wasn't what we thought we were moving into and so for the first probably five years or so, quite frankly, if I could have given the key back to somebody and gone back to the mainland I would have done.

We did the civil partnership the first year we came over here and then when gay marriage or whatever they call it came in we had it, we did that, which is just, I mean, they actually backdate it to when the civil partnership was. We did it on the Island. In fact, we did that, it was the first year we came over here and in a way it worked as a sort of introduction to the Island to our friends and family. We did it as a sort of house-party type thing so a lot of the people that came to the civil partnership hadn't been to the Island before. We did the civil partnership over a weekend, sort of three or four days really, so people came over and stayed with us. When you've got a hotel you've got plenty of bedrooms. So they stayed with us and we went out for meals and drinks and such. Then the civil partnership was at Northwood House and we organised a coach to come to the house and then everybody got on the coach and we all went together to the civil partnership. It was quite nice because by that time everybody had got to know each other so family and friends who hadn't maybe met before, over the weekend they got to know each other and it was very good, it was really good, that was a really positive thing. So we did that thirteen years ago.

Rosa

I was out. I was out from a teenager really. I suppose I was the kind of person that couldn't hide it because I was too much of a tomboy so I think everybody knew before I really did, so it wasn't an issue. My mum was great, I remember she tried to start a dialogue with me and what she said was, "you know, you're my daughter and I love you and it doesn't matter to me what you do because I will always love you and you will always be my daughter", and I thought, "hmm, I'm not ready for that conversation with her just yet". I was about nineteen then. I think I kind of knew from when I was about four because I remember telling my mum when I was about four that, "when I grew up I am going to marry a lady". She started laughing, she said, "oh, you can't, if you're a lady you've got to marry a man; if you're a man you've got to marry a lady", and I said, "but I thought people could marry who they wanted", and she said, "yes, they can", then she kind of went, "well, when you get older you'll understand it". I thought, "OK, maybe she knows something I don't know", but I got older and I still didn't understand it. I think when I was at school I was really focussed on school work because I wanted to get an education, I wanted to get some qualifications. I knew that I wasn't going to grow up and get married and someone was going to look after me and I'd live happily ever after, I knew that I would have to support myself. So I was really focussed on school, I was very involved in school and I worked really hard, got my exams, got a place at teacher training college.

I do remember when I was about fifteen or sixteen my sister wanted to go out and stay out late and my mum wouldn't let her and she said, my sister said, "well, how comes Rosie's allowed to stay out late and I'm have to come home at ten o'clock", and my mum said, "Because I know Rosie's not going to come home in trouble". By that I think she meant I wasn't going to come home pregnant. So I think from then she knew that I was not interested in boys and that I wasn't going to go and get married and have loads of kids. So, it was never actually said, like I say, until that time when my mum made that comment to me when I was about nineteen. It was never actually said but I think it was known.

Jess

I feel like when I was growing up on the Island I'd never even considered... I don't even remember to be honest, I don't think it was something I ever really considered because you just lived with your mum and dad and everyone lived with their mum and dad but then obviously my mum came out as being a lesbian so that was quite a shock. I think I was about six or seven at that point. But I don't remember ever feeling like it was weird even though we all lived in the house with my dad and she would have girlfriends come to stay which in retrospect is a little bit strange now but at the time it was just normal because she just had really cool friends that were coming to visit. Yeah, and then it was just normal and then from that point onwards I just thought people were people and it was just really normal to me. I remember being really protective of that so that every time people would say, "that's really gay", I would shout at them in school and be like, "you can't say that, I have a gay mum!" Or whatever. So yes, it was just normal to me from that point I suppose but before that, I really don't think I ever thought about people being gay or trans or bisexual or anything. It's Wroxall, it's a very small village too so that probably didn't help.

David

My home was very Victorian. We were scared to death of our father and my mother, well, she was a mother but he was very domineering so she didn't get much say in anything. I went to an all-boys school, did all the usual things, in that I was in the band, I was in the school choir and whatever and nothing sexually went through my mind because it wasn't a thing that was talked about at home ... I was seventeen when I changed my religion and became Roman Catholic and I was preparing to go into a monastery. I couldn't do it until I was 21 because I needed my father's signature and my father hated Jews, Catholics, you name it, he hated them all, Black, Chinese. He only liked himself. So I was waiting until I was 21. So I went through seven years, I took my vows after two years and I learnt to be a chef [Laughs], they sent me to a local college to mingle with young people there because I was only in my early 20s. So I took a catering course and walked away with two City and Guilds certificates [Laughs] ...

Left there because things were starting to change too much and they were modernising and I am very traditional. Went home. I was at home for a few weeks and then I got a job in London for two men as their housekeeper because then I was nearly 27 or I was 27 or whatever and things were going through my mind then about sexual things. I still wasn't sure what they meant because I hadn't anybody to tell me. So I applied for this job as housekeeper for two men. So I thought, "I can clean and it is a stepping stone, it's away from home". So anyway, I'd been housed with these two for about a year and a half or whatever and then I made friends with somebody in Hampstead itself who was part of a, erm, he was the cook or the chef for a seminary for Jesuits and I got on very well with him.

Then I came to the Isle of Wight, met my first partner, full-term partner in a sense and we had this hotel on Sandown seafront. Then my father died and I went up to Yorkshire to sort that out and we used to get my mother to come down to the Island then every so often and then we were told that she only had six months to live, when she was 59 and she had been in for an operation and they couldn't do anything. I wouldn't let them tell her. I said, "if she finds out she's only got six months and it is the hospital's fault, I will sue you for every penny you've got", because I thought I could keep her going better without her knowing. So we had to get her to come down about every two months. My sister used to stick her on a train and I used to go up to meet her. We used to start meeting at Kings Cross, then we used to start meeting her at Portsmouth and then I used to meet her in Ryde. She got so, her confidence was, I mean, she was all there, she loved my partner.

My mother died on holiday with us in 79 in Fairlee Hospital which is now the Mountbatten and we sold the hotel thinking we would have a couple of years just to travel and then come back and settle down and open another hotel. That was November when we sold. In January we bought this derelict guest house in Totland and we spent a quarter of a million putting it right – this is 1980. We were open in six months, it was a luxury hotel, we didn't take children, not in the restaurant or bedrooms, and we were full 90% of the year. Anyway in 1984 my partner ran off with the barman. [Laughs] As one does. [Laughs] He went to Guernsey and through a crooked solicitor, when the hotel was sold because neither of us would buy each other out, all the money was transferred to him and out of the £600,000+ we sold it for, I got 19,000. I lost 100,000 then. I couldn't do anything about it because Guernsey is a state of its own. The solicitor got the sack because he was found, because we were a limited company and he was our company solicitor, he'd been doing it to a couple of people already so he got the sack for that. At the end of it I didn't mind anyway. And then, well, before then, I'd advertised for a barman in Gay Times through which I then met my current partner and we have been together now for 35 years this year.

Michelle

I transitioned. I came out, for want of a better word, when I was sixty but I have known about my gender dysphoria for more than 70 years. A long time. When I was four, four and a half, I had a complicated operation at the children's hospital in London. Great Ormond Street Hospital. I was there for a long time and in those days, we are talking about the 40s, in those days visitors could only visit for about an hour or I don't think it was as much as two a day. We lived, my parents and I, way outside London so basically I assumed I had been left alone, I rarely saw my parents. I mention that because it may have some, it may have created an effect which amplified my dysphoria. I don't know, but I did study psychology later when I went to university so it is possible.

My first association with the Isle of Wight was that I learnt to swim because my parents and my various uncles used to come to Seaview on the paddle steamer every summer and my uncle taught me how to swim in the swimming pool in Seaview. I learnt to swim without my feet touching the bottom. So, that was my first association with the Island.

I played, when I was very young, with a tomboy across the road, Marian, and we did all sorts of things like dressing up and I was always the nurse and she was always the doctor. We climbed trees and did various things that kids do. But when we were about, I think it must have been about six or seven years old, we were camping in my garden and discovered that we were different because we were not wearing any clothes. We had taken them off and my mother put her head in through the door and there was Marian exploring the fact that I wasn't the same as her. So that ended camping in the garden and various things but we continued, we dressed up quite often I think over at her house and things.

Michelle

I then went to school, as you do, I won a scholarship to a boys' public school in London at around age eleven but by then my parents, I gather, were worried about me and I suppose because in those days gay or homosexuality was illegal and I discovered all of this later as I will explain perhaps later, but my parents were worried and they wanted to man me up. So at the age of eleven, with another boy aged eleven, we were put on a train to the Lake District and we walked around the Lake District for two weeks in Youth Hostels and planned our route and all the rest of it. I don't think one would send eleven year-olds 200 miles away on their own nowadays but in those days it was regarded as the thing to do. At least my parents thought it was.

Caroline

I'm the eldest of three, my dad was in the army and I was born in Manchester because he was based in Ashton-under-Lyne in the army there. So it was a very traditional family really; he was the breadwinner and my mum stayed at home, she worked part-time, but it was kind of a traditional family in that sense. But, yeah, it was a happy family. I am lucky to have very understanding, supportive parents who have got a lot of humour, always see the funny side of things even when things go wrong and are very loving towards me and my two sisters. We always felt that we were very cared for and they were very happy to have us. They have got a very strong relationship, they are still together now, they've been married for 55 years in June and so I feel quite lucky to have that supportive, stable family background. They've had ups and downs like couples do but in the main it was a very supportive environment.

We did move around a lot; my dad was in the army which meant that he moved every two and a half years and he spent quite a lot of time away from the family and these were the times when there was no internet and he would, at times, go away for six months. We might get a letter, we might get an odd phone call so I did feel quite a lot of separation because I am very close to my dad and I do remember feeling that kind of separation. It was quite an intense relationship between my mum and I because I think she was quite surprised, she is only [a] quite small woman, she is about five foot tall and I was a big 9lb 3oz baby and I always feel as if I sort of took them by surprise in that sense. But yeah, it was a happy family upbringing, very traditional, and there were no real role models in terms of anyone who was LGBT apart from a cousin, Emma.

We moved around a lot, it was very much a kind of patriarchal environment because the army really dominated everything. We would move house sometimes without an awful lot of notice or I might be halfway through my A' Levels for example, and they said, "oh, sorry, you need to move". So I had to go to a new school. So it was quite unsettled but you kind of get into, you get used to it because everybody around you is doing that same pattern of moving around. So that was really how it went and it was all quite a traditional environment, there wasn't anything that I could say was a trauma but we just got into this habit of having to move every two and a half years and to go to completely different places. We went to Hong Kong and Germany and Northern Ireland so it was, you know, it was a great experience to get to know those places and the schools always had other army children in, so although you were meeting new people everybody was in the same position so nobody batted an eyelid when somebody new came to the school because we were all used to that kind of unsettled pattern.

But in terms of LGBT and my first thoughts about perhaps I wasn't heterosexual. I did have a friend – she's actually straight as well which is a little bit awkward because she's on Facebook now and we've sort of contacted each other as friends. I remember that I used to go to sleepovers at her house and we used to be quite intimate and I remember feeling as if this was much more of an exciting thing for me than perhaps it was for her.

THE GIFT

A Mother's Story

I remember the scene vividly: Mum, Dad and (we thought) daughter, standing outside a sunny London pub, glasses in hand. Not prepared for what our middle child was about to tell us – that he had realised he needed to live his life as a man.

I have to admit it came as a shock – I managed not to splutter my beer all over him, but to hug him and assure him we were right behind him and would support him. But once the first surprise was over, I did wonder over and over how I had missed the signs. And could I have guessed and supported him earlier? By the time he was ready to come out he was in his twenties, living and working away from home. What about all those years when I had shared a home with him?

I knew he had been troubled through his teenage years, but I had put that down to a multitude of other things – he was very intelligent and deep thinking; he sometimes found it hard to bond with people his own age; he read voraciously and absorbed ideas from everywhere and just wanted to write. He seemed to blossom at uni – he was with intellectual equals and was more able to be himself, yet when he graduated with a top-class degree he was unwilling to pursue further studies, and still seemed aimless, like he was looking for something that wasn't there.

Except it was. And perhaps he just needed that time to come to terms with his inner self. I could appreciate the courage it took to come to the conclusion he did and to share it with his parents. Only he knows how much.

Over the following weeks I felt several emotions: fear, guilt, apprehension and loss, but also supreme love and respect for my son. Selfishly, I mourned the 'loss' of the beautiful daughter I had held in my arms, imagining seeing her in her white wedding dress, giving birth – all those rites of passage which we parents impose on our offspring. Unfairly. Generously, my son recognised this and apologised for 'depriving' me of my only daughter. I worried about how his life would now go – would he be accepted? Would he be victimised? Would our relationship change? What about all the medical and psychological work he would have to undertake?

In the beginning it was difficult to get used to a new name and pronoun – I made mistakes, all the time. And again, generously, my son forgave me, because he knew I was doing my best. Yes, there were difficulties along the way – other members of the family were at times less sensitive than they could have been and understandably my son was more sensitive about anything that related to his gender. Yet there were some really touching moments when aunts and uncles embraced the change, and when choosing a new name, he not only kept the same initials as he had previously but also chose family names, which meant a lot to me: one being the name of my father's brother who had died at the age of nineteen in World War II. A lovely gesture.

And so, very quickly the positives began to surface. We have always been close but our bond was never predicated on sharing makeup, clothes and shopping – neither of us are really into that – but on a love of literature and theatre, and that hasn't changed. Our relationship stayed the same because, of course, he is still the same person he has always been – except that he is now happy and fulfilled. Watching the way he has handled all he has had to deal with over the last few years has given me a new sense of pride in him and appreciation of his qualities. And I quickly came to realise I had not been 'deprived' of anything – I had gained a beautiful, happy and loving son.

Since that day outside the pub I have watched my son come alive. By the time he went for surgery, I knew he was moving toward the person he needed to be, and although every parent will appreciate the anxiety of watching your child being prepped for an operation and wheeled off, then the hours of wandering round nearby shops and cafes, not tasting the coffee you force down your throat until it's time to go back to the hospital, thankfully to be told all has gone well, all that was more than worth it to see his extra confidence and sheer delight in his new body.

Yes, it has taken time for my husband and me to adjust; yes, the waiting around for diagnoses, counselling sessions, medication and surgery to be approved has at times been difficult – far more for our son than us though; and yes, there have been times when we have had to work at the relationships to adapt to the changing circumstances – but then all parents have to adapt to their children growing up, being independent – this was just another change to cope with along the way.

Today, my son is in his own home, doing a job he loves: providing support for LGBTQ+ people in the area he lives in – and I mustn't forget the other loves of his life, his two gorgeous cats. A few months ago he paid me a great compliment: he told me a young man had come into his workplace distraught because he had told his parents that he was gay and they had reacted very badly. My son told him:

> "Remember, your parents gave you life – but it is a gift, and the giver does not have the right to decide how you use the gift they gave you. It is yours to use in the right way for you."

My son reminded me that I had given him this advice. Not only was I astonished that one of my children had actually listened to something I said … I was genuinely moved that he thought my advice was worth passing on. Most importantly, my son knows he is loved and cared for, I know he is the same lovely person I gave birth to – and he is happy. And that, to a parent is all that really matters.

THIS IS ME

Vicky-Marie Newsome-Hogan

Vicky-Marie Newsome-Hogan is a married, 59-year-old transsexual woman, having completed her transition in 2019. She moved to the Island in 2017 following eighteen years living in Canada. The same year Vicky-Marie met her wife Claire, who founded and operates a wildlife rescue charity on the Island. Vicky-Marie is a trustee of the charity and is medically retired after careers in the fire service, military, civilian police, and social care. Vicky-Marie fulfilled her dream to retire by the seaside but she never imagined it would be on an island, but circumstances brought her to the (sometimes) sunny Isle of Wight. Coming here and completing her transition on the Island, Vicky-Marie described as "such a positive move for her in every way. I met the wonderful woman who is now my wife, here on the Island and we have a lovely life together here in this beautiful part of the country, with our dog Tashi".

What you see before you: this is me.
I may not look or sound how you would expect
and for that I have no choice
      but this is me.
My heart and soul lives within what you see
      and this is me.
I hid in fear inside this shell, tried to be what isn't me.
I have but one life, one chance to be
so I will seize that chance and say
      this is me.
Look beyond what you see and hear. Look beyond my eyes
and see: the tears of a life lived in captivity -
      this is me.

I am a person just like you, but was afraid to show
      that this is me.

One day I could not try any longer to be what wasn't me.
In fear and hope, in a final bid to feel at ease, I said to the world
        look –
                this is me.

I've hidden for so long, afraid of what might be.
So for the time I have left I'll show you
            this is me.
I threw off the shroud I'd worn so long and stepped into myself.
I showed the world
            this is me.
The pain and loss I've suffered since showing you me
has wounded my heart, but set me free.
I'm able to express the truth of me, to feel content
in spite of all. To feel the liberation and calm within my soul.

I've lived my life in a cloudy haze
but now the sun will shine for the rest of my days.
The pain and loss continues, but I now can say
            this is me.
It won't be easy
and some days it's hard
but at least every day I can say
        look – this is me.
So take the time to listen
look beyond what your eyes may see.
Stand beside me, take my hand and tell the world,
I will help this tortured soul to say this is me
        I am free
then maybe others can finally say
        This is also me:
        I too
                am free.

LGBTQ+ ROLE MODELS

David E. Bennett

We asked our oral history interviewees "Who are your favourite role models? Did you know them personally? How have they shaped your life?".

Role models help us choose who we want to become. My favourite role model has long been Dutch artist and resistance fighter Willem Arondeus, who burned down the town records office to protect the identities of Jews and other targets ahead of the arriving Gestapo. Nothing has done more to cement in my mind the capacity of gay people to defy their stereotype and show selflessness, dignity and bravery than his final defiant words when facing the firing squad: "Let it be known that homosexuals are not cowards."[8]

The need for LGBTQ+ role models

Unlike heterosexuals, LGBTQ+ youths who usually grow up without relatable role models in their own homes,[9] are at much greater risk of mental health problems, and are several times more likely to be made homeless, a process that often damages their sense of identity. [10, 11, 12] Young

[8]David Hudson, 'The Gay Man Who Bombed a Building and Deserves to Be Celebrated as a Hero', *Gay Star News*, September 24, 2018, https://www.gaystarnews.com/article/gay-willem-arondeus-building/.

[9]K Bradley, 'Gay History Teaching Generates Debate', *Evening Standard*. October 28, 201.

[10]Emmie Matsuno and Tania Israel, 'Psychological Interventions Promoting Resilience Among Transgender Individuals: Transgender Resilience Intervention Model (TRIM)', *The Counseling Psychologist*,46, no. 5 (2018): 632-655, https://doi.org/10.1177/0011000018787261.

[11]Michael Sadowski, Stephen Chow, and Constance P. Scanlon, 'Meeting the Needs of LGBTQ Youth: A "Relational Assets" Approach', *Journal of LGBT Youth* 6, no. 2-3 (2009): 175-193, https://doi.org/10.1080/19361650903013493.

[12]T. Butchart-Kelly,'Gay Sportsmen Are Good Role Models', *Evening Standard*. August 18, 2015

LGBTQ people with accessible role models become more resilient and report less psychological distress than those without them. Trans youths who still to this day lack public role models benefit most of all, while trans adults themselves often enjoy a greater sense of purpose and wellbeing after acting as role models.[13]

Having both openly LGBTQ+ role models and straight allies growing up helps young LGBTQ+ people 'reconcile their emerging identities with the relationships central to their lives' and make meaningful relational connections that help them to accept and become at peace with themselves and lead happier, healthier lives.[14] Public figures who come out in fields that have been historically male-dominated bastions of homophobia, such as professional sportspeople and business leaders, are particularly useful, especially for men. They help change attitudes, inspire more LGBTQ+ young people to try sports or to take on leadership roles and overcome fear of harassment so that it is no longer a barrier to realising their dreams.[15] Yet, while such distant role models can shape LGBTQ+ identities, they cannot listen or provide the support young people need[16]. Accessible role models who the young person knows and can talk and relate to, such as teachers, mentors and other adults, are the most valuable in helping to maintain LGBTQ+ youths' mental health.

LGBTQ role models before 1990

LGBTQ+ people have been both blessed and cursed with being able to conceal their sexual and gender identities and with some effort conform to the prevailing heteronormative culture. There has long been social pressure for LGBTQ+ people to conceal their sexuality, historically leaving LGBTQ+ youths in particular with few if any role models. The number of celebrity role models who have shaped gay identity has increased from the 1990s onwards. However the availability of warm, available, relatable and accessible LGBTQ+

---

[13]Emmie Matsuno and Tania Israel, 'Psychological Interventions Promoting Resilience Among Transgender Individuals: Transgender Resilience Intervention Model (TRIM)', *The Counseling Psychologist* 46, no. 5 (2018): 632-655, https://doi.org/10.1177/0011000018787261.

[14]Michael Sadowski, Stephen Chow, and Constance P. Scanlon, 'Meeting the Needs of LGBTQ Youth: A "Relational Assets" Approach,' *Journal of LGBT Youth* 6, no. 2-3 (2009): 175-193, https://doi.org/10.1080/19361650903013493.

[15]T Butchart-Kelly, 'Gay Sportsmen Are Good Role Models', *Evening Standard*, August 18, 2015

[16]Jason D.P. Bird, Lisa Kuhns, and Robert Garofalo, 'The Impact of Role Models on Health Outcomes for Lesbian, Gay, Bisexual, and Transgender Youth', *Journal of Adolescent Health* 50, no. 4 (2012): 353-357, https://doi.org/10.1016/j.jadohealth.2011.08.006.

role models in everyday life to young people growing up, that make a real difference to young people's lives, remains a lottery. We are starting to see successful individuals come out as role models at the top of their professions – but not before, because of the sustained risk to their career progression.

The systematic erasure of LGBTQ+ people from recorded history has left history replete only with heroes and rulers who appear to be heterosexual[17]. As a result, previous generations were forced to be out and proud, fighting to be visible and to draw attention to the existence of sexual and gender diversity in order to give a relatable face to the oppressed. LGBTQ+ role models were comparatively few and far between, and they were excluded from classical role-model occupations and the associated values and qualities society was taught to respect, this dissociation being used as another reason to degrade homosexuals and bully young LGBTQ+ people.[18]

Persistent myths that children became effeminate and grew up gay because they attached to homosexual role models or lacked sufficiently strong heterosexual role models played midwife to fears that gay men were a threat to children and civilisation in general. This created a culture in which, until the late 1990s, LGBTQ+ people were actively denied role models, save for those lucky few with LGBTQ+ acquaintances.[19]

Gay and cross-dressing men remained a source of comedy on stage and screen, but like the actors who portrayed them, their sexual diversity was expected to remain safely on stage and screen, one step removed from real life. Characters in dramas were largely restricted to parodies, such as Mr Humphries in *Are You Being Served*, which acknowledged the existence of gay people but at the same time reinforced gay stereotypes. Stage performers such as Danny La Rue and Dame Edna Everage exploited the permissive performing arts to create transvestite comedic personas, but gender diversity and trans icons were absent. Gay people were shown role models that represented how society

[17]Gabriel Gomez et al., 'The Legacy Project: Connecting Museum Advocacy to Gay, Lesbian, Bisexual, and Transgender (GLBT) Role Models', *Journal of Museum Education* 38, no. 2 (2013): 193-206, https://doi.org/10.1080/10598650.2013.11510770.

[18]E. G. Spitko, 'A Reform Agenda Premised Upon the Reciprocal Relationship Between Anti-lgbt Bias in Role Model Occupations and the Bullying of LGBT Youth', *Connecticut Law Review*, 48(1), (2015). 71-117.

[19]Dorothy I. Riddle, 'Relating to Children: Gays as Role Models', *Journal of Social Issues* 34, no. 3 (1978): 38-58, https://doi.org/10.1111/j.1540-4560.1978.tb02613.x. / 'LGBT Travel Leaders Urged to Become "Role Models"', *Travel Trade Gazette UK & Ireland*, 3119. October 16, 2014, 4.

[20]Stephen Moss, '"He Was a Gay Guy Who Won": Why I Wrote a Play about Ice-Skating Genius John Curry', *Guardian* (Guardian News and Media, August 21, 2017), https://www.theguardian.com/stage/2017/aug/21/looking-for-john-curry-olympics-tony-timberlake-assembly-hall-edinburgh-festival.

wanted them to be: submissive, accepting of menial workplace roles, and celibate. Great effort and awareness were necessary to pick out obscure role models, such as 1976 ice-skating champion John Curry.[20]

A handful of LGBTQ+ role models began haphazardly to emerge from the 1980s onwards as the mass media moved from censorship to sensationalism, with scandals such as the lesbian love affair of tennis star Martina Navratilova hitting the headlines in 1981. Reporting remained oppressive and judgemental, and role models were castigated rather than celebrated.

The gay 90s to present

From the 90s onwards, ground-breaking shows such as *Queer as Folk* and Ellen Degeneres' coming out in 1998 marked a watershed, ushering in an increasing number of LGBTQ+ gay and lesbian characters on television[21]. From this time onwards gay and, later, lesbian and, far more rarely, bi characters have begun to appear in mainstream soap operas and dramas. Sexual and gender diversity first expanded within their traditional safe space of drama, one step removed from real life, before real-world role models began to emerge in what became dubbed by the contemporary media as 'these gay times'.

Relatable characters in person, in literature, films, television shows and the media all serve as beneficial role models[22]. Lesbians and bi women in particular benefit from exploring experiences in literature, yet lesbian fiction is scarce and often scattered among other fiction and so is hard to discover[23].

Heroes and other noble characters in television dramas can also inspire and disrupt the association of heterosexuality with heroism in the public consciousness, as John Barrowman commented on his role as bi character Jack from the BBC's *Torchwood* and *Dr Who*[24]. In general, leaders, sportsmen,

---

[21]Sarah C. Gomillion and Traci A. Giuliano, 'The Influence of Media Role Models on Gay, Lesbian, and Bisexual Identity', *Journal of Homosexuality* 58, no. 3 (2011): pp. 330-354, https://doi.org/10.1080/00918369.2011.546729.

[22]Jennifer R. Cook, Sharon S. Rostosky, and Ellen D. Riggle, 'Gender Role Models in Fictional Novels for Emerging Adult Lesbians', *Journal of Lesbian Studies* 17, no. 2 (2013): 150-166, https://doi.org/10.1080/10894160.2012.6914 16.

[23]Jacqueline D. Goldthorp, 'Can Scottish Public Library Services Claim They Are Socially Inclusive of All Minority Groups When Lesbian Fiction Is Still so Inaccessible?', *Journal of Librarianship and Information Science* 39, no. 4 (2007): pp. 234-248, https://doi.org/10.1177/0961000607083215.

[24]Myke Bartlett, 'Outsized Role Models Take a Queer Turn'. *Metro* : media & education magazine. v 172 (2012), 120-125.

soldiers and others in fiction and who come out in real life, who have enjoyed success in roles only heterosexuals were traditionally allowed to hold, defy the stereotype.

While the number of gay characters on television has increased, bi characters are still rare, and trans and LGBTQ+ characters of colour remain conspicuous by their absence. LGBTQ+ people who are black or from minority ethnic (BME) backgrounds suffer from a lack of visible role models in general, at the same time as facing the intersection of homophobic, racist and, in the case of women, patriarchal oppression[25].

LGBTQ+ role models in science, commerce and industry are also still lacking. Although a few prominent leaders have come out, including Apple's CEO Tim Cook and Lloyds of London's CEO Inga Beale, they did so only after their final promotion, recruitment experts warning that being publicly out can still derail a person's career progression[26].

Looking ahead: a bright neoliberal future?

Even with the comparatively greater legal and civil freedoms today and the ability to find love, sex, friendship and romance online and through mobile apps, many younger LGBTQ+ people have adapted by satisfying their relationship needs online and minimising the importance they give to their sexuality as part of their identity. I find this retreat from public view and towards digital intermediation worrying. Young people need to feel secure in coming out in order to grow their confidence and be a visible part of society, to remind others that gay people exist and are in many ways like them. A comfortable retreat will not serve them longer term, and a lack of role models can only isolate them.

Young people might now have access to more LGBTQ+ role models online than ever before, yet we can still all make a real difference by being the accessible friends and informal mentors, the reliable, real-life LGBTQ+ role models and straight allies young LGBTQ+ people need to survive and thrive.

---

[25]Jimmy Nguyen, 'Why We Need More LGBT Minority Role Models', *The Root*, January 12, 2017, https://www.theroot.com/why-we-need-more-lgbt-minority-role-models-1790894443.

[26]C. Hymowitz, J. Kaplan, C. Giammona & T. Giles, 'Apple's CEO Comes Out, Could Fill Role Model Void for LGBT Workers', *HR Focus*, 91(12), 2014. 12-13.

EXTRACTS FROM ORAL HISTORIES

Anonymous

Who were the role models? Well, Ellen DeGeneres was a role model, she was a big one. I don't think I ever had any male role models that I was looking up to. She was a big one and I was so proud of her for when she came out on that TV show and I thought, "well, if she can do it, I can do it". So she was a major one but there was not one male that I went to. That's interesting because I do watch films, I am a big film and movie-buff person. It was like a desert on TV and media, it really was and you were sifting through this desert for stuff to go and watch. The most positive one was probably *Beautiful Thing*. I remember Anna telling me about *Beautiful Thing*, that was a really lovely, fairy-tale play and it had a happy ending and I think that's big … I studied media and I think LGBT film and TV is changing now. It used to be you had gay characters, you'll have a gay character in a film or TV show and as soon as they get with another gay character one of them will be killed off. So, it always happened like that in popular films and TV so it was very hard to find something that you were really … that was LGBT but more than that … that you had good positive LGBT characters in it. So *Beautiful Thing* was really a lovely story. I am just trying to think what else there was TV and film-wise. I mean, a lot of it was Channel 4 late on a Sunday night, because you only had those four TV channels that you'd watch. *My Beautiful Launderette* was another one, but again, I think … it ended up happy actually, but again it was very difficult. I remember a show/film came out back then called *But, I'm a Cheerleader*. That was good, that was about the girl who comes out as gay in America. It was a comedy but it had a serious element, serious issues. This girl comes out in America and she goes to a conversion camp to turn her back to straight and it was a comedy. Since then serious films have been done on that because that problem is still going on worldwide. Back then RuPaul was in it and it was quite funny. It was really good. We watched it, me and Anna, and thought, "this is amazing, this is funny". But I watched a lot of film and TV … and occasionally you'd get gay characters just turning up and it was quite exciting to have those gay characters and you were like, "Oh my God! There's a gay character in this!". But it was never, usually it was never very positive. Even in *Braveheart*, I think there was a point where there were the two gay princes and one of the gay princes says to the father, the King, "this is my love and we are going to be together", and the king just goes,"no you're not", and he throws one of them out the window. So, it was quite harrowing in those days and now it's all changed, now you can't switch on *Eastenders* without two gay guys getting married or something, you know! Yeah, those kind of romantic aspects that come from old-fashioned movies are very much models for us, aren't they? For a lot of the gay community, I do think, since then a lot of relationships are open now and it just keeps growing, the LGBT community, because you think, "right, we've got protections at work, we've got marriage equality", but things just keep growing. The younger generation have now got new terms for pronouns and things like that so it just keeps growing and evolving and changing so I don't think that they will be any time soon, any end to the consistent fight for those rights.

Karl S

Role model? No. Nobody at all, I mean there was Larry Grayson on television, John Inman, people like that. What was he called, he used to do the "ooh, you are awful but I like you" chap? It was all very camp. Danny La Rue, people like that. I knew I wasn't any of those things. I thought they were funny but everybody thought they were funny. I didn't identify with that, there were no real … there was nobody like Russell Tovey or anyone like that where you could say, "OK, I like Russell Tovey, he's a nice guy and he's an actor and he's doing his thing", there was nobody like that to look at. *Queer as Folk*, obviously, was amazing to watch. That was just … we lived for the next episode of that. That was fantastic and we watched it just the other week again and it is still fantastic. All that sort of Russell T. Davies type stuff, we look out for things that he's written and suchlike. Films, and in London the theatres, the King's Head in Islington and such were always doing cutting-edge type productions and we would go along to those and some of the other theatres to see things. It was all quite exciting. There was no sort of stand-out thing apart from *Queer as Folk*, but yes, we watched the films and looked in *Time Out*, studying it line by line to see what's happening; the new bars that are opening or a play or a film or something to go and see. Of course there was lots going on in Brighton, the Komedia and the like, and they were putting on all sorts of different plays and LGBTQ stuff. Then we came here. Bit of a shock to the system really! Bit of a shock to the system and again, you've kind of got to work for it because in London you had *Time Out* and everything was listed there so it was quite easy to say, "tonight we'll go to such and such and tomorrow we will go to so and so". In Brighton it was the same and here, because there isn't anything, you've got to say, "right, we've got to look for it and we have to go through Amazon and see what films are coming out", and sort things out that way. You have to

Karl S

work harder at it I think. That's the thing when you're in the country or when you are on an Island like this, you have got to work at it, you can't expect it to come to you because it won't.

Robert

TV was all stereotypes wasn't it? I mean you had Mr Humphries in *Are You Being Served?* You had Danny La Rue and people of that sort, Larry Grayson, who I remember saying in some interview or other, "oh, but it's so wrong". Then why are you camping it up?! There were no positive role models for homosexuals when I was young, no, or at least if there were I can't think of any. That came much, much later. Again, I would say in the last 20 years. There were homosexuals: Kenneth Williams, Charles Hawtrey. That was acceptable because they were funny. But watch them do anything, they wouldn't be so funny then, they'd be up in court! That's why Williams in his diaries, of course, wrote as he did, "came home, did the traditional", but he would never, ever do it in public and he had a hell of a life as a consequence. I empathise with that, he was older than I am by some thirty years but it didn't change all that much, certainly down here, until about twenty years ago.

Karen

I just kept it all to myself really because when you are growing up in the 70s and 80s there were no role models. You had Martina Navratilova – well, I am so not a lesbian if that's it. Or it was all the women at Greenham Common with donkey jackets and with political attitudes and monkey boots. There were no role models that I could associate with, that I could say, "that's just like me".

Julian

No [role models], I think it was more just from music and things like that because I was always into music and I wanted to be a music producer, a record producer. It didn't really occur to me when I was younger because I got into listening to a lot of progressive rock which I got from a friend. My dad never listened to any music, he wasn't into music at all, he was very 'un-musical' so I didn't really get any musical influences from the family. Most of the music that I got into was classic rock and progressive rock and things like that, plus I was very interested in being a record producer. My heroes then were Stock,

Aitken and Waterman because I was more interested in them than in the acts that they produced. But it wasn't until later that I realised that the music scene was something that being a female I couldn't have, because all my heroes and role models and musicians were all men. Even when I started playing the guitar and started learning music skills when I was probably about thirteen or fourteen, I wanted to look for female role models and I really wanted there to be female role models. I was so disheartened because out of all the music that I liked and out of all the artists that I liked there were enough women that you could count on one hand. It made me feel really bad and it still does. I lost hope in doing this as any sort of career because even when I was looking for bands or groups or the things that I could do, I knew that the majority wouldn't want me anyway and this was really obvious when I started playing drums and guitar. I used to think, "oh, I'd really like to join a band", but then I did actually know damn well that because I was a female, people wouldn't want me. I always sort of hoped that people wouldn't notice that I was a female. That just sounds really stupid because it is so obvious and it is the first thing anybody notices about someone but the women that were in music had to be a certain way and behave a certain way and dress a certain way and all my musical role models were men so in the end I just sort of felt it wasn't worth the effort. So I was just really, really disappointed about that.

Lucy

Well, my main role model is… do you know Rebecca Root? The actress. She was in a sitcom called *Boy Meets Girl*. She was the first trans actress. Everything has happened in the last five years. But trans visibility seems to have snowballed. I just think it's amazing. I've got a friend, she's eleven years old and she looks up to me because she's trans. One of my best friends, it's her granddaughter and she's thinking about transitioning. I think it's lovely because her parents are so supportive, grandparents are so supportive, the school is supportive, she's…you know, she went to her first Pride this year. I think it's just absolutely fantastic for her, like I say, lovely for her.

Robin

There can't have been [any role models] that strong because I can't remember them! Certainly, the blokes I was unfortunately in love with, but they wouldn't be a role model. I think Ian McKellen was very good for me and Christopher Isherwood, I've read his books, very much so, I couldn't believe how open he was; so, Christopher Isherwood meant quite a lot. And I came upon, a bit later I suppose, Edmund White, things that I've read. I've never been much into pop culture to be honest. Not at all really. My musical tastes are almost 100% classical really. I mean you do get gay … I suppose I was very aware of David Bowie, obviously, and I thought, "gosh, how can he … somebody actually", he was bi really wasn't he, David Bowie I think? Anyway, it was something. I suppose I mentioned passingly, Proust. He was actually and a whole lot were, of course, and then you began to realise the sonnets of Shakespeare, some to a dark lady, some to the young gentlemen, and that encouraged me like anything. A lot of it was literary really.

Sydney

There's lots of people I've admired. Writers, musicians and artists generally, so, yeah, with my background being in art. One of the things I look back on and think, "oh yeah, almost all of these people are women". Full trans stuff, I don't know, I have read lots of individual stories of people, their coming outs and things that struck a chord with me. I don't know if there's any people … there were no trans celebrities when I was growing up really. There's people later on that I respect, I have a lot of respect for people like Munroe Bergdorf and Laverne Cox and people like that. Yeah, I find women who pushed things forward and stuff and be loud and I was a big fan of a punk musician called Poly Styrene, the X-Ray Spex, she kind of went a bit weird later on in life and joined a cult and stuff but her kind of music and look at stuff was huge, like a big thing for me. I remember when she died. I was really, really kind of cried all day. And like I already said, various women artists … oh my God, my brain has frozen. There's a woman who … This is why I am embarrassed because I have a really bad problem with names, I always have to look things up on the internet! I can't tell you someone is my role model and then tell you that I can't remember what she's called, can I?! But that's true.

It's the art, she did all this feminist art, it is quite iconic and it is photographs and text, bold text and black and white and red colours. There's this one and it is this woman's face and it is cut in half and half is negative and it is just this slogan, 'your body is a battleground'[27]. I think of that quite a lot. She was talking about abortion and things like that and I think it maps very well to the trans debate a bit as well because so much is contested about the medical care and things and our genitals and things like that. Barbara something I think. And other artists and writers like Ursula Le Guin, the science fiction writer, an absolute icon of mine. I very much admire her writing and thought and stuff. Loads of people. Not just women, it's writers. In terms of role models, no one specific, not specific, I mean specific people. Obviously I am still trying to come to accept my identity as a woman so for a long time admiring women seemed like there was something elicit or weird about it because I have always been very interested in feminism and stuff but I was like, "do I have a right to be interested in feminism, or to call myself a feminist as a 'man'"? These are questions I ask myself.

---

[27] *Untitled (Your Body is a Battleground)* is an iconic 1989 silkscreen portrait made by artist, feminist and activist Barbara Kruge

HEALTH AND WELLBEING

Franko Figueiredo-Stow

The World Health Organisation, in 1948, defined health as a state of complete physical, mental and social well-being and not merely the absence of disease or infirmity[28].

Our interviews and the past two years of research have uncovered two main topics under the theme of health: the first being that mental-health issues were, and still are, a common occurrence in the LGBTQ+ community, and the second that there is still a lot of progress to be made in providing medical support to LGBTQ+ individuals.

Stonewall produced a Health Report in 2018 which has found that 'LGBT people are at a higher risk of experiencing common mental health problems than the general population'[29]. Many of our interviewees explained how experiences of discrimination and harassment in day-to-day life, rejection from one's family and friends, and being subjected to hate crimes or just the fear of not being accepted can have a negative impact on their mental well-being[30].

LGBTQ+ health projects on the Island and the access to healthcare by LGBTQ+ individuals has been a rollercoaster journey. Access to healthcare is a challenge for many in rural communities, but for rural LGBTQ+ individuals, those challenges are multiplied. Over the years, sexual orientation or gender-identity-based groups faced increased isolation due to anticipated, internalised, or enacted stigmas. Stigma, and the fear it produces, are ingrained early on for LGBTQ+ individuals. A government report from 2017 indicated that 70% of respondents with a minority sexual orientation said they avoided being open about their sexual orientation to strangers (including health services) for fear of a negative reaction from others'.[31]

---

[28]Adam Felman. 'What Is Health?: Defining and Preserving Good Health', *Medical News Today* (MediLexicon International, April 19, 2020), https://www.medicalnewstoday.com/articles/150999#what_is_health.

[29]Chaka L. Bachman and Becca Gooch, 'LGBT in Britain - Health', Stonewall, April 17, 2019, https://www.stonewall.org.uk/lgbt-britain-health.

[30]Caroline Diamond further expands on this topic in the book's next part entitled 'Suicide'.

[31]Government Equalities Office, 'National LGBT Survey Research Report', www.gov.uk, July 23, 2017, 33 https://assets.publishing.service.gov.uk/government/uploads/system/uploads/attachment_data/file/721704/LGBT-survey-research-report.pdf

I could not write about LGBTQ+ health without expanding on the stigma that originated from the legislation adopted in Germany in 1871 in which homosexuality moved from being a sin or a crime to being recognised by medics as mental illness and which gave rise to the medical development of treating homosexuality as a disease of the mind [32].

Oscar Wilde, during his imprisonment, petitioned for release in 1896, whereby he attempted to use the conceptual realm of mental illness, rather than spiritual illumination, to escape from the constraints of legal classification as a criminal.[33] Those found not guilty by virtue of insanity might be released to the care of a private doctor, as Wilde requested, but they were more likely to be detained in an asylum for the rest of their lives.[34] Wilde could not shed the fear that illness had led him into criminality and that he was, in the language of the time, a 'criminal lunatic', since in that letter he came to conclude that 'desire at the end, was a malady, or a madness, or both'.

A National Opinion Poll extracted from the *Daily Mail* in October 1965 stated that '63% of people polled disagreed that homosexual acts in private should be criminal, although 93% believed that homosexuals were in need of medical or psychiatric treatment'.[35]

Over a century later, we still encounter individuals who hold such beliefs; some psychologists and psychiatrists still hold negative personal attitudes toward homosexuality. Extracts from oral histories at the end of this article show these LGBTQ+ individuals have had difficulties when visiting their GP, sometimes resulting in an inappropriate referral to mental health services.

I should point out that, during our research, we haven't unearthed any significant health activities directly aimed at the Isle of Wight LGBTQ+ community pre-80s.

---

[32]Jeremiah J. Garretson. *The Path to Gay Rights: How Activism and Coming Out Changed Public Opinion*. New York: NYU Press, 2018. 69-95.

[33]Oscar Wilde. *The Letters of Oscar Wilde*, edited by Rupert Hart-Davis. London: Rupert Hart Davis, 1962, 423-511

[34]Ralph Partridge. *Broadmoor: A History of Criminal Lunacy and Its Problems*. London: Chatto and Windus, 1953, 86

[35]https://blog.nationalarchives.gov.uk/sexual-offences-act/

The 80s UK HIV epidemic prompted a number of government health initiatives, with the Isle of Wight receiving substantial funding towards sexual health awareness and prevention projects. *The Isle of Wight County Press* reports:

> Being a popular holiday destination the IOW attracts people from all over the world, including areas where there is a greater prevalence of HIV infection. It is therefore essential to continue to educate and inform everyone who is sexually active both about the HIV virus and about how we can avoid being infected by it. Education of young people remains a priority and there are initiatives in place to continue to develop this.[36]

Previously, in 1986, the World Health Organisation, had added further clarification to its definition of health to:

> a resource for everyday life, not the objective of living. Health is a positive concept emphasizing social and personal resources, as well as physical capacities.[37]

In November 1991, the Isle of Wight hosted 'Sharing the Challenge', its first World AIDS Day event heralding a new era for the Island in terms of recognising and supporting its LGBTQ+ community.[38]

Above ∧ *Image of volunteer wearing a 'Captain Condom' campaign T-shirt, circa 1994. Courtesy of Karl Love.*

In 1992, a switchboard for people wanting help and advice on homosexuality was set up by the Island Lesbian and Gay Group. It was estimated the Island had a population of approximately 12,000 people who identified themselves as LGBTQ+ and Ms Pamela Vinnycomb, Health Promotion Adviser and district HIV prevention coordinator, supported the creation of a switchboard as part of the Health Authority's duty to promote messages about sexual health and offering advice to prevent the spread of sexually transmitted diseases and Aids. In an interview with the *Isle of Wight County Press*, Vinnycomb said: "We are also thinking of the emotional health of people who are anxious about their sexual identity. This has an enormous spin-off in mental health."[39]

In 1993, The health commission announced its 'Captain Condom' campaign as a versatile initiative, which is employed in a variety of settings to get messages across and provide information.

> Through Captain Condom we are able to approach young people, the tourist population, working establishments, prisons, the gay community. Further education settings, and the general public through popular public events[40]

By May 1996, the Island's lesbian and gay switchboard is reported to have taken its 3,000th call since it was first set up. An interview with one of the switchboard volunteers reveals: "Most callers are in the thirty to sixty age range, many feeling lonely and isolated, unable to admit their sexuality to friends and colleagues".[41]

From then on, we would see a number of initiatives such as the Students Health Advisors Group (SHAG), the Island Gay and Lesbian Youth Network (IGLYN), the Switchboard became the WightOut Helpline promoting LGBTQ+ awareness through social events, newsletters and a dedicated website[42], and as Anna Murray, one of our contributors explains "the switchboard, the newsletters, the social gatherings were a major lifeline, even for the most anti-social of us, because being around other gay people made you felt like home more than anything. It felt safe and although not without drama, it was a place to be yourself."[43]

---

[36]'Campaign to Halt Spread of Aids', *Isle of Wight County Press*, November 26, 1993, sec. Healthwatch, 56.

[37]Adam Fellman, 'What Is Health?: Defining and Preserving Good Health', *Medical News Today*, MediLexicon International, April 19, 2020, https://www.medicalnewstoday.com/articles/150999#what_is_health.

[38]Kay Marriott, Speaking Out, Gay Men and Lesbians on the Isle of Wight Write about their Lives and Early Experiences. Isle of Wight: Delta Press,1997, 5

[39]'Helpline for Gays Gets Health Authority Cash', *Isle of Wight County Press*, November 13, 1992, 16.

[40]'Campaign to Halt Spread of Aids', *Isle of Wight County Press*, November 26, 1993, sec. Healthwatch, 56.

[41]'Callers Keep Gay Switchboard Busy', *Isle of Wight County Press*, May 10, 1996, 44

[42]'www.iowgayguide.org.uk - Redirection Service Provided by Easyspace', www.iowgayguide.org.uk - redirection service provided by Easyspace, accessed September 20, 2020, https://web.archive.org/web/20050307053351/http://www.iowgayguide.org.uk/.

[43]Anna Murray, email message to author, August 15, 2020.

In 2006, WightOut stopped, as funding dried up and the Isle of Wight LGBTQ+ Golden Age came to an end. For the next decade, the Island was barren in terms of initiatives geared towards the community, both funded and voluntary.

In 2010, the Medical Association's LGBT Companion to Healthy People booklet highlighted the need for more research to document, understand and address the factors that contribute to mental and physical health in lesbian, gay, bisexual and transgender communities. The Institute of Medicine pointed out that most studies on LGBT people have been conducted among adults, with a modest number on adolescents, yet there has been comparatively less attention on LGBT elders. The 2018 National LGBT Survey commissioned by the UK Government Equalities Office reveals that 'only 8% of respondents were over 55 years old'.[44]

From 2010 onwards, we observed a rise in complaints towards healthcare providers. This is confirmed by Stonewall's Unhealthy Attitudes research with healthcare providers and 'revealed that LGBT people face discrimination and lack of understanding of their specific health needs when accessing services'. Ten years on, and LGBTQ+ people continue to face similar barriers in accessing healthcare treatment.[45]

Unsurprisingly, the strains of living a 'closeted' life put too much pressure on one's health and one could say that, in many cases, lack of health, as defined by WHO, and being queer go hand in hand.[46] Records show that LGBTQ+ youth are four times more likely to commit suicide than their heterosexual counterparts.[47] Existing research suggests that homophobic, biphobic and transphobic bullying remains a problem in schools. Furthermore, widespread assumptions in educational institutions that students are heterosexual and cisgender leave the specific support needs of LGBT students unaddressed.[48] More than half of individuals who identify as transgender experience depression or anxiety.[49] It's a gloomy point to make, but it makes sense that we, the LGBTQ+ community, have struggled disproportionately.

From 2015 onwards we also observe a rise in homophobic attacks, both locally and nationally; and in this context, it seems natural that the Pulse massacre in Orlando has had such an impact on the LGBTQ+ Island community, igniting them back into fight mode, and proving to be the unlikely catalyst for the Isle of Wight's first ever Pride event.

Happiness, measured as positive health, is not homogenous within the LGBTQ+ community. Many LGBTQ+ individuals, elders in particular, not only fear societal discrimination, but may also have to contend with health providers who have limited knowledge about specific LGBTQ+ general medical needs. We need a holistic health system that provides an environment free of prejudice, only then we will succeed in preserving the mental and physical health of all LGBTQ+ patients.

(From Left to Right) ∧
Trish (deceased), David Barnard and David Froud on the floating bridge helping to promote the Isle of Wight Gay Guide, 1997. Courtesy of Karl Love

[44]Battle, Juan, Jessie Daniels, Antonio (Jay) Pastrana, Carlene Buchanan Turner, and Alexis Espinoza. 'Never Too Old To Feel Good: Happiness and Health among a National Sample of Older Black Gay Men', *Spectrum: A Journal on Black Men* 2, no. 1 (2013): 1-18. Accessed July 28, 2020. doi:10.2979/spectrum.2.1.1.

[45]Chaka L. Bachman and Becca Gooch, 'LGBT in Britain - Health', Stonewall, April 17, 2019, https://www.stonewall.org.uk/lgbt-britain-health.

[46]World Health Organisation, www.who.int. Accessed July 28, 2020.

[47]Alexander Leon, 'LGBT People Are Prone to Mental Illness. It's a Truth We Shouldn't Shy Away From', *Guardian* (Guardian News and Media, May 12, 2017), https://www.theguardian.com/commentisfree/2017/may/12/lgbt-mental-health-sexuality-gender-identity.

[48]Nathan Hudson-Sharp and Hilary Metcalf, National Institute of Economic and Social Research, 'Inequality among Lesbian, Gay, Bisexual and Transgender Groups in the UK: a Review of Evidence', July 2016, 10-17

[49]Chaka L. Bachman and Becca Gooch, 'LGBT in Britain - Health', Stonewall, April 17, 2019, https://www.stonewall.org.uk/lgbt-britain-health

EXTRACTS FROM ORAL HISTORIES

Robin

I have forgotten to tell you, after I had been to Tavistock, I had a bit of a breakdown again and this was locally, it was in Portsmouth because I lived in Portsmouth for a while. So I was sent down to the mental hospital as it were and they put me on drugs, hormone ones, do you know what I mean? Anyway, I began to start developing breasts and I was impotent and all the rest of it until I thought, "no, I won't go along with this". But I mean, you see, that again was the case. You would treat, the liberal position was that you were ill. 'That' was liberal! And, of course, people were very understanding, the professionals by that time unlike my bloody GP who chucked me out of the surgery, the professionals were very understanding because you were a sick man. When I say there has been such a journey, there really has.

Karl S

I think the problem comes, and I think this is where having a gay community or maybe coming from Pride, Pride can really help, is if you're a couple or if you're a single person and you are very happy with that, fine. But if something happens, maybe to your partner or to yourself and suddenly you find that maybe your relationship has broken up or something or you've got some sort of illness or something, actually, where do you go? How do you get help and support? Now obviously there are the standard ways that anybody would do it but if you are a gay person maybe you need different kind of support, different kind of help, and where do you go to? How do you access that sort of thing? I suppose personally I probably wouldn't have a problem, I know enough, I know who to go to and what to do but I think a lot of people might have a problem so it would be quite good if there was some sort of, somewhere that they could go, some group that they could contact.

Anonymous

There was a sexual health awareness group at school, at college, and I came up with the name to be honest because I remember voicing the name and it was called the Student Health Advisors Group (SHAG). It was good, we gave out free condoms and we advised on pregnancy and safe sex and it was really good, and on general health really, mental health and coming out and things like that. It was really useful, really helpful and I worked with a friend on that and it was a really nice group. She, we met Prince Charles at one point, I don't know if I've told you this story?

Prince Charles came to the Isle of Wight and he greeted lots of different groups and he came up to our group and me and my friend were standing next to each other. He saw that our badges or our T-shirts said SHAG and he said, "so what does this 'shag' mean then?" And we were like, "oh my God, Prince Charles has just said 'shag'", so we were obviously really quiet and I said, "well, we sort of help and advise on teenage pregnancy and safe sex and general health", and he said, "does it help?". And we said, "well…". And he said, "I guess not", and then he walked past us. So, yeah, it was quite funny. But it was just a really nice time and I felt really supported in that group because it was about being out and being supported. I left the Island when I went to university when I was 21, and then I did come back every now and then.

So that would have been when I would have been nineteen or twenty or something like that. To be honest, I mean I can't remember if that Prince Charles incident happened before coming out or after coming out… So I think I am pretty much sure I was out before I was in the group.

I can't remember how it all came about. It just came about, there were two health advisors there and one of them was very friendly and we just became friends with her and she started talking about having a group and getting a group together. My friend was one of the people who was very close to her and then we just started work on it. There was a sexual health hut on campus and it would be manned by us volunteers and it was good so it was quite useful.

Yeah, I remember moving off the Island. I should say a bit about what life was like when you are gay on the Island because I haven't mentioned that. There wasn't really anywhere to go, there was an LGBT switchboard, telephone I think it was, but it only operated on certain days of the week at certain times like two hours every Monday or every Wednesday, something like that.

Sydney

The GP is, she is tolerant, understanding, she has worked with me on it, also kind of doesn't know what she's doing and they screwed up my referral initially and so delayed it by several months which was … It's spilt milk now, but that was kind of, I am pretty confident that wasn't malice, it was just not quite understanding the procedure, that's partly a problem of the way the system is set up as much as anything. GP has been pretty good, they have worked with the private people and I have a shared care agreement so basically my private endocrinologist suggests the medicines that I should be prescribed and the blood tests that I should have to my GP who then orders them which means I don't have to pay private fees for everything just for the consultations which does keep the costs down quite a lot. It still sticks. It does stick in the craw a little bit that I have to resort to private medicine at all.

I think there's the matter of training and it's an institutional problem because trans medicine isn't covered in basic medical training. It is seen as a very specialist and arcane sub-area and even then there is no specialist, specialism. You can't just go to medical school and learn about trans medicine in this country. It is something that people pick up, they are trained on the job at gender identity clinics normally or somewhere or in one of the private practices. So, yes, there is a kind of lack of, there is a lot of timidity about it because of the environment in the press, the sensationalism I think about it, GPs. GPs on paper are perfectly within their rights to prescribe cross-sex hormones to people, they can't obviously refer people for surgery or anything like that but if someone comes in and they are trans they are perfectly … Now some, very few, GPs will do that because it is so controversial and because they are liable for anything that might happen, I think they're scared. It is not normalised in any way. There are some schemes to possibly kind of make it that but as I say, there is all this sensationalism in the press unfortunately.

Karl L

It was clear that they wanted me to be here on the Island. I was obviously, I won't say a commodity, but a resource that they hadn't had and even today we still struggle from the same scenarios with recruitment that we had then, which was about importing people with the skills necessary in order to move the Island forward into the future. At that time, you know, I was one of the few people that was working specifically in education; I was never into the treatment of HIV, so my job was to come and do detached work on the streets to try to support young people in terms of having safer sex, but looking at their sexual health and well-being generally, their drug use and so on, to try guide people away from those kind of behaviours so that society was protected more and that people could take their own, you know, look after their own health.

Oh, I can remember some almighty rows in Cowes about bringing Captain Condom on the High Street because of the sailors that come from all over the world and what images might be sent back to Australia and New Zealand of us giving out condoms and having Captain Condom on the High Street and the fear of tarnishing the reputation of Cowes.

I mean, my job at that particular point was quite complicated because I had just arrived on the Island from the point of view of health and where there were some hidden agendas if you like, within that, which was, one, my sexuality because my sexuality could be used to inspire and support those who were not out and reach a hidden community so I always described that the LGBT communities at that time were hidden in the shadows.

Well, not just the indigenous population but some of those who had moved here and there's definitely a difference, in my opinion, between the indigenous population of the Isle of Wight and those who are Overners who have come from the mainland, like myself, we were much more out. You have to remember that David and I came from a large, well, David came from a large industrial town, I was in a much smaller place called Elland in West Yorkshire, in the Pennines, so I've got a very thick accent, Yorkshire accent, which I have never tried to lose, that's part of who I am. We were going out clubbing and pubbing on the gay scene in Manchester and Leeds and so we had access to everything and anything and then we came to this island and discovered that there was nothing. But do you know something? We had so much fun, we made so many friends, it was a very different way of being out.

So, the hidden communities were very much about word of mouth and people knowing. On a small Island like this word spreads quickly. If somebody new comes out in Newport within a couple of months everybody knew that there was somebody new in Newport, particularly for those people who were single or on their own that was, you know, "we'll go up there and we'll have a look around and we'll try and meet this person to see if that is a potential partner for the future". So, it was all about that networking and it was very different from Manchester and so on. We were literally 20 or 30 years behind.

So the first part of my experience, the first two years I worked for the Youth and Community Service here and then for the remaining six years that I was here, I worked for health directly in a gay men's role that we started, the Island's Gay Men's Health Project, at that time of which there were some volunteers, in fact there was about eight or ten volunteers, and that continued up to more or less when I left because things changed quite dramatically then because of the funding. So the economic impacts on HIV then saw the money going away from prevention and into treatment.

Caroline

I met Anna Murray, can't remember how we got in touch, but anyway I think somebody said, "you need to talk to Anna", and we saw an advert on Facebook for funding from an NHS project called My life, a full life, and I said to Anna, "look at this, shall we apply for it and see if we can get some money up together and set up a group?". We applied for £3,300 and we put a two-line advert in the *County Press* in the personal column for lesbians and bi women on the Island and we set up a group which we called Wight Lesbians which seemed like a good idea at the time! Not so much now when I get bank statements through the post with Wight Lesbians on the front! Anyway, we set the group up and the funding provider said that they wanted us to meet at various locations on the Island so we met in Newport, Ryde and Cowes.

The thing that shocked me most was the number of women who had mental health problems ranging from quite severe to loneliness, isolation and anxiety. I think nearly all of them had some level of anxiety and I really felt a lot of empathy for certain people within that group because I just thought, "I would hate to feel like that", because I remembered how emotional I'd felt coming out and how fortunate I was that people were OK.

So we worked really hard at getting the group going and we met up in Cowes and Newport and met some really interesting people and formed some great friendships and I just found it really rewarding, just getting to know these people, hearing their experiences, looking at the different relationships; some were married, some were single, and that kind of evolved on its own and that was just before Pride. Now people actually ring up. I had a situation recently where somebody phoned me and they said, "we know two lesbians; one of them is not very well and the other one is her carer and would you be able to talk to them because they don't know anybody?". So it's been fantastic to be able to get in touch with people.

David

I belonged to a group which met in St Mary's conference room and it was a group for gay and lesbian people to come together to seriously talk about the way things were going on the Island. It was there to socialise as well and at the time, I think we had been going for about eighteen months and the person who was chairman of the group had been approached by Pam Vinnicombe, because then the Health Authority was run by commissioners. It wasn't like it is now but it was a group of only four commissioners who ran the Isle of Wight health service.

One of those was Pam Vinnicombe, [who] was very interested in developing things that had been happening on the mainland for all gay people; there was a phone line where if anybody had a problem they could phone this number. It was like Samaritans in a way but this was for gay people. She approached me and said that she'd had been asked to start a group call the Isle of Wight Gay Men's Health Workers Group. Would I be interested in developing this myself and choosing a number of people to join it? So I said, "well, let me just think about it first", because I had a business that I was running anyway. I agreed, and said, "well, it is only going to be for a few hours certain evenings of the week", and that's how we went.

Pat Vinnicombe was absolutely fantastic. Virtually anything we asked for we got. She developed all the systems that went into these groups, and she was there supporting them with money and advice and various other things. She paid for me to go on a course to become a bereavement counsellor. The lady who took that post was based at Mountbatten Hospice, but she taught it to nurses in Portsmouth University. I think she was called Wendy. She's gone now, a long time ago. She was such a nice lady.

There were only two of us doing this course; it was thirteen weeks and she kept saying to me, "you shouldn't really be doing this", and I said, "why do you say that, Wendy?" She said, "well, if you were in a monastery for seven years and you were counselling people for…", I said, "yes but not for HIV and AIDS", I said, "this is what I was going to be counselling people [for], anybody who had lost somebody through this illness", and she said, "you are still counselling people". She said, "I feel I am learning more from you because I didn't know anything about gay people really and I am gaining knowledge from you". I said, "well, we are working together, that's all that matters". But she was ever such a nice lady. So I did that, the Health Authority paid for that.

Then I found a group of certain people who are friends as well, that we could all work together, and there were about six of us. We used to meet either every two weeks or every month and we used to go to discos and we used to have our boards there telling everybody to be safe and we had condoms and lube to give out and so that was the start of the Gay Men's Health Project.

I went over to Netley four times a year with Mark Rees, the support officer, and we went to Netley to the training centre for the Hampshire Police and we used to meet all the others there. There used to be about a hundred of us altogether including police officers. So apart from being a great social day out in a sense, it was good with the groups we were talking to and taking ideas from them about how they worked. So they funded that as well. She funded so many different things. It was all lost once it became what it is now because they were needing the GUM[50]. It's had its budget slashed by half; you can't run a hospital like that, you can't just cut departments in half. So yeah.

I can't think of how long I did it and then Karl became the Gay Men's. He was then the AIDS Gay Men's Health Worker for the Isle of Wight. We worked with him and he was our leader [and] in that sense. I used to go out and do outreach work with him twice a week. He was so funny! He was from my part of the world, Yorkshire, as well, he used to say, "I'm sure I should have been at a meeting this afternoon. I can't find my diary". As I was getting into the car, because in those days there were filofaxes. So as I was getting into his car, I said, "what's that under that rubbish on your back seat?", "Oh, it's my diary!". [Laughs] He said, "no, I didn't miss a meeting actually". But his memory was appalling!

But we got through. He was very nice and he did his job, that was the main thing. … The thing I should have said that I was very proud of was: I had a letter from a Chief Constable which said that I was out working for the Health Authority and he was aware of the work that I was doing and if any officer stopped me they had to have good reason for it and let me carry on with whatever work I was doing.

Julian

I think I just feel very disappointed because I listened to a lot of people who I believed knew better than I did. I remember going to my doctor when I was about thirteen or fourteen and saying that I should have been a boy. I didn't really know what the words were, whether it was transgender or transsexual or whatever because nobody ever talked about it. I did know vaguely about people having gender reassignments but it was always kind of treated as a joke. It was always a little bit more acceptable for girls to be tomboys than boys to be cissy boys, so I thought it would be OK. But my doctor basically said, "oh, you're a pretty girl, just go and get on with your life and don't talk such rubbish!" It was the same with my school counsellor who I tried to talk to. I don't know if he thought this was the cure or what it was but he said, "oh, you'll have a baby in a few years and you'll forget you ever said it". So I just felt like those were people who were older men who I should have been listening to but I think as it turned out, I was right and they were wrong.

---

[50]Sexual health clinics are often referred to as genitourinary medicine (GUM).

Julian

I hope that whoever our next MP is [it] somebody who is very open-minded and we can get over a lot of the bigotry and a lot of the institutionalised bigotry. I hope that people within the health service can be properly educated so that they don't ask awkward questions. I would really like it if the Island had its own gender identity clinic because the gender identity clinics like Tavistock have got two-year-plus waiting lists and now there's such an influx of people, especially young people, who aren't getting access to the services. I think that it needs to be opened up across the board, across the whole country. It's quite worrying that I know from other people who are trans who have had to educate their doctors themselves and have had to sort of explain things to doctors because that hasn't been part of their training. Even triage nurses and people at the hospital don't know the basics, they don't know the basic terminology or anything and I think that there has got to be a lot more open dialogue on that and a lot more education. So hopefully that's a good thing for the future of the Island.

Michelle

I still was a closet crossdresser but I met a very brilliant and very helpful lady as a counsellor, not a psycho-sexual counsellor but a counsellor, who every week I used to see.

I became quite a vocal supporter of transgender rights in both direction male/female and female/male and I eventually became, I was elected to be Chair of the transgender stakeholder group and we began to set up a proper group in the NHS to address the issue because before it had been a Catch 22, it disappeared into a black hole and there was a vast waiting list of people who couldn't move further. So we managed to get that going. I then got onto the escalator at that point at Charing Cross [Station, London] because there were those services in Wales. I was put on the, well, it wasn't a waiting list, I guess it was a waiting list but I wasn't on it for very long and I went through the process of transition. That was on the Island and I used to drive over. It started, really my initial intention was to see what I could do to rebuild my marriage because we were separated but we didn't divorce for quite a while. But then it moved on to discussing my gender dysphoria, what turned out to be a diagnosis of gender dysphoria, which took about six years under the system, the system didn't really work very well.

Well, after I first came out it was six years before I got onto the escalator, it was about three years after that. Escalator is a term I am trying to use because there was, call it a waiting list, it was not a waiting list, there was a totally inadequate system for dealing with transgendered people. It just didn't properly exist. There was a lot of words spoken but very little activity and by then I had got my PhD and discovered that if you're a doctor you get listened to in the NHS and you get more access and I was able to get a lot more access and eventually I had started the process, I was part of starting the process of addressing this issue. That's still going on and I have a good friend who still lives in Wales with her partner and she is still at it, she's even got an MBE for it, but she deserves it because she is more diligent than I ever was, but we got it going.

Perhaps I should say, dealing with the Isle of Wight, having been in the NHS or inside of the NHS in Wales, I was interested in what resources there were on the Island and the NHS trust here talked about transgender and the rest of it and I tried to get involved. I used to come down from Wales and spend the night and going to meetings and all the rest of it but it was, I think, much more of a talking shop and it was put together more as a device to get chartered status for the, they don't call it chartered, what do they call it? The NHS Foundation Trust status, and that eventually dropped and I sensed that the support for the LGBT side of things evaporated. It has come back a bit now but I am not entirely convinced that the NHS trust here on the Island is particularly supportive of transgender and probably not of LGBT people in general.

There's a much more comfortable, reassuring community atmosphere about the Island. Yet, you'd think, wouldn't you, that actually in our sort of enlightened ways in 2019 and our acceptance of everybody being individual, we are more able to be ourselves now.

SUICIDE

Caroline Diamond

> Inside you, you just do not see the point of anything. Nothing has flavour or savour. Nothing has any meaning. Everything is just hopeless.[51]

Stephen Fry talks about his numerous suicide attempts, the most recent in 2012 on the *Art of Change: Nothing Concrete* podcast. He was diagnosed with bipolar disorder aged 37 and is a poignant reminder that mental health does not discriminate, indeed as our research shows, anyone can suffer.

In our oral history interviews and research we found links between suicide and fear of coming out, suicide and facing homophobia within both families and the wider community, suicide and poor physical and mental health, and suicide due to loss of a partner.

It would be impossible for us to document the suicide of every LGBTQ+ person on the Isle of Wight in the last 100 years. This is partly because the sexuality and gender of the deceased is not always documented and acknowledged for reasons of privacy and sensitivity. Also because that person may not have been 'out', their sexuality may have been hidden for fear of rejection or because of their own self-loathing and internalised homophobia. Karl Love, the Island's first Sexual Health Worker and Isle of Wight Councillor explains: "There are times particularly pre self-acceptance of one's own sexuality and when leading up to coming out that many LGBT people feel suicidal."[52]

LGBTQ+ people, particularly young people, are at a higher risk of completing or attempting suicide than straight people. There are also links with suicide and mental health issues, another area where LGBTQ+ people suffer worse than their heterosexual counterparts. Is it any wonder when sex between men was illegal in England and Wales until 1967, until 1981 in Scotland and 1982 in Northern Ireland? In 2015, a survey carried out by mental health charity PACE found that LGB young people were almost twice as likely to have attempted suicide as their heterosexual counterparts, with transgender people even more likely to have tried to take their own lives. As Alan Downs stated in his book *The Velvet Rage*, "Back in the 1950s and 60s, it wasn't all that unusual to hear that a gay man had committed suicide. For a lot of men, it was just too disgraceful."[53]

"The NHS is weighed down by people, mostly heterosexual, suffering from illnesses that are self-inflicted by behaviour of medicating painful feelings …

regardless of sexuality"[54] writes Matthew Todd in his book *Straight Jacket*. However, it is fair to say that LGBTQ+ people often have difficulty finding appropriate services and support where they can voice those difficult feelings and be heard. In a paper entitled 'Why Identity Matters', Peter Molyneux, Chair of Sussex Partnership NHS Foundation Trust interviewed LGBTQ+ young people, and writes: "So many of them talked about the anxiety, the depression, the trauma, the shame and the body dysmorphia they experience. The link between poor mental health and being LGBTQ+ for today's young people was really strong and worrying".[55] Peter talked to a number of LGBTQ+ NHS patients about their experiences. I was struck by how 'don't ask, don't tell' they said the NHS can still be. Visiting an LGBT patient group and talking to a young man who had attempted suicide when his boyfriend had left him, he said that when he tried to talk to his nurse about this the reply had been: "I am not interested in your private life". One psychiatrist said 50% of attempted suicides in one London Borough were by young people who are LGBTQ+, adding: "We know that because we know our patients".

We cannot pinpoint suicides where the individual's sexuality was rumoured to be a factor but not recorded. This would not be appropriate and could potentially 'out' the individual and be upsetting to that person's friends and family. However, our findings, over the period of our research and interviews, reveal that suicide is a far more common issue than we were aware of and often goes unreported. For men, being gay was illegal until 1967 and often taboo for many years after and any suggestions of homosexuality are not evident in public records until very recently.

[51] Chris Gunness, *The Art of Change with Stephen Fry - Episode 1*. Barbican, accessed September 22, 2020, https://www.barbican.org.uk/read-watch-listen/the-art-of-change-with-stephen-fry-episode-1.

[52] Karl Love, email message to author May 26, 2020.

[53] Alan Downs. *The Velvet Rage: Overcoming the Pain of Growing up Gay in a Straight Man's World*. Cambridge, MA: Da Capo Life Long, 2012, 60.

[54] Matthew Todd. 'Straight Jacket', in *Straight Jacket: Overcoming Society's Legacy of Gay Shame*. London: Black Swan, 2018, 12.

[55] Peter Molyneux, *NHS Choices*. NHS, accessed August 20, 2020, https://www.england.nhs.uk/blog/why-identity-matters/.

Mark Fear and Alan Stafford lost their lives to suicide and, unusually, their stories were clearly documented revealing that they had same sex partners. Mark Fear was former television newsreader Kenneth Kendall's partner. Tragically, Mark took his own life less than a year after Kenneth's death. In a suicide note he had written, Mark said "I simply cannot face the future without Kenneth".[56]

Life can be lonely in rural, isolated areas like the Isle of Wight with the absence of professional or community support networks and finding a same sex partner can be difficult. The suicide of 58-year-old Alan Stafford was another example of someone who, like Mark Fear, felt that his life was over when his relationship broke down. Alan jumped off a Wightlink ferry and, such was his determination, he tried once and slipped over before attempting again, climbing the railings and jumping to his death. Alan's sister said:

> Alan had suffered from depression since he came out as gay as a child but had a long term relationship as an adult… They were together for twenty five years, then he left him for a woman and I do not think he got over it. We think he felt that there was nowhere he could go with his life at his age. Being gay, it is not easy to find a partner.[57]

In 2020, some LGBTQ+ people are thriving, enjoying visibility with the parity of same sex marriage and the efforts of certain employers to be mindful of equality and diversity. There are also many retired LGBTQ+ people, usually couples, who have moved to the Isle of Wight and live happy lives albeit discreetly. Instead of using their years of experience to challenge homophobic views and to support younger generations, they feel that they have 'done their bit' and their years as LGBTQ+ activists are over. However, on the Isle of Wight, the need for acceptance within the family and community and signposting to effective local support services, where available, is still glaringly apparent across the LGBTQ+ spectrum. Our research found that some young Isle of Wight LGBTQ+ people were victims of homophobia and transphobia and moved to the mainland to urban areas with increased support and the proximity of social groups. As interviewee Karl Love explains:

> Older age can be challenging for LGBTQ people when living an independent life becomes more difficult. Having lived in a same-sex relationship for many years there are limited choices about living in a retirement home where some people may feel that they have to supress their sexuality in order to appease others. I hear less these days about

this aspect of LGBT life, being forced back into the closet in order to live in close proximity to others, that can cause depression particularly where there may be no close relatives or friends having lived a long life.[58]

At the time of writing, in July 2020, Ben Hunte, the BBC's LGBT Correspondent, produced a report on suicide within the LGBT community.[59] During the lockdown, due to Covid-19, from March to July 2020, he found that calls to charities across the UK from LGBT individuals were higher than ever before. The lockdown exacerbated feelings of isolation and meant that access to community groups, services and medical appointments, in person, was extremely difficult. In another example of the plight of LGBTQ+ people being ignored, Ben Hunte reports 'Two years ago the government said it would launch a "rapid review" to look into LGBT suicide and create a plan to look into LGBT deaths – it hasn't.' In the same report, Ian Howley, CEO of Health, Equality and Rights organisation LGBT Hero, highlighted how this absence of recorded data erases the traumas experienced by the LGBT community saying 'Unless we are counted, we don't count'.

40 County Press Friday, February 1, 2019

Man leapt overboard from ferry

By Ben Mitchell
Press Association

WIGHTLINK ferry passengers were screaming as a man deliberately leapt overboard to his death, an inquest heard.

Alan Stafford, a port crane operator at Portsmouth Naval Base for BAE Systems, suffered from depression and had 'never got over' splitting with his partner.

He jumped from the St Cecilia ferry, which left Portsmouth for the IW at 10.30am on August 29 last year.

DS Marcus Mills, from Hampshire Constabulary, told the Portsmouth inquest: "A male was seen to jump from the ferry into the water. Coastguard and other craft assisted with the search but no body was found."

The Bembridge RNLI lifeboat assisted in the rescue effort, together with the Portsmouth RNLI and Portsmouth and Hillhead Coastguard Rescue Teams.

The body of 58-year-old Mr Stafford was spotted in the water on September 3, about a quarter of a mile from Gilkicker Point at Gosport, and recovered by a Ministry of Defence Police boat.

Witness Victor Thanayagam, who was travelling on the ferry with his family, saw Mr Stafford jump over the railings.

He said: "I saw this guy coming, the first time he tried to jump, he slipped, the second time he jumped, he climbed over the railings.

"My wife and everyone was screaming. It was very fast."

Mr Stafford's sister, Katherine Upsall, told the hearing her brother had suffered from depression since he came out as gay as a child but said he had a long-term relationship as an adult.

She said: "They were together for 25 years, then he left him for a woman and I do not think he got over it."

She added: "We think he had felt there was nowhere he could go with his life at his age. Be-

ing gay, it is not easy to find a partner.

"We knew him as happy Al and I feel we should have picked up on that."

Coroner David Horsley's post-mortem examination showed Mr Stafford died as a result of drowning and concluded he had taken his own life.

He said: "Quite clearly he had enough and intended to his life. We must recognise emotional and health issues. I think he was suffering long-standing depression.

Mr Stafford, from South had five sisters who have tribute to him, saying he lovely and a 'kind-hearted and caring' man.

a's sister ferry, the St Faith, coming into [W]ashbourne.

[56]'Former Newsreader's Partner Took Own Life', *Isle of Wight County Press*, November 1, 2013, sec. News, 11.

[57]Ben Mitchell, 'Man Leapt Overboard from Ferry', *Isle of Wight County Press*, February 1, 2019, 40.

[58]Karl Love, email message to author, May, 26, 2020.

[59]Ben Hunte, 'Lockdown: Suicide Fears Soar in LGBT Community', *BBC News*, July 2, 2020. https://www.bbc.co.uk/news/health-53223765.

EXTRACTS FROM ORAL HISTORIES

Robert

I was eighteen in '68, that's when I went to a grammar school and I was quite ill at that time, I had a form of epilepsy so that [I] didn't do a lot, and I got depressed. I got very depressed and I had to leave the school because I couldn't handle it any more because the travelling was exacerbating my physical problem and that made me more depressed than ever and I couldn't sleep and, of course, there were these young men, you see, and well, I was more interested in them, I'm afraid, than in Chaucer.

Well, eighteen-year-old young lads are very attractive. I was too knackered basically to really attend to my academic studies. I had to travel eleven miles in a bus every day and if you are not sleeping very well to start with that is very difficult to do and you've got epilepsy on top of that. So I was fairly shattered and I had a few fits at school and the only good thing about that was that I tended to be picked up by great big hulking sixth formers! Otherwise the charm of it eluded me, so I left and I spent two years more or less catatonic suffering from depression. I got over that eventually but I committed, attempted, obviously had not committed suicide otherwise I wouldn't be here, but I had attempted to commit suicide at the age of sixteen and I think, I am pretty sure, that was because I knew that I just wasn't ever going to be like the rest of them. I took a lot of phenobarbitone but fortunately, or unfortunately, not enough.

Karen

So I was obviously married to a man at that time, we got married for tax reasons but we weren't even in the same bed. He had his room and I had mine. I'd had boyfriends but nothing had happened because I never wanted it to. I'd been to the doctor at one point because I was really concerned and they sent me to The Gables to try and sort out why I didn't want to sleep with men and she said either I was a lesbian or I had been abused as a child. And it's like, "oh God, I can't be a lesbian and I don't remember being abused as a child", so that didn't really help. No one suggested I might be gay.

Then I worked with a girl called Donna and I knew that she was gay because we just used to talk. I don't know what happened, I was getting to a point where something was going to have to happen. I need to sort this out. She

Robert

lent me a book called *Curious Wine*, and she just said, "read this, it'll either make your mind up one way or the other". I read it in a day and a half and I remember closing that book and thinking, "crap, I'm gay!". That's how I got to where I was.

Well, I had seen the doctor because, obviously the man that I married, Garth, we had started off as girlfriend and boyfriend but it didn't really pan out because I couldn't, and I was really concerned that I had got to my early twenties and I had never slept with a boy and it was like, "God, I must be frigid, there's something wrong with me". I went to see the doctor and she said, "this is a mental health issue, we will just refer you to The Gables to see a psychologist, there may be a mental block". I remember, I only had one session with her and she asked me lots of questions and she said, "have you ever considered that you are a lesbian?" I'm like, "no, no!", "Well, maybe you were abused as a child, tell me about your childhood". So I did but, no hang-ups or anything about that. It was like, yeah, just she didn't really explain; "you're a lesbian or you have been abused as a child". No advice really. I didn't have another session and that kind of left more questions than answers for me.

When I came out I had a lot of mental health issues, I couldn't really cope with this change and I ended up, well, I was going to go and drive my car off the end of Ryde pier I was so depressed, not living anywhere in particular, sofa-surfing and I ended up being referred to the mental health team and I had a clinical psychiatric nurse and that helped a lot. I just couldn't cope with the fact that you think you're straight and you grow up very straight and then, whoa, there are, how do I do this? And I just cracked. But that was a really difficult time but I kind of got through that and I think coming out can affect your mental health.

I ended up going to a community psychiatric nurse. So that was, I think, that was a big impact because I just lost it. I had moved out of the house, I didn't have anywhere proper to live which probably didn't help. I was getting into sticky situations with women that I shouldn't have been getting into and suddenly all the rules had changed. It was like a storm, the perfect storm of all these things going on in my life just created this massive, "I really can't do this".

The Isle of Wight at that time had really good mental health services and I saw my GP and she was really nice and I think within two weeks I'd had a referral up to the clinic and I had eight or nine sessions with this woman and she was really good. It was the whole parent/adult/child balance that had gone wrong. Yeah, coming out as gay caused me a lot of mental health issues.

It was a very difficult time, but the mental health services, you know, I saw my doctor, I told my doctor I had come out as gay and she said, "that's fine, you're allowed to change your horse halfway through the race", she was really understanding and she said, "we'll refer you to the community psychiatric nurse", and she was really understanding, my doctor.

Sydney

Even though I had sort of gone back into depression/denial, I think because I was not trying not to actively explore it, actually a lot of things did fall into place in my head in my late twenties and I kind of got over a lot of the neurotic circular things I had been going through. What precipitated my, there was a big emotional crisis type thing that made me ... A friend of mine, a very good friend of mine killed himself in early 2018. He went missing and they found his body months later. He wasn't living on the Island, he was living up in Bristol at the time. He was a very good friend of mine and my wife so I know that he, not necessarily about gender and so on, but I know he had a lot of struggles about his own identity and things and I didn't really know why, no one really knew, he kind of snapped. He was okay, I remember talking to him on the phone around Christmas time and then he killed himself, on like, January 13th or something like that. It just kind of, it made me feel, it made me think that something had to, feeling kind of like, "God, what if that happens to me? What if I, by all this repression and all this kind of thing, but not facing up to what I know?". Because, I now had this sense almost in the back of my mind that I had actually decided I was trans and that I would transition but it was at some point way in the future when, I don't know, when technology, when you could just jump in a booth and nano-machines would remake you! Back to the sci-fi stuff, you know!? But I sort of thought (a) what if this repression makes me snap like he did and do something horrible to myself? And (b) that made me think about the fragility of life and how absolutely terrible it would be if, you know, I could get knocked down by a bus tomorrow and I would never have been me, essentially.

Robin

And there you are. What it meant is that I came back, I went very much into myself. I can remember going to the GP, this was the early 60s, 1963, because I had some physical problems there and he just told me to get out – I was filthy and get out – and that was how it was in those days you see. I mean if it was another place I expect there would have been enlightened people. This is in the 60s.

And a bit later I did get referenced because I was upset. I was banished, you know. Yes. And, oh yeah, I did get some help. I went to the Tavistock Clinic, I was referred there. Very briefly I went and lived in London and stayed for a while and, of course, I bloody fell in love with a young man. I know it is all very muddled up, but anyway, a friend of mine here. Oh no, I met somebody when I was hitching back, a girl, Shona, and we would stay together, no sexual relationship. We became good friends and went up and visited with a friend and she was married to a Sri Lankan man and I became very involved and eventually moved in with them. There was about fourteen of us there, most of them were Sri Lankan, and I fell in love with this really gorgeous young man called, funnily enough, Garvin, not Gavin! And that was alright, I thought Garvin was great but he didn't think I was great and then I went completely bonkers and took an overdose. I was whizzed off to some ghastly hospital in Surrey, one of those old-fashioned loony bins. He was so hostile to me and I came back to the Island. So I had a series of rather unfortunate incidents. He wasn't gay at all I don't think, anything but.

Jude

I know at one point, and this is why I don't ever buy a *County Press*, the police apparently, the building was a single storey building with an apex roof and apparently two coppers, two male coppers, were laid up as far as I know, this is what I was ... were laid in there. I think there was probably holes in the roof so they could see down, see where people were, two of them going into a cubicle. I think that was, sorry, I feel quite choked at this, they had a really successful raid one night and got thirteen people arrested. Later on one or possibly two committed suicide, there was another guy who was married, he lived just up from me in the village, married, got three daughters, and they put, the *County Press*, and there was a newspaper called, maybe it was called the *Isle of Wight Post*, I'm not sure, I can't remember, I should because we used to deliver it to all the shops in West Wight. They published full names of the blokes, they published in inverted commas 'addresses' but the guy up in our village, they said he lives with his wife and daughters in a cottage with roses around the door in Newbridge. The cottage was called Rose Cottage. I mean he didn't top himself, his wife and his daughters still were his wife and daughters, whether they had known beforehand I don't know. But he did actually die of cancer a few years later which my belief is that that situation won't have helped or will have helped the cancer, let's say. I think they were the ones at Carisbrooke but there were other cottages as well that were well known. I am not sure if they were all arrested in one place or in several but those two papers printed details that identified the blokes. Like I say, two guys, one killed himself, the other one I think killed himself or may have just had a blooming good attempt. I know one of them died because he was one of my older son's partner, her family knew this guy.

LGBTQ+ PEOPLE IN THE *COUNTY PRESS*

David E. Bennett

Up until the 1990s, the only mentions of homosexual behaviour and homosexuality are derogatory, condemning it as lewd, divisive, deviant and socially corrosive. From the early 1990s onwards homosexuality begins to be talked about more regularly in the *County Press*, but only in the last six to seven years has the tone warmed towards homosexuality and the message changed to one of supporting minorities and celebrating diversity. Letters and reporting of LGBTQ+ issues have become much more frequent; articles and letters longer and more nuanced, and reporting more supportive over the time period investigated.

The newspaper has only consistently celebrated diversity since 2017. One columnist has written articles openly supportive of LGBTQIA+ people and social inclusion and articles have celebrated children being taught about sexual diversity. Almost all the articles report on interviews, letters, events and groups supporting social inclusion.

A brief chronology of LGBTQ+ reporting: 1918 to 1969

With the exception of the debate within the Anglican Church, no records of sexual diversity could be found until the 1950s. All reporting in the 1950s, a time when sex between men was a criminal offence of gross indecency, consisted of brief factual reports of criminal convictions taking place on the Island. Several chillingly dispassionate accounts describe how repeat offenders were sentenced to psychiatric treatment to 'cure' their persistent homosexual tendencies and repeated criminalised sex with other men. All were very brief. Only one mention of homosexuality could be found from the 60s. Entitled 'Queers, weirdies, hippies, tramps,' it reported on the moral horror expressed by local residents in the immediate aftermath of a music festival on the Island.

Helpline for gays gets health authority cash

1970 to 1979

The 70s featured a number of brief articles chronicling criminal offences including youths arrested for singing "He's a queen" as a policeman passed by. Articles ridiculed a play featuring a gay Richard I, a voter wrote to the local paper to express shock (and wanting to warn others) that they had discovered their MP was a liberal who believed in equal rights for homosexuals, and one indignant local wrote to tell the world that it was no wonder that society was 'in chaos', its moral backbone having 'collapsed into "tolerance".'

1980 to 1989

Reporting on stories involving homosexuals in the 80s was more expansive, its stories now containing more salacious detail. Tales focus on crime, violence and murder. While homosexuality is being more freely discussed, the reporting appears somewhat slanted, continuing to associate homosexuality with crime.

1990 to 1999

The debate on the morality of homosexuality reached fever pitch in the 1990s, with both church and secular parties recycling the old arguments fiercely in the Letters section on numerous occasions. HIV and AIDS reporting on the Island appears to have started in 1990, almost a decade later than in many parts of mainland Britain. Across the 1990s, there was a trend in HIV/AIDS reporting that perpetuated the 'othering' of gay and bisexual men, seeking to portray them as deviants who spread HIV/AIDS and perpetuating harmful myths that sexuality and promiscuity were lifestyle choices freely and wilfully entered into that should be disregarded or suppressed. But there was also a greater appreciation that all these social problems were driven by social conditions, loneliness and a lack of support and information. Once again, the lay clergy led the way, pointing out the dangers of the public and medical profession's trend in blaming the HIV pandemic on promiscuous homosexual men, and pointing out that all were at risk, however infrequently they were unfaithful. Other clergy were quick to blame the usual suspects – immigrants, deviants and other undesirables – for the latest social disease.

Throughout the 1980s and 1990s, we find a war among churchmen and members of secular authorities between progressive people who embrace diversity and who prioritise public and mental health and those who either wish for religious absolutism or who continue to maintain, in the face of ample scientific proof to the contrary, that homosexuality is a lifestyle choice and therefore undeserving of any additional support. Only in 1990 does reporting become more sympathetic to gay people, outside letters from social activists and the clergy. An article sensitively and in some detail chronicled the last days of a 'gentleman gay' whose life ended in suicide following prolonged loneliness and depression, apparently triggered by a verbal attack from a man he knew in a local public house.

While evidence for the existence of the Lesbian and Gay Switchboard has been found dating back to 1972, it appears not to have been featured in (or at least was not indexed by the archive search engine for) the *County Press*

County Press   January 16, 2009

Force is top of the cops for gay staff

By Richard Wright
richardw@iwcpmail.co.uk

GAY PC Michael Hughes has spoken of his pride at Hampshire Constabulary being ranked the UK's top force for lesbian, gay and bisexual employees.

Hampshire police were second overall in a national league table, behind Lloyds TSB.

PC Michael Hughes, 26, who is based at Newport Police Station and has served for three-and-a-half years, spoke of the support he received from the force.

"When I first thought about joining the police, I thought my sexuality might have been a problem. But I'm very pleased to say it hasn't," he said.

"Hampshire Constabulary has been very supportive throughout my career, as have my colleagues, and I've never had a problem speaking to my sergeant, inspector or other line managers.

"What also put my mind at rest is from day one, the vari-

their roles explained in detail. Working as a PC is the first job I've done where I've felt comfortable enough to be 'out' to my colleagues.

"In previous jobs, this has always been difficult. If you're not 'out', it's near impossible to talk about life at home with colleagues and friends at work and you have to choose your turn of phrase very carefully.

"To be open about my sex-

much easier because I'm happier and being happier motivates me to get on with the job of being a police officer: to catch, disrupt and detect criminals.

"I've had nothing but support from my colleagues about my sexual orientation. If anything, I'd imagine it's almost seen as a skill area. Historically, the gay community has been distrusting of the police and it can be difficult for members of our com-

munity to speak to the as they're fearful of th tion they might receive

"As an openly gay of I or anyone else can make a report to the then that makes it but for the constabu whole.

"This is why the services are there, s actively reflect the c ties we serve."

PC Michael Hughes, above, said he had received full support from the force. CONTRIBUTED

Hampshire police is top gay-friendly force

OR the fourth year running, ampshire Constabulary has ken pride in its gay-friendly edentials.

It has again been named as the 's top-performing police force lesbian, gay and bisexual peo-

fter coming fourth overall in th year's Stonewall Workforce ality Index for all types of nisations, chief constable Alex hall, who is the force's leader

on fairness and equality, said: "It is testament to our commitment to providing an excellent service to every one of the diverse communities we serve.

"Naturally, having come second nationally in previous years, we would have liked to have made the top spot this time round but to remain in the top five, and to do so consistently, is a huge achievement.

Although H

ulary's score increased this year, the competition was also much tougher.

A record number of organisations entered the index, up from 352 in 2010 to 378, and the threshold score to get into the top 100 increased from 66 to 73 per cent.

For a fourth year, Hampshire Constabulary's officers were permitted to march in th

event in August by police officer, police community support officer and police staff, led by assistant chief constable Steve Dann.

Police say they have policies in place that make sure staff can do their job to the best of their abilities and lesbian, gay, bisexual and transgender people who com

Member Hampsh Constabu take part the Bright Pride para CONTRIBUTED

until 1992, when it controversially received funding from the local health authority at a time of severe financial deficit. The local authority defended the spending as necessary for mental and sexual health support, while a former Medina Mayor tried to appeal and stop the funding on the grounds that it was unaffordable and morally wrong to support a charity he maintained was set up to promote a deviant lifestyle choice.

The Island Gay and Lesbian Switchboard attempted to draw up a list of gay friendly hotels on the Island in 1993 but found hoteliers almost universally afraid of being inundated with enough gay people to alienate their usual clientele but not enough to book every room in their hotel, reducing their profits. By 1998, the Switchboard had produced its own gay tourist guide for the Island to counter the popular impression that no gay scene existed there. While the Island's tourist information service declined to distribute the Switchboard's guide, it supported the effort to increase tourism to the Island.

2000 to 2019

From the late 1990s onwards, articles began predominantly to celebrate diversity and increasingly so in the last decade, although it was only from the turn of the millennium onwards that any mention of trans people appears.

As recently as 2016, *Diva* magazine reported that the Island remains 'conservative and old-fashioned'. In the same year, a local councillor took it upon himself at a meeting at which pigeon droppings at public toilets were being discussed to make a sweeping statement that homosexuals, paedophiles and pigeons were nuisances that could all only be dealt with by employing toilet attendants. Although more gay and lesbian support and activity groups now exist, there are no longer any gay clubs or bars on the Island.

Such attempts to assert a spurious association between homosexuality, paedophilia, immorality and criminal behaviour has been made many times over the decades, mostly by local politicians and in letters from the general public. These attempts have variously sought to demonise homosexuals, to prevent them from adopting children or taking on positions of responsibility. Perhaps this is because once homosexuals hold positions of trust, it becomes obvious that they are largely trustworthy and more similar than different from the public at large.

There is some evidence that while there have long been voices raised from all quarters in support of equity and inclusion, in keeping with other isolated communities the Island remains comparatively conservative. LGBTQ+ people on the Island reportedly continue to feel isolated. In some quarters at least, it appears that the more things change, the more they stay the same.

The great church debate

From the 1960s onwards, the Anglican and other Protestant churches are shown to have been very active in the public debate over the morals of gay rights (the recognition of bisexuality and trans people was still some decades away) in the *County Press*. However, an article from decades earlier showed that the Church of England had been threatening to tear itself apart over the moral debate over homosexuality for a much longer time.

In 1988, an openly homosexual Anglican priest made light of an already longstanding debate at the General Synod by suggesting that perhaps the Church of England should return to the biblical ethical ruling that lifelong celibacy was the natural and proper state for everyone. He felt compelled to withdraw his tabled amendment after it became clear the Church was about to take it so seriously that there was a real risk that it might tear itself apart in the ensuing debate. While this was reported in the *County Press*, it was not clear whether the priest was from the Isle of Wight.

The debate raging from the 1960s into the 1990s was fiercely contested by ordained priests, the lay clergy and other impassioned locals. Erudite and learned priests painstakingly constructed arguments for the liberalisation of Christianity and argued for a socially inclusive and equitable society that celebrated diversity and afforded everyone equal dignity and rights.

Brittle, waspish and occasionally venomous, the conservative counter-arguments all relied heavily on the conviction that the Bible could not and should not be interpreted, because it was necessary for the Church to hold any moral authority that the word of God thus revealed to be unquestionable and free from interpretation. They were in turn accused of driving the faithful to humanism and making the Church appear archaic, bigoted and irrelevant to the modern world.

Lay supporters of conservative values strongly resented suggestions that the Bible comprised books that contradict one another, were written from different perspectives, for different purposes and at different times. They claimed instead, at times verging on moral hysteria, that were the Church to sanction consenting homosexual acts in private, it would void its authority to speak out on any moral issue. It was claimed that if society were to sanction the same, that all morality and law would be rendered immediately and universally null and void, after which chaos would reign. Perhaps these same people look at the world of today and feel vindicated that their prophecies have come to pass, and that the appearance of ongoing religion, morality and law is only illusory. Churchmen themselves were, on the whole, more conciliatory than their parishioners, albeit with several notable exceptions. Both sides routinely accused the other of poor scholarship and deliberately misinterpreting religious scripture.

Witnessing the immediate, impassioned and often very personal attacks these letters provoked, the reason these arguments were so carefully constructed and watertight quickly became apparent. The battles were frequently vicious, with priests who defended gay liberation having their fundamental faith, piety and required obedience to the canonical articles of faith they had sworn to uphold called into question. One reactionary made the familiar plea that they were in fact the oppressed party, condemning liberal priests with fundamentalist arguments while claiming in the preceding breath that they dare not be seen to judge anyone for fear of censure. This battle for the Island's soul raged throughout the twentieth century, drawing in priests, lay clergy and their friends from as far afield as London.

In 1999, the Anglican Church's opposition to gay adoption prompted a dismayed outcry and criticism from a local priest who supported the Children's Society's advocacy for gay adoption. He warned that such socially divisive religious bigotry would primarily hurt the children involved and argued that as a heritable trait, homosexuality was a natural state ordained by God and not – as had been traditionally assumed – a perversion condemned in religious scripture.

As in previous arguments, the liberal wing of the Church celebrated unfolding scientific understanding as a continuing revelation from God, with conservatives apparently maintaining that all meaningful communication from God had been suspended since the compilation of the Bible, pending the second coming of Christ. The latter position provides the comfort of complete and unwavering certainty at the cost of upholding ancient tribal judgements and beliefs over all subsequent human learning. As one liberal priest commented, the arbitrary selection of ancient judgements that support popular prejudices while other supposedly unquestionable truths are allowed to sink into obscurity has meant that the comfort afforded by fundamentalist belief invites unjustifiable and entirely avoidable bigotry and a wilful persecution of others.[60]

Winds of Change

The history of reporting on the Island, the role of Christians on both sides of the great moral debate on sexual mores and morality, and the slow but comparatively objective local reporting reflect politics elsewhere in Britain in the 20th century. On the Island, gay rights appear to have suffered more from a sustained lack of visibility that helped perpetuate the status quo and from selective reporting of salacious articles that associated gay people with crimes

---

[60]Rev. Hugh Wight, 'Acts of Perversion World away from Homosexuality', *Isle of Wight County Press*, February 4, 1994, 8

and violence than they did from any direct attack. It might surprise some that the church was so active and engaged on both sides of the great moral debate. Many of their letters from the 1970s still feel as fresh as if the newspaper ink was still wet.

Sadly, the Island appears still to be struggling to accommodate change. With a small population isolated by the natural moat of the Solent, the Island often feels like a world lost in time. The wheels of history feel as if they turn more slowly here. On these grounds, we might be cautiously optimistic that understanding and appreciation of diversity will increase over time. Many LGBTQ+ people on the Island today continue to feel isolated and lonely, networking online more than meeting in traditional bars and clubs, while some local politicians behave as if the last fifty years had never happened.

And yet, schools are teaching children to understand and celebrate sexual diversity. The experiences of the LGBTQ+ islanders who led local gay liberation are being recorded for future generations and the hidden LGBTQ+ history of the Island rediscovered. With more opportunities to travel, organise, and participate in global online communities, LGBTQ+ islanders are now citizens of the world as much as locals of a small island. Local journalistic reporting has become supportive and progressive.

Change has been hard won over many years, by both religious and secular allies as much or more than by LGBTQ+ people themselves. The fact that this project has been possible shows minds are now opening, and as journalist and writer Katharine Whitehorn observed, 'the wind of change … blows most freely through an open mind.' The LGBTQ+ community owes a sincere debt of thanks to all those who have helped us come this far, and to those who help us towards complete and lasting respect, dignity and equity.

COMING OUT

What We Talk About When We Talk About 'Coming Out'

Melissa Gilmore

It's a whole genre of videos on YouTube, a feature of almost every LGBTQ+ storyline on television and there's a whole day dedicated to it on October 11th each year. But what exactly do we mean when we talk about coming out?

It's frequently referred to like a one and done affair; the first time we knew it ourselves, the first time we told a friend, when we told our family. And often the discussion centres around these larger moments and ignores the little ways we come out every day. When I casually say 'she' instead of 'he' when I talk about whom I'm dating, I am coming out. When I choose to wear a pride flag badge out in public, I am coming out. When I listen to nothing but Janelle Monáe on repeat until my co-workers riot, I am coming out.

So, when we talk about coming out, are we talking about saying the words "I'm gay"? Or are we talking about the things we do and say every day to signal our identities? Each are equally valid ways to come out, but one is subtler than the other. Is the coming out question only reserved for the grand gestures? And that's to say nothing of the timeline conundrum!

When I first tell someone that I'm bisexual, one of the questions they'll ask me is when I came out and I find myself wanting to ask, "Which time?" I came out to myself when I was fifteen, my Dad when I was twenty and my grandparents when I was twenty-one. I came out at work when I was sixteen, then again at twenty-four, and again at twenty-eight. At age thirty, I came out in an entirely new way as non-binary. If I say I've been out for fourteen years or six months, both of these things are true. So what is the answer? What do they want me to say?

The truth is, coming out is a much more complicated and continuous process than we're led to believe – it's a discussion we have to have with ourselves our whole life. I come out nearly every week. Whenever I make conversation at the bus stop, meet a new friend or start a new job, I have to decide whether to come out or not. We live in a strange world indeed when we have to weigh honesty against safety, a little voice in the back of your head asking "Is it safe? Is it safe? Is it safe?" like a skipping CD. Is the relief of not having to edit my words and behaviour worth any homophobia I might encounter?

There is a trend in certain areas of the media (both mainstream and LGBTQ+ publications) to criticise closeted members of the LGBTQ+ community for choosing not to come out. 'You need to be a good example for young people', 'keeping secrets is bad for your health', 'you're lying to everyone'; these are just a few of the reasons why people are being told to announce their identity publicly. Being able to be open about your identity is a blessing and a relief that I hope everyone in our community gets to experience – on their own terms.

In my coming out journey, I've been met with love and acceptance or at least tolerance on all fronts. Yet despite this incredible luck, every single time I've come out there has been a knot in the pit of my stomach and my pulse pounding in my ears because I know that my experience has been exactly that. Pure luck. Being able to make the choice of whether to come out or not is a right that we all should have as members of the LGBTQ+ community. Defining your own boundaries and advocating for yourself is one of the healthiest and most honest things a person can do, which I believe sets an excellent example.

I dearly hope that one day we live in a world where coming out is a source of nothing but joy for our community. Until that day, we get to choose how and when and with who. Whether we're leading the parade at Pride or remaining fiercely private, we each get to define what coming out means to us.

In this chapter, I have created a timeline of sorts, tracking coming out in Europe and America from the beginning of the notion through to the present day. I hope to offer both a history of the concept and its various meanings, as well as a little historical context on how society and certain events have shaped it. While I will draw from events and experiences outside of the United Kingdom, my focus will be on British history as it has the most relevance to the experiences of the personal histories of those from the Isle of Wight.

The First Coming Out

In 1867, German lawyer Karl Heinrich Ulrichs stood up in front of the Association of German Jurists to speak about same-sex attraction and protest the laws in place against it. As recounted by Ulrichs in his pamphlet 'Gladius Furens' (Raging Sword), he read from a prepared speech. In the speech, he referred to a motion previously proposed by himself and a collaborator which requested the removal of anti-sodomy laws:

> This proposal addresses the revision of the existing material penal law, especially and finally to repeal a specific unlawful paragraph in the

penal code handed down to us from past centuries. It is directed to abolish this paragraph of the penal code which discriminates against an innocent class of people.

[...] Gentlemen, the matter also concerns a group of persons whose size numbers in the thousands in Germany alone. Many of the most eminent and noble persons have belonged to this group of men, which is discriminated against for no reason other than [...] because creative nature has implanted in this group a sexual nature which is inconsistent with the common, vulgar one...[61]

Since 1864, Ulrichs had been publishing pamphlets under a pseudonym, in which he wrote that queerness was a natural state of being which should be respected. At this point in his life, Ulrichs had already lost his career due to his homosexuality becoming fodder for gossip and had taken the step of telling his family of his attraction to other men. The publication of his work was faced with public outrage and legal threats, with both Ulrichs and his publisher, Heinrich Matthes, being taken to court over the pamphlets. Viewing queer people as a class of people with shared interests and sensibilities was considered a fairly radical belief in nineteenth-century Europe. In an 1864 letter to newspaper *Deutsche Allgemeine*, Ulrichs wrote:

By publishing these writings, I have initiated a scientific discussion based on facts. Until now the treatment of the subject has been biased, not to mention contemptuous. My writings are the voice of a socially oppressed minority that now claims its rights to be heard.[62]

While his attempts at removing legal barriers for LGBTQ+ people ultimately failed, it is through Ulrichs' work that the western understanding of homosexuality as a distinct orientation – rather than simply 'deviant' acts – came to be developed. Indeed, the term 'homosexuality' would not exist until 1869 when it was created by Karl-Maria Kertbeny five years after the publication of Ulrichs' first anonymous pamphlets.[63]

---

[61]Karl Heinrich Ulrichs (translated by Michael A. Lombardi-Nash). *Araxes: a Call to Free the Nature of the Urning from Penal Law*. Los Angeles: Urania Manuscripts, 1981), 11-14.

[62]Liam Stack, 'Overlooked No More: Karl Heinrich Ulrichs, Pioneering Gay Activist', *New York Times*, July 1, 2020. https://www.nytimes.com/2020/07/01/obituaries/karl-heinrich-ulrichs-overlooked.html.

[63]Robert Beachy. *Gay Berlin: Birthplace of a Modern Identity*. New York: Knopf, 2015, 51.

Writing prior to Kertbeny's work, Ulrichs created the term 'Urning' to describe gay men, drawing from one of the myths about the birth of Aphrodite. The myth went that she was born from seafoam created by the Greek god Uranus' genitals being thrown into the ocean. What Ulrichs noted was that in this version of Aphrodite's birth 'the female played no part', hence his inspiration for 'Urning'.[64]

Another Greek myth about Aphrodite's birth goes that she was the daughter of the Greek god Zeus and the Oceanid Dione. Therefore, Ulrichs created the term 'Dioning' to describe heterosexual men and 'Dioningin' to describe heterosexual women. Ulrichs later expanded his terms, using 'Urningin' to describe lesbians, 'Uranodioning' to describe bisexual men, and 'Uranodioningin' to describe bisexual women. 'Zwitter' was the term he came up with to describe intersex people.[65]

In modern times, we have many words with which to self-identify our sexuality. For Ulrichs and his contemporaries, using a term to define their sexuality was a new and freeing concept. In his early pamphlets, Ulrichs advocates for 'Urnings' to reveal themselves and claim their right to be treated equally to 'Dionings':

> The class of Urnings is perhaps strong enough now to assert its right to equality and equal treatment. To be sure, a bit of courage is required. Fortified with the shield of the justice of their cause, they must bravely dare to come out of their previous reserve and isolation. Herewith let the ice be broken.[66]

In 1868, after his speech to the Association of German Jurists, Ulrichs began writing under his own name. This in itself was a revolutionary act, laying claim to his work on sexuality whilst also declaring to the public that he was – in his own terms – an 'Urning'. This is perhaps the first documented occasion of a person 'coming out' in our modern understanding of the phrase. In an interview, historian Robert Beachy is quoted as saying, 'There is nothing comparable in the historical record. There is just nothing else like this out there.'[67]

In his 1870 work *Araxes: a Call to Free the Nature of the Urning from Penal Law*, Ulrichs lays out his desire for legal equality plainly:

> The Urning, too, is a person. He, too, therefore, has inalienable rights. His sexual orientation is a right established by nature. Legislators have no right to veto nature; no right to persecute nature in the course of its work; no right to torture living creatures who are subject to those drives nature gave them.

The Urning is also a citizen. He, too, has civil rights; and according to these rights, the state has certain duties to fulfil as well. The state does not have the right to act on whimsy or for the sheer love of persecution. The state is not authorized, as in the past, to treat Urnings as outside the pale of the law.

[…] Uranian love is in any instance no real crime. All indications of such are lacking. It is not even shameful, decadent or wicked, simply because it is the fulfilment of a law of nature. It is reckoned as one of the many imagined crimes that have defaced Europe's law books to the shame of civilised people. To criminalise it appears, therefore, to be an injustice officially perpetrated.[68]

Ulrichs' work was influential for a number of sexologists. Richard von Krafft-Ebing, for example, cites Ulrichs in his pioneering 1886 text *Psychopathia Sexualis*, which led to his receiving letters from people who read about Ulrichs in his book. Krafft-Ebing later published a number of these letters in revised editions of *Psychopathia Sexualis*. One man wrote:

I cannot describe what a salvation it was for me to learn that there are many other men who are sexually constituted the way I am, and that my sexual feeling was not an aberration but rather a sexual orientation determined by nature…. I no longer attempted to fight this orientation, and since I have given my Urning nature freer reign, I have become happier, healthier, and more productive.[69]

By 1900, the term 'Urning' had entered German society and was commonly used describe gay men. It was even cited in the German encyclopaedias Meyers and Brockhaus in their entries for homosexuality. Notably, Ulrichs was cited by the ground-breaking sexologist Magnus Hirschfeld in his 1914 work

---

[64]Robert Beachy. *Gay Berlin: Birthplace of a Modern Identity*. New York: Knopf, 2015, 51.

[65]Salvatore Licata and Robert P. Petersen. *The Gay Past: A Collection of Historical Essays*. New York: Routledge, 2013, 106–107.

[66]Hubert C. Kennedy. *Karl Heinrichs Ulrichs: Pioneer of the Modern Gay Movement*. Concord, CA: Peremptory Publications, 2005, 70.

[67]Liam Stack, 'Overlooked No More: Karl Heinrich Ulrichs, Pioneering Gay Activist', *New York Times*, July 1, 2020. https://www.nytimes.com/2020/07/01/obituaries/karl-heinrich-ulrichs-overlooked.html.

[68]Karl Heinrich Ulrichs (translated by Michael A. Lombardi-Nash). Araxes: *a Call to Free the Nature of the Urning from Penal Law*. Los Angeles: Urania Manuscripts, 1981, 12-13.

[69]Robert Beachy. *Gay Berlin: Birthplace of a Modern Identity*. New York: Knopf, 2015, 43-44.

Homosexuality of Men and Women. Hirschfield is known for coining the term 'transexual' and was the founder of the German Institut für Sexualwissenschaft (Institute for Sexual Science). The Institute was open from 1919 to 1933, when the building and its archives were seized by members of the Nazi party. In 1973, a spiritual successor to the Institute was opened under the same name at Goethe University in Frankfurt. Its director, Volkmar Sigusch, called Ulrichs the 'first gay man in world history'.[70]

The Golden Age

By the onset of the twentieth century, Europe and North America were experiencing a population boom. With this came the growth of cities like London and New York, drawing in people from rural areas with the allure of money, work and anonymity. Such a concentration of people allowed homosexuals – as they were starting to be known – to more easily find each other, socialising via whisper networks and designated meeting areas.[71]

However, the spectre of Oscar Wilde hung heavy over the LGBTQ+ social scene in the early 1900s, particularly in London. The moral outrage triggered by his trial had yet to fade and police raids on known meet-up spots were frequent and brutal. Society was, to quote English writer and actor Quentin Crisp, 'stumbling about in search of a weapon with which to exterminate this monster [queerness] whose shape and size were not yet known or even guessed at'.[72]

Discretion was of the utmost importance in order to avoid prosecution and scandal. Unsurprisingly, it was during the early 1900s that Polari – a form of cant created from a mix of Romance languages, Romani and London slang – crept into the queer community in England's capital. It allowed a coded form of communication that those not versed in the language were unable to decipher. Dropping a Polari word or two into conversation to see if someone understood could be a way to figure out whether someone was also queer.

This period also saw the beginnings of research into medical treatment for the trans community. Between 1917 and 1918, American physician Dr Alan Hart who was assigned female at birth, began hormone therapy and underwent gender confirmation surgery at the University of Oregon Medical School before legally changing his name to Alan. He married his wife, Inez Stark, in 1918 and in an interview with a local paper declared that:

[I felt] happier since I made this change than I ever have in my life, and I will continue this way as long as I live [...] I have never concealed anything regarding my [change] to men's clothing [...] I came home to show my friends that I am ashamed of nothing.[73]

It was around this time that the terms 'transvestite' and 'transexual' were coined by German sexologist Magnus Hirschfield.[74] In 1919, he founded the Institut für Sexualwissenschaft (Institute for Sexual Science), which became the first clinic to regularly treat transgender people.[75] He carried out numerous gender confirmation surgeries for trans patients during this era, including overseeing the confirmation surgeries of artist Lili Ebe – now known from the book and film *The Danish Girl*.

It was in the 1920s that began what is considered by some to be a 'golden age' of LGBTQ+ culture which lasted well into the 1930s.[76] Cafes, bars and pubs had begun opening up in abundance in the major cities of Europe and the USA during the First World War, catering to the demand created by the flood of soldiers and sailors looking for places to let off some steam. That a number of these establishments catered to the LGBTQ+ community is unsurprising. As historian Peter Ackroyd put in in his book *Queer City*, 'in the face of death and destruction, an instinct for self-expression, or liberation, became visible.'[77]

After the War ended, a number of those who had found themselves in a city decided to stay there, taking advantage of the opportunities there. It was during the 1920s that the expression 'coming out' entered into the vocabulary

[70]Volkmar Sigusch, Karl Heinrich Ulrichs. *Der Erste Schwule Der Weltgeschichte*. Berlin: Verlag rosa Winkel, 2000, 20.

[71]At this time, there was little public awareness of those who experienced attraction to multiple genders, let alone the terms to describe them. 'Homosexual' was something of a catch-all term for those who experienced any same-sex attraction, regardless of their attraction to any other genders. It is used here for the sake of noting contemporary terminology.

[72]Hugh David. *On Queer Street: a Social History of British Homosexuality 1895-1995*. London: HarperCollins, 1998, 130.

[73]'Dr. Hart Explains Change to Male Attire'. Albany Daily Democrat (No. 259). March 26, 1918, 1.

[74]As covered in our chapter on the evolution of language throughout LGBTQ+ history, terms have changed substantially over time. 'Transexual' was – and remains for some – the preferred term for those in the trans community, while 'transvestite' is now largely considered to refer to cisgender men who cross-dress. However, I am conscious that others now consider it to be outdated or offensive. Going forward I will be using the terms 'trans' or 'transgender' except where 'transexual' or 'transvestite' is the term used in quotes.

[75]Robert Beachy. *Gay Berlin: Birthplace of a Modern Identity*. New York: Alfred A. Knopf, 2014, 211.

[76]Hugh David. *On Queer Street: a Social History of British Homosexuality 1895-1995*. London: HarperCollins, 1998, 129.

[77]Peter Ackroyd. *Queer City: Gay London From the Romans to the Present Day*. New York: Abrams Press, 2018,196.

of the LGBTQ+ community, although primarily used by gay men at this point in time. The purpose of the phrase was also somewhat different to how we use it today. Historian George Chauncey explains:

> Like much of campy gay terminology, "coming out" was an arch play on the language of women's culture – in this case the expression used to refer to the ritual of a debutante's being formally introduced to, or "coming out" into, the society of her cultural peers. … A gay man's coming out originally referred to his being formally presented to the largest collective manifestation of pre-war gay society, the enormous drag balls that were patterned on the debutante and masquerade balls of the dominant culture and were regularly held in New York, Chicago, New Orleans, Baltimore, and other cities.[78]

The distinction between coming out then versus now was a matter of audience and purpose. For gay men in the 1920s, coming out was a communal action, achieved either through entering gay society at large or being initiated into gay practices via a partner, the latter more commonly being referred to as being 'brought out'.[79] The intended audience for this entrance into the gay culture of the time was other members of that culture, rather than mainstream society. The idea of the 'closet' had not yet entered into LGBTQ+ parlance at the time and would not do so until the 1960s. So rather than 'coming out of the closet', coming out into gay society was not so much about revealing your sexuality to yourself and others but about 'proudly joining a community'.[80] One man commented, "What was criminal was … denying it to your sisters. Nobody cared about coming out to straights."[81]

It is important to note that even during an age in which LGBTQ+ culture flourished and the community was more connected than ever before, the threat of prosecution, blackmail and violence remained prominent. Ackroyd states:

> [LGBTQ people] were subject to a level of prejudice and intolerance not seen before in Western history; entrapment, imprisonment and sudden police raids became familiar characteristics of London. … If you were arrested, taken up and taken away, your family, your employment, your prospects were gone in an instant.[82]

The coming of the Second World War began a strange period for the LGBTQ+ community. In the face of yet another massive loss of life, among blackouts and the threat of imminent invasion, a certain loosening of the moral hysteria around sexuality took place. Oral historian Allan Bérubé quotes Stuart Loomis, an American army psychologist during WWII, as saying:

People sort of did with their gay behaviour what they did with everything else. Which was to take chances and risks and try to enjoy things because who knows where you might be sent tomorrow.[83]

In London, the blackouts were something of a boon for the LGBTQ+ community. Low visibility and few people on the streets offered an advantage for the queer community, for whom avoiding being seen was so important. Ackroyd, quoting Quentin Crisp, captures the atmosphere of those chaotic, uncertain times: "Never in the history of sex was so much offered by so many to so few."[84]

A Danger To Others

This sense of openness and risk-taking did not last. After the War ended, the moral panic returned with a vengeance. After the horrors of war and the upheaval of daily life, the renewal of 'traditional life' and its values was venerated by society as proof of safety; that the War was really over and things were returning to normal. The LGBTQ+ community, therefore, were a threat to this safety.

The onset of the Cold War only increased the already suspicious social atmosphere. In the context of a world in which spies and Communist agents were the boogieman under the bed, the common practices developed by those in the queer community to avoid being caught could be misinterpreted as signs of treason. Journalist Peter Wildeblood recalls:

[78]George Chauncey. *Gay New York: Gender, Urban Culture, and the Making of the Gay Male World, 1890-1940*. New York: Basic Books, 1994, 7.

[79]Ibid.

[80]Kasandra Brabaw, 'What We Mean When We Talk About Coming Out (Of The Closet)'. *Refinery29*. Vice Media Group, October 12, 2018 https://www.refinery29.com/en-ca/2018/10/213864/coming-out-meaning-history-origin.

[81]George Chauncey. *Gay New York: Gender, Urban Culture, and the Making of the Gay Male World, 1890-1940*. New York: Basic Books, 1994, 276.

[82]Peter Ackroyd. *Queer City: Gay London From the Romans to the Present Day*. New York: Abrams Press, 2018, 201.

[83]Allan Bérubé. *Coming Out Under Fire: The History of Gay Men and Women in World War II*. Chapel Hill: University of North Carolina Press, 2010, 98.

[84]Peter Ackroyd. *Queer City: Gay London From the Romans to the Present Day*. New York: Abrams Press, 2018, 198-199, 203.

It was necessary for me to watch every word I spoke, and every gesture that I made, in case I gave myself away. When jokes were made about 'queers' I had to laugh with the rest, and when the talk was about women I had to invent conquests of my own. I hated myself at such moments, but there seemed nothing else that I could do.[85]

Already viewed with suspicion and loathing for their sexuality, the idea of the LGBTQ+ community as traitorous was only furthered by the Cambridge Spy Scandal. In 1951, the British public became privy to the revelation that a group of men had been spying against the UK since the 1930s. This revelation came only after Donald Maclean and Guy Burgess fled England and defected to the Soviet Union. They and their fellow spies – Harold Philby, Anthony Blunt and John Cairncross – had been recruited while studying at Cambridge in the early thirties. Both Burgess and Blunt were gay men, although Blunt's identity was not revealed to the public until 1979. He and Burgess became '[symbols] of the "evils" of homosexuality: predatoriness, blackmail, betrayal, mistrust.'[86]

The police were harsher and more inquisitorial than ever in their pursuit of 'criminals'. British writer Colin Spencer recalls:

I can remember people sending me letters which had little bits of sticky paper on the back to show if they had been opened or not… They were terrified of the knock on the door in the early morning or late at night; the idea that the bed sheets might be inspected for semen stains – which was something that actually happened! There was suddenly a police state in England in the Fifties.[87]

Books masking homophobia with pseudo-science were being published en masse. While same-sex attraction between women was not illegal, queer women were still subject to the same psychiatric interventions faced by queer men. There is evidence that early conversion therapy was carried out on a number of women during the 1950s and 1960s, with methods including electro-shock therapy, LSD and induced vomiting.[88] One woman recalls:

It was appalling to have to go through something like that. The treatment went over six weeks and the idea is you are given injections and made to feel physically ill at the sight of women doing anything. For about three months I felt dreadful about it, I mean, I couldn't face being anywhere near the proximity of women. But what it doesn't do, you see, is make you like men any more.[89]

The appointment of Sir David Maxwell Fyfe as Home Secretary in 1951 dealt a massive blow to the LGBTQ+ community. In Parliament in 1953, he stated:

> Homosexuals in general are exhibitionists and proselytisers and are a danger to others, especially the young. So long as I hold the office of Home Secretary I shall give no countenance to the view that they should not be prevented from being such a danger.[90]

He implemented tactics described by writer Francis Wheen as 'neanderthal' and was responsible for the terrorising of the LGBTQ+ community by police. Hugh David quotes an anonymous gay man from the West Country as saying:

> … one particular member of our gay community was caught 'cottaging' by the police. They threatened him with ten years in prison if he didn't tell them the names of all the gay men who lived in the area. So he went round in a police car to everywhere we worked or lived and a dozen of us ended up at the Quarter Sessions in Exeter Assizes.[91] [92]

After the Cambridge Spy Scandal, the Special Branch of the Metropolitan Police had begun compiling what was referred to as a 'Black Book', which was a list of known members of the LGBTQ+ community – mostly gay men – in positions of authority. It was about to be opened. In 1953, Lord Edward Montagu – along with Michael Pitt-Rivers and Peter Wildeblood – was arrested and charged with 'gross offences' due to what police alleged were 'wild orgies', but the three men testified was actually just a friendly party. Nevertheless, all three were found guilty and sentenced to prison. In a letter sent to his mother before the verdict, Wildeblood wrote:

---

[85]Hugh David. *On Queer Street: a Social History of British Homosexuality 1895-1995*. London: HarperCollins, 1998, 158.

[86]Dusko Doder, 'Of Moles and Men.' *The Nation*. June 29, 2015. https://www.thenation.com/article/archive/moles-and-men/.

[87]Hugh David. *On Queer Street: a Social History of British Homosexuality 1895-1995*. London: HarperCollins, 1998, 157.

[88]Sarah Carr and Helen Spandler, 'Hidden from History? A Brief Modern History of the Psychiatric "Treatment" of Lesbian and Bisexual Women in England'. The Lancet Psychiatry Insight 6, no. 4 (2019): 289-290, https://doi.org/10.1016/s2215-0366(19)30059-8.

[89]Rebecca Jennings, '"The Most Uninhibited Party They'd Ever Been to": The Postwar Encounter between Psychiatry and the British Lesbian, 1945–1971', *The Journal of British Studies* 47, no. 4 (2008): pp. 883-904, https://doi.org/10.1086/590173.

[90]Hugh David. *On Queer Street: a Social History of British Homosexuality 1895-1995*. London: HarperCollins, 1998, 177.

[91]'Assizes' here means a court held in a county's main town by a visiting judge from London's higher courts. The Crown Court of England and Wales would not exist until 1972.

[92]Hugh David. *On Queer Street: a Social History of British Homosexuality 1895-1995*. London: HarperCollins, 1998, 164

Whatever they decide, I do not want you to be ashamed of anything I have done. Be glad, rather, that at last a little light has been cast on this dark territory in which, through no fault of their own, many thousands of other men are condemned to live, in loneliness and fear.[93]

Light had indeed been cast. In 1954, the Wolfenden Report – chaired by Sir John Wolfenden, whose son was gay – was commissioned to look into the legal status of homosexuality. Published in 1957, the report found that 'homosexual behaviour between consenting adults in private should no longer be a criminal offence.'[94] This was followed by the formation of the Homosexual Law Reform Society in 1958 and the publication of Michael Schofield's *A Minority: A Report on the Life of the Male Homosexual in Great Britain* (1960). While Wolfenden's recommendations were not passed into law until 1967, the seeds of change had been planted.

The Closet Emerges

The late 1950s and early 1960s saw trans rights in the spotlight in the UK. In 1958, naval surgeon and heir to the baronetcy of Lismullen, Michael Dillon, was outed as a trans man in the *Daily Express*. His outing came after the discovery of a clerical error – *Debrett's Peerage* listed him as male while *Burke's Peerage* listed him as female. Fearing the public's attention, Dillon fled to India. The 1961 outing of British model April Ashley was a more personal affair. A friend sold her story to the tabloids which ran it under the headline, 'The Extraordinary Case of Top Model April Ashley – Her Secret Is Out'.[95] The event significantly damaged her career and she struggled to find work; all of which led to Corbett v Corbett, the court case that would define trans rights in the UK for over thirty years.

In 1966, Ashley filed a petition requesting maintenance payments from her estranged husband, Arthur Corbett. Despite knowing Ashley was a trans woman when they married, in response to her petition Corbett filed a suit to have the marriage annulled. He argued that the marriage should not have been allowed to take place since Ashley was legally 'male' at the time. In 1971, the court ruled that a person's gender was legally defined as their biological sex and granted the annulment.[96] This ruling would stand until the Gender Recognition Act of 2004.

The 1960s saw the start of the modern LGBTQ+ liberation movement, one led by members of the community themselves rather than sympathetic allies. In 1963, the Minorities Research Group – an organisation which advocated for lesbians and bisexual women in the UK – was founded in London.[97] They took part in scientific research aimed at educating the public and changing attitudes towards lesbians and bisexual women at the time. From 1963 to 1972, they published the monthly journal *Arena Three*, later known as *Sappho* which had a readership of up to 1000 at its height.

Buoyed by the Stonewall Riots in the USA and the subsequent political undertaking, the Gay Liberation Front (GLF) was formed in London in 1970. Born 'out of rage, and defiance, against harassment',[98] the GLF's manifesto demanded equality and rejected the discrimination and harassment that had become par for the course of daily life in the LGBTQ+ community. It 'marked what seemed to many to be the first assertion of gay identity without apology or equivocation.'[99]

It was during this period of revolution that the idea of 'the closet' arose. Before this time, language was used to describe the experience of being 'in the closet'. George Chauncey writes:

> Many gay men, for instance, described negotiating their presence in an often-hostile world as living a double life, or wearing a mask and taking it off. Each image has a valence different from 'closet', for each suggests not gay men's isolation, but their ability – as well as their need – to move between different personas and different lives, one straight, the other gay, to wear their hair up, as another common phrase put it, or let their hair down. Many men kept their gay lives hidden from potentially hostile straight observers (by 'putting their hair up'), in other words, but that did not mean they were hidden or isolated from each other – they often, as they said, "dropped hairpins" that only other gay men would notice.[100]

[93]Hugh David. *On Queer Street: a Social History of British Homosexuality 1895-1995*. London: HarperCollins, 1998, 174.

[94]Peter Ackroyd. *Queer City: Gay London From the Romans to the Present Day*. New York: Abrams Press, 2018, 205.

[95]Christine Burns. *Trans Britain: Our Journey from the Shadows*. London: Unbound, 2019, 30.

[96]Ibid, 119-120.

[97]Clare Summerskill. *Gateway to Heaven: Fifty Years of Lesbian and Gay Oral History*. London: Tollington, 2013, 114-115.

[98]Peter Ackroyd. *Queer City: Gay London From the Romans to the Present Day*. New York: Abrams Press, 2018, 208.

[99]Ibid.

[100]George Chauncey. *Gay New York: Gender, Urban Culture, and the Making of the Gay Male World, 1890-1940*. New York: Basic Books, 1994, 6-7.

The very first Pride parades were held in the USA in 1971, with London Pride following in 1972 and countries like Italy, Australia and France following soon after that. In 1972, *Gay News*, the UK's first queer newspaper, began publication and in 1975, the groundbreaking film *The Naked Civil Servant* – based on Quentin Crisp's memoir of 1968 and starring John Hurt – was broadcast on ITV. The following year, Hurt won the Best Actor BAFTA for the role.

However, the hardships of the post-war years had led to a feeling of increased isolation among those in the LGBTQ+ community. The strictures placed upon them by the need to keep their sexuality a secret had become suffocating; thus, the fitting metaphor of a small, dark and cramped space such as a closet.

The association with the 'closet' was possibly a mash-up with the notion of 'skeletons in "the closet"'– a dark secret someone was hiding. Coming out of the closet was therefore a denial of the idea that queerness was something so terrible that it needed to be kept hidden. The audience for coming out had shifted from LGBTQ+ society and its members to the straight mainstream. It became a politicised act, a way to force straight society to confront and accept the fact that the LGBTQ+ community would no longer be forced underground but instead demanded their due as equals.

A famous speech by out gay politician Harvey Milk includes a section which goes:

> Gay brothers and sisters, you must come out. Come out to your parents. I know that it is hard and will hurt them, but think about how they will hurt you in the voting booth! Come out to your relatives. Come out to your friends, if indeed they are your friends. Come out to your neighbours, to your fellow workers, to the people who work where you eat and shop. Come out only to the people you know, and who know you, not to anyone else. But once and for all, break down the myths. Destroy the lies and distortions. For your sake. For their sake.[101]

Coming out became an imperative, something you did to further the cause and bring the LGBTQ+ community into the light. Tom Robinson's 1978 song 'Glad to Be Gay' became an anthem for this new era. However, not everyone was happy with this change. Some found the idea entirely unnecessary and preferred to continue living under the radar; others saw it as a source of unease, the fear of backlash still a very real risk. And then came the virus.

AIDS/HIV emerged in the early 1980s, leading to the deaths of at least 32 million people worldwide by 2019, with 37.9 million currently diagnosed with the disease. Initially thought to be a kind of cancer, the virus was officially identified as such in 1984 with effective antiretroviral drugs developed in 1996 cutting the mortality rate in Europe and the USA by more than half by the next year.[102]

This progress was hard fought for. Dismissed as a 'gay plague' by the public and the tabloid media, the LGBTQ+ community were largely left to fend for themselves.[103] A 1980 edition of *The Mail on Sunday* declared, 'Britain threatened by gay virus plague', while a 1985 copy of *The Sun* ran an article with the headline, 'I'd shoot my son if he had AIDS, says vicar!'.[104] Betrayed by their government and faced with doctors who refused to treat them, the LGBTQ+ community organised once more. In the USA, the Gay Men's Health Crisis was formed in 1982 with the aim of raising money for research on AIDS and providing support for those suffering from AIDS. From this group, some members splintered off to form AIDS Coalition to Unleash Power in 1987, popularly known as ACT UP. ACT UP's confrontational and politically active approach to the AIDS crisis was mirrored by the UK faction of the group, with 'die ins', protests and marches being common tactics.

The introduction of Section 28 – legislation against 'homosexual propaganda' – took place in 1988 and led to the founding of Stonewall, arguably the UK's most prominent LGBTQ+ charity to this day. This period is covered elsewhere in this book by Robin Ford and others, but suffice to say that it was a source of both great strife and great motivation for the LGBTQ+ community.

Onwards and Upwards

From the mid-1990s through to today, we have seen a lot of change and progress for the LGBTQ+ community in Europe and the USA. Legally, we have come a long way from 1900. There are now protections against discrimination in education, the workplace and healthcare. Same-sex marriage is now a reality. The legal right to adoption, surrogacy and IVF has been equalised for

[101]Harvey Milk, 'That's What America Is'. Speech, San Francisco Gay Freedom Day Parade, San Francisco, June 25, 1978.

[102]Shilts, Randy. *And The Band Played On: 20th Anniversary Edition*. New York: St. Martin's Griffin, 2007.

[103]Peter Ackroyd. *Queer City: Gay London From the Romans to the Present Day*. New York: Abrams Press, 2018, 198-199, 210.

[104]Ella Braidwood, '"Gay plague": The Vile, Horrific and Inhumane Way the Media Reported the AIDS Crisis', *PinkNews*, November 30, 2018. https://www.pinknews.co.uk/2018/11/30/world-aids-day-1980s-headlines-tabloids/

LGBTQ+ people. LGBTQ+ identities have been decriminalised and are no longer classified as psychological illnesses.[105]

Socially, we have also made progress. More people are coming out than ever in Europe and the USA, including those in the public eye, from athletes to politicians to actors to even royalty. What was once only a scandal has come to be seen as a celebration. Notable comings out from the past thirty years include: Justin Fashanu in 1990, Elton John in 1992, Ellen DeGeneres in 1997, George Michael in 1998, George Takei in 2005, Jodie Foster in 2007, Janet Mock in 2011 and Caitlyn Jenner in 2015. Peter Ackroyd offers an interesting observation on coming out. He argues that the continued relevance of coming out is itself an indictment of how far we still have to go:

> Where sixty years ago homosexuality itself was a crime, homophobia has now taken its place, and the very expression 'coming out' testifies to lingering societal prejudice.[106]

In the media, LGBTQ+ representation is on the rise. *Brokeback Mountain* and *Moonlight* both took home the Oscar for Best Picture, while at Cannes Film Festival, *Blue Is the Warmest Colour* won the Palme d'Or and *Portrait of a Lady On Fire* snagged Best Screenplay. Andrew Sean Greer's *Less* was awarded the Pulitzer Prize for fiction in 2018, with Bernardine Evaristo's *Girl, Woman, Other* winning the Booker Prize in 2019. LGBTQ+ characters are becoming a common sight in television, while shows focusing on LGBTQ+ culture such as *Queer As Folk* and *Pose* have enjoyed praise from critics.

This shift is not altogether welcomed by all those in the LGBTQ+ community. As we are becoming more accepted – or merely tolerated – by mainstream society, establishments built for LGBTQ+ people are being shuttered, or are sanitising themselves in order to not offend the sensibilities of straight 'tourists'. Being forced to play into respectability politics offers a different kind of closet. The bowdlerising of queer politics and identities in order to achieve acceptance into 'polite' society is a tactic that has its benefits, but comes with the cost of self-censorship. An article published by *The Goose Quill* about the widely used phrase 'love is love' sums up this dilemma:

> More often than not there seems to be a need to repeat sentiments such as "We are just like you" or "We love just like you" accompanying the use of the slogan, rendering the transformation of the lives of lesbian, gay, transgender, and queer people into devices of acceptance. This necessitates assimilation by queer individuals into heteronormative society. LGBTQ love then must prove its likeness to the love of

heterosexual and cisgender people. In contending that gay people love the same, the slogan places heteronormative love as the standard in the simple formulaic fashion that most all slogans contain.[107]

As with all progress towards equalities for minorities, the reigning class is inclined to push back. We are currently experiencing a wave of transphobic and homophobic sentiment in the UK, fed by both mass media and social media. These tools which allow us greater visibility and connection to people around the world also offer a medium in which we are made vulnerable to attack. Lawyer and activist Richard Akuson writes:

> Social media can be a delightful way to connect with loved ones far away, but for me it has also become a space where my own family and friends have turned into censors, distorting my life, denigrating my being gay from thousands of miles away.[108]

A hate crime is defined by UK law as 'a range of criminal behaviour where the perpetrator is motivated by hostility or demonstrates hostility towards the victim's disability, race, religion, sexual orientation or transgender identity'.[109] Hostility is further defined as 'ill-will, spite, contempt, prejudice, unfriendliness, antagonism, resentment and dislike.'[110] From 2018 to 2019, police recorded 14,491 LGBTQ+ hate crimes committed in the UK, more than double that recorded only five years early for the period between 2013 and 2014. Trans hate crimes alone rose by 37 per cent from the 2017 to 2018 statistics.[111]

[105]Stonewall. 'Key Dates for Lesbian, Gay, Bi and Trans Equality'. Stonewall, August 25, 2020. https://www.stonewall.org.uk/about-us/key-dates-lesbian-gay-bi-and-trans-equality/.

[106]Peter Ackroyd. *Queer City: Gay London From the Romans to the Present Day*. New York: Abrams Press, 2018, 217.

[107]Ezgi Demir, '"Love is Love": Queerness and Respectability Politics'. *The Goose Quill*, May 1, 2019. https://medium.com/the-goose-quill/love-is-love-queerness-and-respectability-politics-e57f8777f2ba

[108]Richard Akuson, 'Opinion: "This Is Quite Gay!"'. *New York Times*, July 6, 2019. https://www.nytimes.com/2019/07/06/opinion/sunday/social-media-homophobia.html

[109]'Hate crime'. Crown Prosecution Service. https://www.cps.gov.uk/crime-info/hate-crime

[110]Ibid.

[111]Philippa H. Stewart, 'UK LGBT Hate Crimes Stats Make Shocking Reading', *Human Rights Watch*, October 23, 2019. https://www.hrw.org/news/2019/10/23/uk-lgbt-hate-crimes-stats-make-shocking-reading.

These statistics emphasise the need for a project such as *Out On An Island*. Our project aims to tell the stories of the Isle of Wight's LGBTQ+ community, to explore and bring to life the rich history of our community here on the Island. We want to share with you the joys and struggles that we have lived through and to invite you to learn about our community here. As American basketball player Jason Collins wrote in his coming out article, 'Openness may not completely disarm prejudice, but it's a good place to start.'[112]

---

[112]Jason Collins, 'Why NBA Center Jason Collins Is Coming out Now', *Sports Illustrated*, April 29, 2013.
https://www.si.com/more-sports/2013/04/29/jason-collins-gay-nba-player

EXTRACTS FROM ORAL HISTORIES

Robert

My mother who is 94 still isn't aware, although I think she must know at some level, she just chooses not to acknowledge it. My father never did and he was fairly homophobic, "it's not natural is it?!". That's what he used to say. I had friends who knew, yes, very close friends, one or two, not many but they did know because I told them. And my brother, who was seven years younger than I am, he knew as well. But it wasn't much help them knowing, because none of them were interested in doing anything about it and I obviously couldn't!

It became clear to my brother certainly, and to my best friend that I was not after the girls and was not interested in sport, was interested in arty things, painting and all that sort of stuff and they said, "are you um...er...?" "Yes", I said. [Laughs] So that was that conversation, that was coming out circa 1968. Yes, it probably was about then, perhaps a little earlier than that but I was seventeen, eighteen, something like that.

[I felt] embarrassed. Angry because it wasn't their fault and I wasn't angry with them, I was angry with me, for having to make a confession, as it were of what actually seemed to be perfectly. It was me! I wasn't confessing to some terrible crime, but I needed somebody to know and so I told them. There was no problem with that, I mean, it was all perfectly friendly about it, not happy about it I wouldn't say necessarily, but friendly about it. But it was difficult because the West Wight and the Isle of Wight generally are a wee bit on the backward side and they were then too. We are talking of church schools and all the rest of it. My best friend was called out in the middle of the class because his mother was an atheist and he said, "you mean to say you have never been to a place of worship?" That was the sort of attitude that prevailed and coming out there against that background, forget it, you wouldn't. You'd be damned to hell and back. So they took me to the doctor. My mother, my father, sort of thought, "there's something strange going on here". Doctor said, "are you interested in women?" "No". "Men?" "Not especially". "Oh, good!". And that was that, that was that, he was an ex-Army doctor.

I never had to [come out again], I never have had to, other than when I was after a particular person, of course, so would they hopefully, so that was OK. But, no. I have done a number of fairly public jobs on the Island over the last thirty or forty years: I was Chairman of the Housing Association, I was agent for the Labour Party and at that time, less so now I think, at that time say 1990, you would do yourself no favours and your Party no favours if people knew as opposed to suspect, which they might well do. But if they knew you were gay, not that that's a word I'd ever use, but still, they would. It would hurt the organisation in some way. It wouldn't have hurt me necessarily, but it would have hurt the organisation and I cared about the reputation of the organisations. So I was sort of lurking around the edges of society basically and picking up what I could where I could but publicly maintaining this picture of relative, what's the word I'm looking for here? sobriety and responsibility. It was a bit of a struggle because, of course, my instincts were going one way and what I needed to do was going the other way and I was being torn down the middle to a great extent.

My brother has always been perfectly relaxed about it, yes, I've never had any difficulty there but my mother, as I say, really if she knows she keeps quiet about it. I think it's just embarrassment more than anything else. My mother is a very, not a very emotional person, she doesn't like sharing emotions generally speaking so she knows I think what she might un-tap if she were to talk about it. Now she's so deaf anyway its very difficult to have conversations, one isn't going to start saying, "BY THE WAY MOTHER, I'M GAY!!". That would be really difficult. So there we are.

Karl S

I didn't. I didn't come out. I never told my parents I was gay or anybody else really, I just was me and I have been with my partner for thirty years. I suppose it was easier because I was in the South of England and my parents were in the North, so it is quite easy to keep things separate, but they knew I was living with a man and they knew that we were going on holiday together and doing things, it wasn't just 'flatmates'. I mean, they came to visit and they loved him like a son really. It was never an issue. I am an only child, now whether it is an issue with other family members I don't really know. I know it wouldn't have been an issue with my grandparents. I was just kind of me really, I never did have a girlfriend. Well, I had girlfriends, but I didn't get through the 'straight' bit, I was always me! At work as well, I didn't come out as such, people either knew or they didn't know, I've never made a meal of it.

I suppose partly it was a conscious choice. I come from the North-East where men are men and you drink copious amounts of tea and beer and you like football. I don't like beer, football or tea particularly so I was always an odd-bod. But it wasn't really a problem. At school I was bullied, not because I was gay or camp or whatever, not that I was really camp, but because I was tall, although I am probably not particularly tall now because there are lots of people over six foot two around. But at the time, when I was six, I was quite tall and I was always quite tall as a kid so I was bullied more for that than not liking football or whatever.

There was no reason not to be out on the Island; we'd been together thirty years so yeah, we have always been out. I don't think ... we're not overtly camp or gay, we don't sort of shout about it or anything like that. I think a lot of people wouldn't know, wouldn't bother, wouldn't care, but there is a sort of undercurrent amongst some people. It's very difficult ... I think it's very difficult anyway moving to a new place when you don't know anybody to actually get to know people. We were working together 24/7 really which worked fine, but it did mean that it was difficult to get out and about and meet up with people. We had to make a conscious effort to join things and meet people that way and form relationships and develop friendships and things with people. But we had to make a definite conscious decision to do that.

Caroline

I did have a burning question for years and years, "am I a lesbian? Am I just bisexual? What's going on?" And it did cause me a lot of... It was one of those things when you are lying in bed at night, it was one of those things that used to go through my mind; "am I? could I be?" And because I wasn't tomboy-ish and I never really wanted to look like a boy – although I didn't feel feminine – I questioned it within myself.

Then the marriage kind of fell apart because it was never ... it was always about being parents rather than being a romantic attraction, so I started to get increasingly unhappy and got divorced in 2011 and moved to Ryde. I thought, "right, OK, it's been difficult going through the divorce and now is your opportunity to explore whether or not you are actually gay or what is going on". So I went on a dating site and it said "are you interested in men, women or men and women" and I put "men and women." I think I was worried that somebody would see me on there and think, "ooh, I'm sure she's not lesbian because she's got three children, I don't know".

So I went on the website and I met somebody and she decided that she wanted to come to the Island even though she lived in Yorkshire and she said, "I really want to see you!" She was very enthusiastic and all the time I was thinking, "this is going to be either the best thing you've ever done or the worst thing you've ever done, because you are going to open up a whole can of worms if you meet this woman." And then I thought, "well, maybe I can just discretely meet her," and she decided to come on a coach from Yorkshire from Monday to Friday and we got together, it was a very, very, very powerful relationship, probably the most powerful relationship because I came out and I just knew without any shadow of a doubt that I was a lesbian. I wasn't bisexual, meeting her and having times with her and everything, I just knew.

But I really, really struggled emotionally; I was very tearful and it wasn't really anything that anybody else was doing, it was all from within me. I found it really, really hard to accept it, because I am a fairly private person and I didn't really want to have to tell people but I knew that if I was going to live life as a lesbian I had to tell people. I'd worked for the *County Press* for five years and had my photo in the paper every week so I knew quite a lot of people and they were mostly older people, none of them were LGBT and I thought, "how am I going to tell those people? how am I going to tell my parents and my three children?" And it all became emotionally completely overwhelming.

But then when I told people everybody was fine. My children were a little bit...I think they thought, "oh, here she goes again, this is a phase!" Because they are quite protective because the three of them are close together in age and I think they thought, "what the hell is she doing? And why is she doing it?" My son, though, was fantastic and I remember him going to school one day and saying that his religious studies teacher had been talking about same-sex marriage and he'd said he was against it and my son said that he put his hand up and said, "can you tell me why you are against it?" And then he came home and told me and I was so delighted that he had the courage to do that in front of all of his classmates and that he was mature enough to sort of think it through. My daughters eventually were OK, my mum and dad were absolutely brilliant, I can't even remember what they said. My dad had always, I think, wanted a son and he always talked to me about football. I love football, and that's all because, I think, he would have liked to have had a son to have had those conversations with, but he always used to talk to me about women quite a lot as well. If there was a really attractive woman walking down the road he would comment to me about her and to this day I wonder how much influence that had. I don't know why that relationship existed because if he'd have done that with one of my other sisters they probably would not have appreciated it at all. So, yes, that was emotional and there was a lot going on.

I remember somebody once saying to me about coming out: you have to think about what you are prepared to lose. I didn't know what she meant and she said, "well, you could lose your friends, you could lose your family, you might lose your job, so when you come out this is what has got to cross your mind". I think now that is a fairly old-fashioned view because people are generally more tolerant, but there are still occasions when people are homophobic. I think it's also about making heterosexuals, straight people, aware that life isn't easy and that it is not a choice, it is about human beings being their true selves and being able to live their life the best way. I probably could think of more but I think that's the general thrust of it really. And for people to be more open-minded and tolerant of each other.

Joanne

Well I grew up in Ireland and I didn't come out. It just so happened that my best friend stayed over and she jumped me and I thought, "we'll have some more of that!" And then it made a lot of sense as I was a bit scared of men and that made sense to me. So we were together but we weren't, we were just friends and it is quite easy to have a best friend as a girl and … do you know what I mean? She would stay at mine, or whatever, and there was no issue but she had boyfriends because that's what you did. I didn't because I just couldn't be bothered to be quite honest, it just wasn't something I was going to do. But we, yeah, we were together but we weren't that sort of a way. And then… I would have been about sixteen and she was the same age as me and we just sort of bimbled along like that. No one else knew, not one person knew about us, it was just me and her.

We were quite happy in our little bubble. We would go out with friends and everything but we'd hold hands under the table. If you were sat on the sofa watching a film you'd have your arms crossed. But it wasn't an issue, we didn't sort of worry about it because no one knew. So no, it was fine, and that was back in 1982-ish.

We moved here [Isle of Wight] in 1984. I was eighteen, didn't want to come, my girlfriend Joan stayed in Ireland. Obviously we were devastated. I could have stayed in Ireland because I was eighteen but I was very close to my family and my mum begged me to come. So I did and Joan came over.

[When we were over here, we didn't seek out the LGBT scene]. No. You just didn't. Like, I, I was ashamed really, didn't want my parents to know, thought I was odd, that I was the only one and, no, you just didn't. And when, cause I lived, came here and then Joan moved over here who was my first girlfriend, and we worked in a factory, this would have been 1985. It is still there now but it is called something completely different, and we worked there together and there was obviously other [lesbians]. I never say lesbian, I don't like the world, I say lebanon. It's just that I don't like it, I never have done. So there was other lebanons there and Joan told one of them. I went nuts. I was like, "you can go back to Ireland, it's me that lives here!" I was scared, I was scared, and I remember we were taken into the office, this is God's honest truth, there was six of us – I won't say the other names – it was me and by that time I had finished with Joan, she was a bit feisty, and I was with another girl, Sue, who was lovely, I loved her, she was lovely. But we were taken into the office, me and Sue and these other four who were couples and we were told we were disgusting, our lifestyle was disgusting and if we wanted to hang on to our jobs we needed to sort it out. And that is God's honest truth… and we were not allowed to speak. I was in shock. I was only nineteen then and do you know why I didn't tell them to poke their job? Do you remember when microwaves first come out, they were like this size, they were about two hundred quid weren't they? They were, and I'd gone in and put a deposit on a microwave for my mum for Christmas and that was all I kept thinking, "you have to pay the microwave off". But yeah, we were disgusting, that's a true story. Yeah. I hadn't admitted to anyone that I was gay and then… and my parents didn't know, it was when me and Sue split up that Sue told my mum. I hadn't told her. So Sue… she didn't do it in a malicious way… she was very upset and she went to see my mum and my mum, oh, it was awful. I think she had started her menopause so she was… My dad threw me out, but he did phone me that night. I think it was just the reaction, he didn't get it, he never got it. And he… there was a big family meeting, the Irish lot. They were all going to club together to send me to Australia to be cured and I was like, "well, it doesn't work like that". I should have taken them up on the offer really and just gone! In all fairness, I could have had a holiday couldn't I? But it was very traumatic to see my mum in such a state because she loved me but she didn't know how to deal with it. But I think she was dealing with a lot anyway, so, yeah.

But once they knew, I was out, I didn't care. And then I went, there was an LGBT … it was called The Social Group that was advertised in the *County Press* and they held a meeting and I went along to this meeting.

Joanne

Jess

It was fine at home for the most part. I don't think my grandparents were overly happy from what I can remember. I think they made lots of comments to my mum about me being gay because she's gay and it being some kind of genetic thing which obviously my mum went back and was sarcastic about the fact that she's gay and does that mean that my gran was gay? Which I don't think went down very well. But, I don't really remember them saying anything to me about it. My family were fine. People at school were not as fine to begin with, yeah, a lot of people would call me, "dirty bisexual", or, "fucking lesbian", or whatever but then after about a year, maybe less than that because I must have left school by then, a lot of people were like, "oh, I think we like gay people now because we don't mind you". I was like, "Um, okay, that's good to know". I was kind of invisible in school to be fair, I normally kept myself to myself so people in other years didn't know that I was gay or anything. My girlfriend wasn't in my school so that was fine, I suppose it would have been different if she was. So the coming out bit was fine because I don't feel I really had an elaborate coming out, I just went home and told people I had a girlfriend and I probably did the same thing at school really. It was more difficult just with random people in the street but that wasn't really coming out that was just being gay in public which people really didn't seem to appreciate very much. I wish I had a good coming out story. I just don't, it's pretty boring.

Anonymous

I was, I think I was twenty when I was, when I came out and it must have been around then that I realised that I liked guys. I fell in love with someone in my class and they were straight at the time, but since then they've come out, but I totally fell for this guy and it was unrequited but I was obsessed with this guy and I think that was the kind of… I'm missing a bit out here… back in High School I did mess about a few times with a local friend sexually and experimented a bit with another boy but I was deeply in denial about who I was and I just sort of kept pushing it back and saying, "this isn't happening, this isn't happening". I messed around, yes, sexually active I would say, around fifteen or sixteen or somewhere like that, with other pupils, yes. There was a big (my goodness, this is why I want to remain anonymous!)… There was a big field behind my house near where I lived and we messed around in this field behind the house, me and a local friend. Yeah, that was mainly where it happened and it was just sexually experimenting really.

I think I was aware, it is really interesting because there is no set point where I go, "oh, that's when it was". It's kind of like, because I think a lot of the time you're in denial and you sort of, especially during that time, it was pushing, pushing it back and going, "no, this isn't happening". I do think it's intrinsically there and I remember reading, as a kid I remember reading *Where the Wild Things Are* and I think Maurice Sendak is gay and there was an element of masculinity in that book with the whole kind of big hairy creatures. So I think that was quite attractive. But there were times when I messed around in High School and then just sort of denied it in myself. It was not until I was in my teens, late teens, until I was twenty that I really came out and said, "this is who I am". It wasn't until college when I fell in love with this boy that it really came out and I realised that I was gay.

Then I think for a period I didn't really know how to do it, how to go about coming out and I – I'm just trying to remember – I remember the Ellen DeGeneres TV show was coming up and it was advertising in the TV issues, I had been watching it and I had heard that she was coming out on this episode. Little did I know how powerful this episode would be and then one night on Channel 4, on Friday night, they had this, they were going to air it and they showed the show about 9 o'clock, 9.30, and they had all these other different shows, different TV shows and pieces on Channel 4 about coming out, about being gay, about how to, The Coming Out Guide, it was amazing. It was one night of all these, um, along the lines of coming out programmes and how-tos, and it was centred around Ellen DeGeneres coming out. Graham Norton was interviewing Ellen DeGeneres that night, thirty minutes before, and then he'd keep cutting back to her, and they'd watch the episode and come back to her, talk about it, talk about her experience, how she was fired from the network company and then she'd had to grow her own business again. But it was such a powerful episode because it was really, it was a really funny episode but it was also very powerful because she was the very person to do it, she was the first out LGBT person on a major sitcom or TV show. So that was very strong and I remember watching it and going, "oh my God", you know, "this is amazing".

I was so inspired that I came out to my mother and father the next day and I did that, I wrote a long letter to my mum and, um, it was like a page long, explaining everything. I thought if I could see it, I am very much into movies and TV shows and I thought if I could see it like a sitcom or a film I could probably do it because if you put yourself as that kind of main character in a sitcom it kind of feels like … like Ellen DeGeneres, it was really weird but I mean that show was so positive in my life. So I wrote this long letter and I gave it to my mum the next night. My mum has a bit of an alcohol problem so she was a bit drunk but she, so she, it is quite funny, she sort of read the letter and went, I mean she is very religious so she sort of read the letter and it said, "I'm gay", at the bottom and she went, "ah well! Never mind!". Because of the drink and she was very drunk and I didn't think she'd taken it in.

The next morning she came and spoke to me about it and she said, "I don't know if I can handle this, I don't know if I can handle this, I am going to have to tell your father, I am going to have to tell your father". I said, "don't tell my dad", because my dad [is] from East London, he'll chuck me out the house and I was so worried, so scared. She went, "I'm going to go, I have to tell your father", and she went off to tell him and I just looked around my room thinking, "oh God, what can I take with me when I'm chucked out? What can I take with me?". It was so terrifying, and then my dad comes in the room and he says, "I love you and you will always be my son", which was really nice and surprising. Then he said, "give us some time to get through this". It was very difficult.

My mum has always had a problem with it, has always had an issue with it and she comes from a religious background, she was brought up within a religion and, you know, I think for like ten years afterwards she just kept asking me if I would meet a nice girl and all this sort of stuff, which is like, "it's been ten years now, I don't think that's going to happen" [Laughs]. So it was just, it was very difficult, a very difficult time. I am very glad I did it at that time, I'm glad… I don't think if the Ellen DeGeneres TV show, *The Ellen Show*, wasn't on and that episode didn't happen I don't think I would have come out then, I think that would have… I would have it in a bit longer. I think that was such a positive thing. Yes, so that's my coming out story.

I started with my mum and dad because I knew that that would be the hardest, the most difficult, so I wanted to get that out of the way first. I thought, "if I can get that out of the way then I can do everyone". And it was, after that it was so easy just to tell everyone else and I was in college, I think on the Monday because it happened on the Friday, the Ellen DeGeneres TV show, I came out on Saturday to my mum and then on Monday I think I started doing it in college and I started, I was with a friend outside and it was sort of quite nice actually, I was with a friend and she was standing there and I said, "I've got something to tell you", and she said, "go ahead", and I went, "I'm gay", and she went, "I know" and then I was like, "oh, okay". [Laughs] And then she was like, "are you going to tell the others?" And I said, "yes", and she said, "let's do it now, together", and I was like, "okay".

So I felt a bit led at that point, but I went up and told people I was gay and she was there holding my hand which was really nice of her and a lot of people were like, "I don't believe you are", and stuff like this. It was quite interesting. One friend thought I was just attention seeking by saying it and said, "I don't think you are, you're just attention-seeking". So it was quite interesting, it was quite interesting, and then my friend said, one of my friends, my good friends, said to me, who I thought, he was one of the hardest so I didn't tell him till last and I think he was a bit pissed off because I didn't tell him till last. I ran up to him and I said, "I'm sorry I didn't tell you first of all!". He said, I think he tried to make a joke of it, he said, "it's okay Anonymous, I'm black", and then sort of walked away and I thought, "that's not very funny", but yeah. So that was how I came out to everyone else.

Then I think after that it was just so easy to just tell people and I think when you come out your personality sort of jumps in the air doesn't it? Because you are sort of, "well, this is who I am now", and because it's in the air who you were, there's pieces of that still in the air and so you are picking pieces of your personality out from the air. When you come out you cling onto things and you think, "oh well, I'm gay so I have to be like this and this and this", when actually you have to learn that your personality is still there and you are still you it is just this other aspect is part of you now. So I was kind of proud and I was telling a lot of people. I did get one time, I did get a little bit, there was a sort of group of guys at college and they were really lovely and I hung around with them and one time, I was living in East Cowes and I was going over to West Cowes and I was on the bus and just before I got off the bus this guy, this other young teen was looking at me funny and giving me nasty looks and saying stuff to me and I just walked past them and went into West Cowes. Later I saw my friends and they said, "oh this guy was going to come after you in Cowes and he was going to beat you up but we took care of it". They'd confronted him and said, "you're not chasing him", and they pushed him away from following me. So that was quite nice I thought. So things like that did happen.

Michelle

I came back, married briefly, managed to produce a son, but the whole thing fell apart, it was not a successful marriage. She didn't want to live in Italy when my company sent me to live in Italy so I stayed in Italy and three years later we had divorced and I lived with and then married an Italian girl. By then I was cross dressing quite regularly. She knew, she put up with it at that time.

And we produced three girls. We were married for 26 years, so during that time I gradually, I was going to say, 'came out', I think 'came out' was rather exaggerating. But I came out of the complete closet, for many transgender females at any rate, start in some form of transvestite/cross dressing and gradually, or some of them, gradually realise their true identity. I gradually, gradually came out but then that marriage began to fall apart. I had signed on to do a PhD in management, part time, so-called part-time PhD and I was up to my ears in work and travel and everything and our marriage didn't really… it was beginning to fray around the edges. We went to counselling to try and resolve it, we shared the counselling with our children so they knew what was going on but it wasn't working out. We separated. I came to work and live… oh, by then I had taken early retirement, I took early retirement and went into the academic sector. But, while I lived on the Island I found a counsellor who was very supportive and I used to cross-dress to go and visit with her. But I was still too far off… I was earning money, I was doing OK and I was scared, frankly. This was pre-internet and it was extraordinarily difficult to find out about what was going on. But after three years on the Island I went to live back on the mainland and I crossdressed most of the time. I was in a relationship. I went into a relationship with a woman who didn't like it, I tried to stop but after a couple of years I couldn't and didn't. That relationship ended and I went to live in Wales up on the mountainside and I decided, and by then I was able to live on a pension, I decided to come out and I came out to discover that in the village there was a very nice lesbian couple who lived up the hill and I came out and gradually came out and the village was very supportive.

I mentioned before, I played the guitar, my son is a very talented pianist and we used to play in the pub so it was just a simple and very supportive route out. Or coming out, that worked extremely well and then I decided I really did want to transition. I began to find out a bit more about things. It was the beginning, the very beginning of the internet, there wasn't a lot. But I went to my doctor and she was very supportive, she said, "well, I think you probably know more about this than I do, what shall we do?" And I went on a, it wasn't counselling, it was, well I guess it was it was Sex-Orientated Psychology. I went there for six months and my counsellor agreed that I needed to move further and I started to try and get into transitioning to discover that in most places, but certainly in Wales, it was virtually impossible.

Melissa

I never worried about telling my friends at the time I just kind of came out to them kind of slowly one by one and one of my best friends I told on the bus home from school one day, I turned to him and just said, "I like men and women", and he just goes, "oh, okay", and then he kind of said, "oh so, oh I can't call you bisexual as a joke any more because it's true!" And I was like, "no you can't do that, that would be homophobic!" So, then he came out later in life as well so it was like one of those things.

Then I told two of my other best friends after we got our GCSE results at school. I just pulled them aside and said, "I need to tell you something", and then I told them, I said, "I'm bisexual", and one of them screamed and gave me a big hug and they were fine with it, they were just happy for me that I'd told them. So I never really worried about telling them and I never worried about telling my mum either, like I never worried that she would reject me or feel uncomfortable or anything, I just went home from school one day and just said, burst into the kitchen and just said, "Mum, I like boys and girls", and she was just like, "Okay, that's fine, what do you want for dinner?" and just kind of moved on from there.

But as a teenager on the Island specifically it was really, it felt really isolating to be honest. I know that we, me and my friends, felt like us and the teenagers that we knew were also out, we felt like we were all that there was. We didn't have any kind of larger community that we felt we could turn to because we were underage so clubs were out of the question; we couldn't get into them. We had no idea where to get fake ID – that's nothing that every passed our minds – we just felt like, "oh, we'll just do our own thing and then we'll leave the Island", because we really felt that there was nothing here for us and we literally had no idea that there was any kind of community here that we could access. We felt quite like we were the only ones so we kept ourselves and had our house parties and went down Appley and hung out in various parks in Newport and did our underage drinking and had our fun and there was this idea that in order to access any kind of wider community we would have to leave, we would have to leave the Isle of Wight and I think we were also really quite aware that the Isle of Wight was very conservative.

I didn't come out to my dad for a long time. I told my mum when I was fifteen, sixteen and we kind of talked about my dad but I knew the type of language that he used and I wasn't sure, I wasn't sure how he'd react. I didn't think he'd react badly, logically, but at the same time I was very nervous to tell him because his sister, my aunt, she's bisexual and she had come out to my grandparents in the '70s/'80s and they had reacted very badly. It really didn't go well at all and it took them a long time to come around and accept her and accept her partners and embrace her in that way and I know that my dad had had struggles with it as well but I wasn't sure how much of that was homophobia and how much of that was him just not liking her girlfriends because you don't always like your sibling's partners, sometimes you're just like, "oh, alright, that's fine, each to their own!" So with my dad I was very nervous to tell him.

I went away to university, on the mainland. I did find my identity and grow a lot, kind of more confident in my identity and in knowing that this was who I was and accepting that and embracing it and learning about my own community and our history and meeting people who also identified in the same way or who were a part of the community, and feeling stronger in it and educating myself about the community as well and educating myself on what it meant to be this way in the society that we had at the time.

Then I realised that I would be coming home from university for a bit to stay with my parents again and I realised that if I didn't tell my dad then I would have to go back into the closet because at the time I was out with my housemates and quite comfortable with talking about my attraction to people who weren't men and talking about queer politics and activism and characters on TV shows or whatever. It was really liberating for me to be able to do that and I felt really free and I didn't want to go back to having to weigh my words when I went back home, I didn't want to have to be put back in the position where I had to hide part of myself and pretend that I was something I wasn't.

So I decided in my last year of uni, I decided that I wanted to tell my dad because I was out to my mum already so I called her and said, "I want to come out to Dad", she was like, "Okay, you can do that, that's fine, how do you want to do it?" I was like, "I want to do it over the phone before I come home just in case he reacts badly", because my mum had always, when I said to her, when I came out to her she was like, "well, if he reacts badly then he can leave, I'll just kick him out!" So I've always felt supported by my mum, there's not anything in my life that I've felt I couldn't tell her because that's just who she is, she's just, "these are my kids, I'll do anything for them".

So I said, because my dad liked to ... after work he'd like to go to the pub and talk to his friends and just have a drink and chill out and decompress so I was like, "Okay, well, I need you to text me when he comes home from the pub and just let me know when he is in a good mood so that I can, I have the best chance of him being receptive to it", essentially and we had a code word

Melissa

which was 'Project Unicorn', or 'Operation Unicorn' and I was going to get her to text me that to indicate that now is a good time.

So she did that and I rang him and I remember being really nervous and I couldn't get the words out for quite a long time, I was just on the phone and like, "Dad, I need to tell you something", he's like, "Okay", I was like, "Um, um, um", and I was just full of adrenaline and just really nervous and he's like, "whatever you need to say I need you to say it because I am making your brother's dinner and I need to go". I was like, "Dad, I'm queer!" And I don't think he quite understood what I was telling him and he was like, "what?" I'm like, "I like boys and girls", and he was like, "oh, okay", and I was like, "is that okay?" And he was like, "yeah, that's fine, I love you, if that's what you are then that's fine". I was like, "oh, okay", he was like, "okay, I still need to finish making your brother's dinner so can I go?" And I was like, "yeah, I guess, bye".

WRITTEN HISTORIES

Elaine's Story

When it was suggested to me that I might like to write a piece for possible inclusion in this book, I had been given the idea of perhaps doing something about Marion 'Joe' Carstairs. At first I was quite taken with the thought, as I'm a huge fan of many Sapphic figures from the last century. Having devoured many books, especially those written by one of my favourite biographers, the incomparable Diana Souhami, I had discovered the enigmatic and fascinating 'Joe' by following a marvellous linked trail. It led to Kate Summerscale's book, *The Queen of Whale Cay: The Extraordinary Story of 'Joe' Carstairs, the Fastest Woman on Water* (I highly recommend it if you haven't read it yet). I was reminded of *The L Word's* chart, Alice Pieszecki's visual representation of the myriad ways in which lesbians are inextricably bound, in a labyrinthine interconnectedness that would make even the most liberal of minds boggle.

'Joe' Carstairs' links to the Island were forged in the 1920s and very far from hidden. Her fabulous wealth and famous lovers, including Marlene Dietrich, ensure her light was never hidden under a bushel. As her extraordinary tale is told so well in *The Queen of Whale Cay* I have decided to take a different tack, if you'll excuse the sailing reference.

So I am going to recount a little bit of my own 'herstory' to explain how I came to be 'out' in this very special Island.

I am what is sometimes known as an 'overner', that is someone who resides here in the Island but who was not actually born here. The name 'Caulkhead' applies to those folk who are 'Island born and Island bred, strong in the arm and thick in the head'. I'm not casting aspersions, it is Caulkheads themselves who proudly quote such rhymes or share wonderful examples of Island words' meanings. In the same way that they're inherently proud of their shared heritage and experience of living in such a beautiful place, I'm proud of the many varied and diverse (I know, a word that's become common currency in many companies' HR brochures) people who make up what I'll call the Gay Community (GC). I don't set any stall politically, gender or orientation-wise, it's simply because the ever-increasing number of letters needed to try to honour the inclusivity requirements takes up too much of the limited character count quota I'm allowed!

Apart from a childhood camping holiday in the late 1960s or early 1970s, my real Island experience began in late Spring of the year 2000. I came over here to live with my then partner, very early in a relationship that would last for nearly ten years. When I arrived, I was fully out, having been pretty much forced out of the closet in 1988. I had been thrown out of a very happy and successful career as an Army-trained nurse, having fallen foul of the ban on openly-LGB personnel serving in HM Forces. I'd subsequently co-founded Rank Outsiders and led the challenge that eventually led to the lifting of what was known as the military ban in January 2000. As part of that campaign, I had appeared in documentaries, TV and radio news features, newspaper articles and books. All my family and mainland friends knew I was lesbian.

I used to describe myself as a dyke then, very much in the vein of 'reclaiming' a negatively associated word and imbuing it with a sense of strength and pride. Even back then I yearned for a time when labels would become obsolete and we could simply give our chosen name, without feeling obliged to expand/explain upon various other aspects of ourselves, to somehow justify or validate our existence.

My partner, another overner who had been living in the Island for many years, was completely closeted. She knew my story, I have always been totally open and honest, believing it really is the best policy. But it was a bone of contention between us from the start. She is a very private person and even though we remain great friends to this day, my writing articles such as this cause her great worry. I tease her that she fears 'guilt by association' but her anxiety regarding people 'knowing' makes me very sad.

So, it was in this atmosphere of stressing about inadvertently 'outing' her, that I began living my Island life. I wasn't overt and I didn't flaunt my sexuality in any way, other than by not wearing make-up, having short hair and nails (I was still nursing then, so that wasn't necessarily much of a give away) and usually preferring to wear trousers and comfortable shoes. As I settled into my new job at the hospital, I initially answered colleagues' questions about husbands, boyfriends, partners with the undoubtedly suspicion-arousing non-gender specific pronouns that invariably gave it away. Eventually, one friend I worked with just asked me directly if my partner was a woman. Having no sense of shame or embarrassment, I of course said yes. This caused no end of arguments at home.

I never experienced any homophobia at all. In fact, most people's reactions were of utter shock and horror at the way in which I had been treated in the Army. I was supported and the few friends that eventually met my partner got on really well with her and liked her. There was no reason not too, I had wonderful taste in women, so why wouldn't they?!

One workmate, an older male nurse, came out to me and I asked him if there was any type of 'scene' here. He told me that there was a pub in Shanklin and part of a beach that had a section designated as nudist/naturist, but which was widely known and accepted as being the 'gay beach'. Apparently, it was mostly men at both venues, so I never went to either. He and I did see the fabulous Bette Bourne playing Quentin Crisp in *Resident Alien* here at Quay Arts in Newport – a deliciously queer evening!

After my partner and I split up in 2010, I wasn't worried about whether or not there was a 'scene'. I never investigated whether there were many other like-minded women here. I went home to North West London to live with my widowed dad at the end of 2012, returning once again to the Island in the Spring of 2015. Dad had had a stroke in 2014, necessitating the sale of our family home to cover the cost of his nursing home fees. He lived in Havenstreet and I returned to Ryde.

When the Island held its inaugural Pride Festival in 2017, I'm a little embarrassed to admit to hesitating about attending. I had an image of a few dozen marchers being heckled by lager louts outside Wetherspoons. I'd bought into the notion of this traditionally conservative, older population being very resistant to the whole idea. When I saw that Peter Tatchell and Linda Riley were coming over, I knew I had to go. I'd met them both in my previous role as an activist and campaigner with Rank Outsiders. The fact that they felt this was a significant moment worth supporting, I couldn't have lived with myself if I'd been too lazy to show up. It was an absolutely superb day and was also when I was first introduced to *Out On An Island's* instigator, Caroline Diamond. We attended a talk together at the Classic Boat Museum in East Cowes shortly afterwards. It was backed by the National Lottery Heritage Fund, which is when the seeds of this project were well and truly sown in Caroline's mind. We also got to meet Alison Child that evening. She wrote *Tell Me I'm Forgiven: The Story of Forgotten Stars* Gwen Farrar and Norah Blaney – another wonderful story, well worth reading.

Caroline's sterling efforts to establish a supportive network of events and groups that welcome members of the GC but lesbians in particular, is truly inspirational. Rather than having to spend a lot of time and money getting across the Solent to other scenes such as in Portsmouth, Southampton, Brighton, London etc, we now have much more choice available to us. And stretching the net wider, with projects such as this, will hopefully continue the vital process of breaking down barriers and prejudices as heteronormative people get to know that we're not a threat.

Having got to know Caroline, Franko, Michael (of Bar 74) and members of the Bendy Book Club, I am enormously grateful and happy to know that I can be out here and enjoy the freedoms that so many others are denied the world over.

I just want to end by saying that being out on this island is an absolute joy and a blessing. But the most important thing anyone from our community can do is to live their lives openly and honestly. It can be scary, but living a lie, hiding what it is that makes us who we truly, authentically are is destructive and wasteful. We only have this one life, so wherever it is, island or mainland, town or country just be true to yourself.

DIFFERENT IS BEAUTIFUL

Laura Franco Henao

Three main reasons have encouraged me to put pen to paper and share a story I had kept to myself. Firstly, I wanted to get to know the main character of this story better. Secondly, to thank many special people in my life and those who have been brave before me sharing their stories. Finally, to tell you that you are not alone. You are beautiful and unique, no matter who you are and who you love. I feel sorry for those who are not yet able to see the beauty in diversity.

I do not feel very comfortable using labels to describe myself. I do not feel like I am 100% of anything and I am constantly changing. For simplicity, I will define myself as a Spanish cisgender queer woman. I came to the Isle of Wight almost two years ago when I was 22. I have to admit that I expected people to be more close-minded because I knew the Island was politically more conservative and the average age of the population was quite high. However, despite some awkward looks and questions, I have not encountered any major issues as a non-straight person.

But when I came to the Island, I was already very comfortable with sharing that I do not only like men. I do not say to people that I am X or Y anymore, just like they do not need to tell me whether they are straight. I just say this is/was my partner, or I like this person.

This story will focus on how I came to feel so comfortable to act like this on the Isle of Wight. My gender identity and sexual orientation are a significant part of who I am but they are not fixed or binary. I have a tremendous respect for people who identify completely with a label and we need to have them to embrace diversity. Where there is no name, there is no visibility, and where you have no visibility, you cannot normalise it. However, it has done me harm to try to fit in one category. I like the term 'queer' because it is an umbrella term which accounts for the ambiguity and fluidity that I experience. I perceive gender identity and sexual orientation like any other thing about me, like a colour I like, a hobby, a music style etc. Unfortunately, in today's world, using these terms still comes with vast consequences about how people perceive you and behave around you but thanks to projects like this one, we are much closer to normalising it.

My favourite thing about writing this is that I have re-lived many memories from my childhood and teenage years. Each person's story is unique. Some people know since they are kids, some find out when they are in their fifties and some might never know. We all have our own pace. In the LGBTQ+ world, there is not one 'coming out' moment. You still need to 'come out' all the time, which is not easy. It is unfair that the default is straight and cisgender and I fight for the day in which it will not be necessary to 'come out' because we will have normalised diversity.

I always knew there was something different about me. Due to what I saw around me, I thought only boys could like girls so I wanted to look and behave like one. I wanted to be that boy that would take care of them and save them. Obviously, women do not need to be taken care of and they do not need to be saved but that was what I picked up from TV, etc. I also know now I do not need to be a man to like a woman.

There are usually at least two very important moments in the life of a person from the LGBTQ+ community: the first time you admit it to yourself and the first time you admit it to somebody else. These moments are powerful and can be scary especially depending on your circumstances because you know you risk losing people that matter to you and in a lot of places, you may be putting yourself at risk.

What have been the hardest parts?

The most frustrating part for me has been facing all the assumptions about it. People do not realise it and I know that most of them mean no harm but it is a constant fight. People suggesting that I am lesbian, that I like women more, or the looks in their faces when I have to remind them that I have never said that and that I like men too. How would they know what I feel better than me? With time, I have realised I do not have to convince anyone and I do not care what most people think but there are people close to me who still do this. I think the problem is that they do not understand the difference between presentation/ expression and identity. The way you present yourself to the world can help you express your identity but your expression is not your identity.

Another big struggle in the beginning was not knowing anything about the community. I was so confused for a long time. Firstly, thinking that I had to be a man to love women; then, trying to fit in liking only men and being feminine;

and finally, that need to choose labels. I did not learn about it in school, I did not have a lot of references in books, films or TV shows and my family did not speak a lot about it to me.

I have realised that many times I only wore make-up, heels or dresses to please some people who wanted me to be more feminine. It is so wrong that we grow up with this pressure. Why? Why do I have to look more feminine if I am already happy with the way I look? I sometimes wear heels, dresses and make-up now but on my own terms; when I want to, because I like it, and not because I am trying to look more feminine to, or for, other people.

In the *Appendices*, Appendix 2, page 210, I have included some of the questions I have been asked when telling people that I was dating a woman. Would a straight person get asked these questions, even from people he/she is not close to? My partners and I have also received many disgusting looks and comments, and I got in some fights for confronting them. This situation concerns me every day and I have always lived in countries with 'high' tolerance. What about the millions of LGBTQ+ people who live in places where it is illegal or where you can get killed, stoned, castrated, raped and suffer all sorts of degrading treatments? Of course, getting legal rights does not mean you can have a normal life. It takes much more than that for something to be normalised in a society.

What am I most proud of?

I am proud of being myself today. I am proud of understanding that I can be whoever I want, love whoever I love and that it is okay if it changes because we are all constantly changing. I am proud of being brave to tell other people, to stand up and raise my voice when I saw somebody saying something that was disrespectful.

It has helped me a lot to become involved in the community, to be part of societies at university that fight to normalise it and to bring other voices to the table. They help you meet other people who have experienced similar challenges. I helped organise the first Pride to ever take place in my city, Valladolid, in Spain. I was in an organisation called 'Plataforma de apoyo al colectivo LGTB+'. Being surrounded by people who understand you has been life-changing.

The feeling of community and belonging is essential in any movement or fight towards equality. You will always have somebody that loves you no matter who you are and who you love.

Change can be slow but courage is contagious. Fight for all those who cannot raise their voices. Fight for all those who have died because of who they are and love. Love is love, love will win and different is beautiful.

MARCHING WITH PRIDE

Isle of Wight Pride, a Short History

John Brownscombe

This is the story behind Isle of Wight Pride, an event no one expected to happen, let alone turn into a huge success. Overcoming prejudice and ignorance to create an event with an unexpected legacy touching many people's lives, and in turn, changing the Isle of Wight forever.

On 12 June 2016 the world was shocked by the tragic events that took place at Pulse, a famous LGBTQ+ nightclub in Orlando Florida. Forty nine people lost their lives as the result of an unprovoked attack by a gunman using an assault rifle and handgun. The shock, grief and sorrow felt by many in the LGBTQ+ and wider community both in the USA and farther afield led to the organisation of a series of vigils, including one held in St Thomas' Square Newport outside of Newport Minster. This took place on the evening of 17 June having been rapidly organised by Hampshire and Isle of Wight Constabulary's Lesbian and Gay Liaison Officer (LAGLO). Many groups, societies, third sector and public sector organisations came together to show their solidarity. It was the first time that such a public event had happened on the Isle of Wight and the attendance and response was overwhelming and very moving. Local members of the LGBTQ+ community were joined by supportive straight allies.

Although much work had already been taking place to support and enable social connection within the local LGBTQ+ community with initiatives such as BreakOut Youth, Age UK, Gay Men's Chorus, Wight Lesbians, Time for T, Sexual Health, various organisations' equality and diversity officers and others, being brought together as one for this sad event had galvanised community support which was more widespread than many of us had anticipated and this became the catalyst for discussions to hold an Isle of Wight Pride.

A small working group was convened to discuss what such an event might look like and to discuss how best to work together to make it happen. Initially many of the people involved in this were also involved in LGBTQ+ support roles either in their day jobs or as part of volunteering. Gradually the group grew in size and started to develop a plan for an event in July 2017. Roles and responsibilities were established and fact-finding undertaken to better understand what legal requirements and considerations would need to be satisfied. In order to ensure that what was being planned would appeal and be representative of the local LGBTQ+ community an online survey was created and advertised through a new Facebook page established for Isle of Wight Pride and through the local media.

The results of the survey were overwhelmingly positive with half the respondents identifying as LGBTQ+ and half as straight allies, giving us the vision for a family-friendly free event over one day, with entertainment, stalls and activities and perhaps most importantly being preceded by a Parade. Ryde was chosen as the venue as public processions had been held through the town over the years including Ryde Carnival and Mardi Gras and a number of other events using the public spaces along the Esplanade and at Eastern Gardens. It also offered the opportunity for Isle of Wight Pride to have a unique element of having the main arena on the beautiful sand at Harbour Beach.

The old adage 'any publicity is good publicity' was put to the test in December 2016 when a columnist in the *Isle of Wight County Press* published her opinion piece. Known for strident and mocking articles this 'journalist' decided to strongly voice her opinion that our event could be 'tolerated' provided that once it was over we would 'shut up'. She continued to generally bemoan the extent of coverage across all media of people sharing their stories of being their authentic selves, seeking to confuse sexuality and gender identity with sexual practice. The homophobia and transphobia weren't even undercurrents.[113]

---

[113]Charlotte Hofton, 'Pride Parade - Do a Deal?', *Isle of Wight County Press*, December 9, 2016.

Deliberately written to be controversial and perhaps offensive in style, the column was met with almost universal condemnation. It received national coverage, suddenly pitching the nascent Pride group into the public eye. Things moved rapidly, resulting in her resignation and an official retraction by the editor who then publicly gave his full support to Isle of Wight Pride. Being propelled into the spotlight left the new Team Pride carrying the banner for not only delivering a successful Pride event, but as vanguards for challenging some local thinking and mores. Isle of Wight Pride had to be a success!

A lot of hard work then followed. Team Pride saw a small group of dedicated volunteers determined to deliver a great event and that it be financially solvent. Sponsorship was obtained from organisations and local businesses who shared our vision belief in the value of Pride to the local LGBTQ+ community, the local economy and also as part of the Isle of Wight's offer as a tourism destination. People were already talking about longevity before Pride had even happened. A series of events and fundraisers were organised to help promote Isle of Wight Pride and provide more opportunities for the community to come together through the year. The knowledge of the event and a general air of anticipation and excitement began to build.

Then Politics with a big 'P' erupted on the Island. In April 2017 the A-level Politics class at Christ the King College in Newport had a longstanding arrangement for a visit by the Isle of Wight constituency MP Andrew Turner. One student decided to ask him if he would be attending Isle of Wight Pride. He replied that whilst he had received an invitation, he would not be going as in his view homosexuality is '"wrong" and "dangerous to society"'[114]. The students, shocked by this response, shared the comments and inevitably it was reported to the local media, being pounced on by national media outlets. Events moved quickly. Roundly criticised for his stance, Turner stood down as MP. Some rallied to support him but the majority clearly felt that his decision to voice his view was inappropriate and demonstrated that he was out of touch with most of his constituents.

On a warm, sunny morning of 15 July 2017, the first Isle of Wight Pride began. With the site barely prepared, the Parade left Ryde School at 12 p.m. and headed through Ryde to Eastern Esplanade. Full of colour and fun with the theme 'Love Wins', thousands of people lined the streets (in particular Union Street), clapping, cheering and waving rainbow flags as those in the

---

[114]Tom Peck, 'Tory MP Standing down after Telling Students Homosexuality Is "Dangerous to Society"', *Independent*. Independent Digital News and Media, April 28, 2017. https://www.independent.co.uk/news/uk/politics/andrew-turner-tory-mp-stand-down-calling-homosexuality-danger-society-a7708671.html.

procession passed by. Individuals, groups, societies, organisations and some businesses were present in the Parade, showing their support for inclusivity and diversity. Many of the shops had decorated their windows to mark the occasion. Over 4,500 people filled Eastern Gardens and Harbour Beach; Isle of Wight Pride was a fantastic mix of entertainment, a community village of stalls with a tea tent and community stage, family activities, and great acts on the main stage.

The impact was apparent almost immediately. Many a tear of joy was shed on the day with stories from folk who had grown up on the Island but chose to leave as they didn't feel welcome, unable to believe that there was now a Pride event back at home. It's a true legacy to hear that people have decided to return to the Island and others are wanting to move here as a result of this public display of support of equality and diversity. Isle of Wight Pride had an unexpectedly wide-reaching appeal, around a quarter of those attending had come from the mainland and some from abroad.

21 July 2018 saw the return of Isle of Wight Pride, bigger and brighter than ever. The organisers had been encouraged to bid to host UK Pride following on from the success of year one and in January 2018 heard that they had been successful in the bid! This along with obtaining Charitable Incorporated Organisation status in late 2017, demonstrating a clear commitment to becoming a sustainable event for the future. With headliners Conchita Wurt (who was also promoting EuroPride being hosted by Austria in 2018) and Gok Wan, the event was truly an international party. The weather was fantastic again for us and we had a crowd of around 14,500 people in attendance. The Parade had grown in size and more and more shops in Ryde and across the Island had decorated their shops showing support for the event and community. The bigger event meant a bigger Team Pride and we were offered a disused youth club premises in the town to act as our temporary HQ in the run up to the day. It was a great success for the volunteers who made it happen and led to a small financial surplus being made to put back into the operating costs of the charity and for 2019.

As all things do, Isle of Wight Pride had to adapt. In early 2019, some Trustees relocated to the mainland for work which meant that the future of the event looked uncertain given the dwindling numbers of people able to commit to what had now become part of the annual Isle of Wight event calendar. Initially a decision was taken to have a 'fallow' year. This was met with disappointment and concern by the local community. A small group formed who stated that they could make something happen in 2019; new Trustees for the Isle of Wight Pride Charity reached out to the group to talk about what might be achieved and consequently a scaled-back event was planned. Working closely with local businesses, we were able to ensure that there was a programme of entertainment, a community marketplace and of course the colourful Parade. Over the day it was estimated that around 3,000 people came into the community market, which was free to enter, with many more enjoying various venues in the town. Yet again, Isle of Pride rose to the occasion, different, yet distinct in character and loved by everyone who came.

In 2020, we had planned to combine the best of the events from 2017 and 2019 to return to the main arena on the beach as a ticketed event to provide an income to pay along with sponsorship for the costs of holding the event, with a free community village on another part of the Esplanade. Preparations for this were well underway when the unexpected Covid-19 pandemic led to the cancellation of all public events due to the need to adhere to social distancing. Although it was disappointing that our 2020 event had to be cancelled, we will be back when the ability to come together as one community will be perhaps more poignant than ever.

EXTRACTS FROM ORAL HISTORIES

Karl S

Pride brought a great deal of change. I was a town councillor for a while and when Pride was first talked about, the Mayor mentioned it in one of our meetings and said this was going to happen and the town council were very positive about it and I was quite surprised. Obviously I was out as a gay man, probably the first Isle of Wight openly gay councillor, or town councillor not Island Council, and one of the town councillors turned to me and said, "absolutely nothing against having Pride, absolutely nothing against it, but I've got to say, there are only a few of you on the Island, why do you feel the need to have a Pride?" And I said, "well, Stonewall", and they all nodded their heads, they knew who Stonewall are, "suggests that there are maybe between 8 and 11,000 people on the Island who identify as LGBTQ. There are thirty or so people in here, that's roughly ten percent of the population are LGBTQ so there are probably two more people as well as me in this room who identify as LGBTQ". I kind of had to pick him up off the floor, he just hadn't realised. People didn't, before Pride, realise that there were so many people over here and I think Pride, if nothing else, brought that to the fore. People actually saw that actually it is more than just half a dozen people on the Island, there are actually quite a few LGBTQ people here and I think that was very positive.

I remember the first Pride, going to the station, going to Shanklin station to make our way to Ryde and the platform was full of people, absolutely full of people, and I'm thinking, "where are these people going?". Then we looked and thought, "she's wearing a multicoloured rainbow skirt, he's got a rainbow T-shirt on, they've got glitter on their faces. My God, they are going to Pride!". By the time we got to Sandown the ticket guy was saying to people on the platform, "you're going to have to wait for the next train because we're full". We got to Ryde and there, flying from the Royal Esplanade Hotel was the biggest gay flag I'd ever seen.

It was just amazing, this is on the Island. And I think things turned amazing then, people had their flags out and posters up and all sorts of stuff and the people out on the streets. To think that something like that could actually be happening here. It was quite amazing. The second one, the UK Pride, was amazing. I mean I will never forget the massive rainbow flag down Union Street. The sight of that was just amazing!

Last year there was talk about whether they were going to have it or not and I thought maybe they shouldn't, maybe do it every other year or something like that, but they said, "yes, we'll do it", and again it was fantastic. It wasn't the same as the first two years but it was still an amazing event. So yes, I think things have changed.

I think it's a pity that there hasn't been a sort of change within… there's still no bar, there's still no club, I suppose that's a lot to expect, but there isn't even a coffee bar or a cafe that people could meet in. I know that in this age of the internet everyone is fiddling about on tablets and phones and things and that's how people are connecting but there is nothing quite like having an actual place that you can go to and pick up the gay press and find out what's going on on the Island… if anything. But there's no a way of letting people on the Island know the kind of events and things that are happening, whether they are necessarily LGBTQ events, specifically or whether they just may be of interest to gay people. I think that's a pity but I think things have changed slowly. Slowly, but things are happening.

Anonymous

My first Pride was London Pride. No, it wasn't. It was Portsmouth Pride and Portsmouth had this Pride and it was lots of, I can't remember who I went with. I think it was the LGBT group on the Isle of Wight and they had this kind of fete area on the Island and it was '98 or '99 or something like that and Mr Gay UK was there. I remember getting a photo with him and having all these stalls and we took the catamaran over to Portsmouth for the day. It was a day event, there was no parade, it was just a pop-up thing in the park and then we got the cat back. That was my first Pride and I remember when I was in uni I went to my first London Pride and that was good.

My first London Pride. It was so big, I remember that, it was really big, it was really massive and it was great and I went with a couple of really pretentious people who didn't really want to go off and have fun. I ended up losing them. It was the first time I have ever been in London on my own having to find my way back, I had to ask everyone to get me back to Victoria train station or wherever it was to get back to Southampton. That was very good. I only heard a couple of years ago that the Isle of Wight was planning Pride when I first went to it. I thought it was amazing.

When I heard about the first Isle of Wight Pride, I was kind of half expecting. I was like, "is this a trap?" Because "are they going to burn us?" It's really interesting because I went to the first Isle of Wight Pride and I was friends with someone who manages the catamaran and he was doing a VIP trip from Portsmouth to Ryde and was going to come on the beach and it was with all the drag queens and there were tents up and stalls up and I thought, "yeah, let's do this!" So we did it and it was fun and it was lovely, it was really lovely.

My god-daughter and my friend were there; my two friends were there and my god-daughter had a sign that said, I think I've still got it actually, my god-daughter had a sign that said, 'Great to see you, happy Pride'. She was about eight or nine at the time. That's how far we've come, you'd never get that in the 90s, a child doing something like that. So the catamaran landed on the beach, we got off and it was Ryde Beach, Appley Beach, so it was a really beautiful, sandy lovely beach and we talked to everyone and it was just great fun. I think it was like, the party continued in a nightclub and we got the last catamaran home.

I went back the following year for World Pride; no, UK Pride, and I did notice that there was a bar down the road and I noticed there were a lot more straight people there which I always think, when straight people attend Pride I'm always like, "well, yeah, come along and celebrate with us but don't take over, this is an event for us, you know, about being proud for one day". It's like our gay Christmas basically. So I am seeing this place full of straight people celebrating and I thought, "Oh God, this is getting more and more about...", but then I thought, "what's wrong with that?" because they're not being homophobic.

I think we have a problem because the LGBT in Pride has been slowly pushed, not pushed out but it just feels as if a lot more straight people go than gay people, I think. And although that shouldn't be an issue, it is an issue because LGBT rights are an issue at the moment, especially trans rights which often get pushed to one side.

So yeah, I went to the Isle of Wight Pride, that was fun but before that Isle of Wight Pride, I'd been to a lot of Prides in Brighton, that was great fun, and London Prides. I even marched in London Pride one year for Football Against Homophobia, and I got to wear a T-shirt and kick a ball about. It was quite interesting because you got some lads who would be like, "good for you, good for you!" And then some people would be like, wouldn't even look at you! Because football is such a masculine sport, isn't it? So, that's the last taboo.

Robert

The Gay Pride events have been on the Isle of Wight, of course. We had one in Ryde and I helped to ensure the Labour Party was connected with that and had its banners and put some money in and so on, but I didn't show myself personally. I don't know why. Partly because it is a bit difficult to get there from here, I don't drive, but that wasn't the real reason, I just didn't feel I wanted to, wrong generation I think.

There wasn't much before. In the time that I was younger you would have got a very adverse reaction anywhere on the Island with a Pride event. Much, much less so now and that's a great thing. But then again, a bit late. Well, I'd give it to other people. One member, a young man, who was keen on doing it, so I basically encouraged him to. You have, I think, to be young to enter into the spirit of that entirely. I think what put me off, actually, was I saw the Chairman of the Isle of Wight Council leading a parade and looking totally absurd. There he was with his chain around his neck going through all sorts of peculiar physical gyrations and I thought, "I'm not doing that, no, that's just silly". So that put me off. But, I dunno, I'd rather encourage others to do that than do it myself.

I think it's remarkable that it happened at all given the territory that has been covered since the time I would be more familiar with, to today. If you had tried to do that in the streets of Ryde in the 80s even, you would get a similar reaction to trying to do it through the streets of Moscow. You'd have things thrown at you, you would be cat-called, you would be insulted, you'd have to have a heavy police presence. That isn't the case any more and that is a very positive thing I think.

Karl L

In the same year that the Gay Men's Chorus ended, the first Island Pride took place, which, I have to be honest, I wasn't in favour of. I was sceptical. I didn't think that the Island was ready for it at that point and I was proved wrong and I am happy to be proved wrong. And you need to then say to yourself, what did that bring to the Island? Well, it brought hope for our young people. But it hasn't actually changed anything in reality on the ground because although there was an attempt to do one or two gay nights again, there was a little bit of competition that existed between different groups and that didn't help the scene move forward.

This year's Pride has been much more community-minded, in my view, than the previous ones because it is being less commercial and that's still allowed the community to enjoy that. But in actual fact what do you do then when people come out of the closet, particularly if they are young, and there isn't anything there for them? The Island does have a youth group, which is running, it is being operated from a group in Southampton, but it does meet. But we don't necessarily need youth groups, what we need is community engagement, community socialisation. A lot of people say to me, "well, we don't need that now because we can go out and sit in a pub", etc. That's great and I am really pleased that people can go out and feel safer and socialise in a way that they want to do, but at the same time we also need to keep our culture and that culture has been lost.

Caroline

There were what I see now as a couple of catalysts that kind of created the success of Pride on the Island. The first one was, well, I am not sure if it was in this order, but Charlotte Hofton, the journalist, wrote an article for the *County Press* and I remember reading it and thinking, "this is outrageous!". The tone was so old-fashioned, the language, the viewpoint was just so stereotypical and all of a sudden people reacted to it in a way I had not really seen for quite a long time on the Island.

On the Isle of Wight there is that community feel, everybody goes along and gets on with their business but as soon as there is something that a lot of people don't agree with, people do club together. Then Charlotte Hofton left the paper and then there was a whole thing with Andrew Turner (the MP at the time) and the comments that he was alleged to have made and all of a sudden Pride got this massive momentum and everybody was really excited about it and it was fantastic. Tatchell and everybody walking down the street and thinking, "this is absolutely incredible!" I'd got up quite early in the morning in the first year and I went to get a paper on Union Street and it was funny because I saw two people walking down the street with a bottle of water, pouring water down the road, and I said, "what are you doing?" They said something about blessing the street because they were religious and they didn't agree with it, but other than that I didn't see any anti-LGBT or homophobic behaviour at all.

David

You see I don't think Pride should be still having the actual parades, because you don't get straight people going down on floats on Union Street saying, "we're straight, we're happy!" We've done the fifty years, we got what we wanted, so therefore we just get on with our lives.

Karen

I went to a few Gay Prides in London, that was quite awesome really, being part of a bigger thing, that was good. Yeah, yeah. I mean the whole Pride thing, I thought it was really good but then, I was quite cynical that all these big companies suddenly came out as being "gay friendly". Although it's good that we have got that support, for me, I suspect it was the fact that they were just after our money.

Then I didn't like the fact that all the straight people were having a good time because it was my day – all the straights with their rainbow flags on their faces and you're thinking, "it's great that you're embracing it", but no. I've been to Brighton Pride and I liked that because it was a big day. On the Island it is good to celebrate, but it is like all my straight friends were really excited about it and they were going along and I'm thinking, "but it's my day". So yeah, that's quite good.

The women's group was really good. When I split up with my ex it was like, "right, I need to see who else is out on the Island", and I found the LGBT group on Facebook and that linked me to the Lesbians on the Island and then to the Bendy Book Club and everybody's been really friendly. It is not as big as it used to be but it's good that you know that there are people out there and you are part of something. So yes, the Prides are good, I thought they were really good but it's just that all the straights can go and have their own day. Then you get people on Facebook saying, "I'm straight, why can't we have a straight day?". I think they are missing the point about our rights and I think it is important that we do stand up for our rights and the Isle of Wight is better now, you know, it is more friendly now.

Sydney

I don't know if I would have been able, if I would have felt like there was any hope of coming out on the Island without Pride. I do wonder about that. Like, because of all the negative experiences I had, I have been in every Pride because I was identifying as a bisexual male before, it is only since coming out that I have actually fully embraced that I am pretty sure I am a lesbian.

So, Pride. I have been in every Pride parade and that was astonishing for the Island, just seeing, like, I didn't know what it was going to be like the first time, I was just like, "what is this going to be like?" I have been in other Prides before and I was like, like, "what, how many people are going to turn up?" I was expecting there to be counter protests. Even at London Pride you get little penned-off sections, you know, "Repent! Repent, sinners!" As the leather twinks sort of dance past them sort of thing, whatever, but there was none of that and there was so many people and it was just astonishing. The positive outpourings of, it seemed like there was, it was so weird because especially as growing up on the Island there was nothing LGBT here at all, nothing, not even a gay night that I knew of anywhere let alone a gay bar or anything like that. There was very little, I wasn't aware of it, there was no trans support group that I knew of, there was possibly Break Out had started maybe, I am not even sure of the timeline of that, I think I was too old by the time I heard about it. There was absolutely nothing; there was no support, no community and then suddenly… you feel like you are completely alone and then suddenly all these people are just there and everyone is cool with it, everyone loving it. Even though it is mostly, you know, just an excuse for people to go out and have a booze-up which everyone likes, but they are there and it was astonishing. Pride was huge, really, really huge. It has had an incalculable effect on the culture of the Island I think. Yeah, it just really has. It's blown the cobwebs away. You can think that maybe the Island isn't quite as closed and conservative, [such a] dreadful place, as you'd think.

I know so many people, quite a few people, not so many but quite a few people who came out because of Pride essentially, especially older people, people who are in their 60s, 70s, 80s even, saying, like, "sod it!" Which is amazing. It allowed people to come out and it showed people that actually there is all this, there are all these people here, there are so many. You know statistically there must be thousands of queer people on the Island, but you never see them.

Callum

I joined Isle of Wight Pride, I think the second year of Isle of Wight Pride, me and my other half and our friends, we just went, our LGBT friends, we went to the second year it was on. I had been to Brighton Pride probably about four or five years before my visit to Isle of Wight Pride. On the Isle of Wight, it was still fairly new, it was, "wow, this is happening on the Isle of Wight, it's amazing". So that was obviously my first experience of a Pride on the Isle of Wight.

It's interesting, I have only recently associated Isle of Wight Pride with a political movement, and as I've learnt more about the history of Pride, I begin to think of it that way. I think last year I kind of wanted to do some volunteering and try and get involved locally in something that I could relate to. There was a local call-out for people to help with Isle of Wight Pride otherwise it might not go ahead and so I live in Ryde, I grew up here, I have got that grass-roots connection to the town, so I felt compelled to in some way help out initially with marketing and then on to help with traders and stall holders.

In fact Brighton and the Isle of Wight Pride are the only Pride events I have been to. I think that I have taken advantage of the fact that I have got a Pride event on my doorstep and consciously deciding to volunteer at Isle of Wight Pride last year was something that was more out of trying to help the community event to happen rather than identifying as gay and I must volunteer.

Brighton Pride has been around longer, it is more established, getting more commercial whereas Isle of Wight Pride is still fairly new. I feel like its values are perhaps based in needing to offer an event which is, I say more inclusive but I just feel it is more grass-roots in the sense that its values are still based upon the origins of what Pride stands for. Obviously, like I said, I am fairly new to the more historical side of Pride and the political statement that is Pride and obviously learning about that has made me more aware of what it stands for. When you look at how other Prides like Brighton are reported in the media it's clearly a very different sort of event.

And from what I know from speaking to people [and] there's Prides popping up all over the country. I think it's fantastic that an event like this promotes equal rights for everyone across the UK, not just in these population hotspots. It's dispersed and regardless of whether it is a party on the beach or a small pop-up event in a town centre in the middle of nowhere, it is still symbolising equality.

And Pride on the Isle of Wight was well received. I think a lot of these things, stuff's been generational, of course, you are always going to get people whose views don't match my own and I think that's equally important that we have that. I think people have been generally very supportive of the event but I think, obviously you are drawn to things on social media and you see some of the comments that people leave. I think, to be honest, that doesn't surprise me, I think Pride is still a very new event for some people and I think it is important that we embrace everyone within the community.

Rosa

I really enjoyed the Pride. I did think, though, that we were kind of herded a little; we had this sort of narrow corridor where this Gay Pride event took place and the beach was cordoned off and I was bit upset about that because I thought to myself, "wouldn't it be nice to just walk along the beach, take my shoes off and walk in the sand and enjoy this wonderful atmosphere?" But we were kind of restricted to this very tight, narrow corridor, which I felt was a bit over-crowded. There were too many people in a very small space and there was a completely empty beach where we could have had a lot more space, we could have sat down and had a picnic, you know, could have made it a bit more enjoyable.

I didn't go to the second one, I have to say, I didn't go to the second one. But it's interesting; on that very first Pride I was there with my little flag, waving it around and I had some friends around me and stuff and I saw somebody that I know from a different event (she's not a lesbian, she's a straight woman) and her husband. So I waved, "hello!" And, "oh", she said, "very nice to meet you here, glad to see you've got your flag". She was very friendly and then her husband started making some, what I thought, quite offensive comments. He was saying that, you know, having sex with children, that a lot of these men have sex with children and I said, "I beg your pardon?" He said, "well, they're all paedophiles, aren't they?" I said, "I don't think so, paedophiles are heterosexual as well, you know!" And I was actually quite shocked that he was trying to say that gay men are paedophiles when I am thinking to myself, "no they're not", I said, "that's actually not gay", I said, "a lot of straight men have sex with children, young girls", I said, "it's not a gay thing". But anyway, she sort of ushered her husband out of the way and off. He obviously didn't understand at all what he was saying or realised even how offensive he was. She knew and so she ushered him out of the way. That was the only thing I thought to myself, "I am really sorry I bumped into them now".

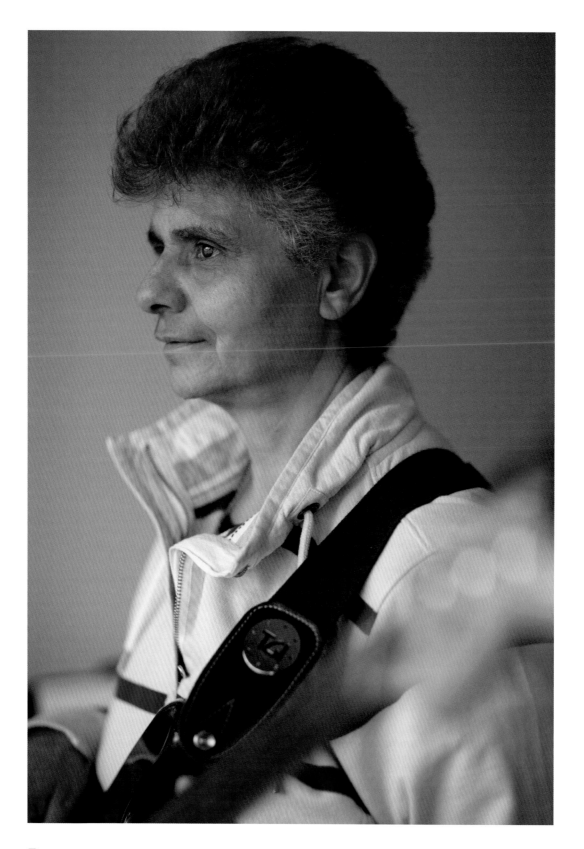

Rosa

I think it is lovely that we've had Pride and I think that, because when I remember years ago the very first Pride I ever went to, it was about 2000 people and there was no advertising of it. We walked through streets, people stared, it was something that was, it was, "oh, look at that weird lot walking through". Some of the guys were dressed in dresses, some of the girls dressed in tuxedos and things and so people were looking at us as if we were very strange. That improved over the years to the point where you got 250,000 people merging at Marble Arch ready to walk along the Embankment and then have your party in, wherever it was. So that grew and it became an event that people started to celebrate and not just gay people, not just lesbians, not just transgendered people and bisexuals it was something that they brought friends and family to. That was really nice, to see that, to see family supporting someone and coming along and turning up. That was nice, but here on the Island it is still very much in its infancy. It is still kind of growing, it hasn't grown into that acceptable space. What made me think that was the way that we were all herded in that little corridor, that very first Pride, which is why I didn't go to the second one. Maybe I'll go to the next one and see how it works out.

WRITTEN HISTORIES

Alan's Story

15 July 2017 is a date that will be etched in my memory forever. It was roughly fourteen months after returning to the Island with my husband to live. I had moved to London in August 2009, thinking that I'd probably never return, apart from visiting family and friends.

The excitement and anticipation in the air was palpable as I stood on Ryde beach watching the entertainment onstage. The weather was being kind, warm and sunny, just as it should be for this sort of occasion. This was the day of the very first Pride event held on the Isle of Wight. Recalling those words, I still pinch myself. Certainly, it was history in the making, and I felt it, I felt excited and nervous (nervous being the operative word) to be part of it.

As I stood there, taking in all the sights and sounds of celebration and happiness, a simple but quite profound realisation came to me as I happened to glance up at one of the many rainbow flags fluttering high on a flagpole along Ryde

Esplanade. In that moment, a photo was taken in my head and stored away. I remember thinking, "OMG! I can't believe they're really flying rainbow flags, and this is a gay event... in Ryde... on the Isle of Wight! Shock horror!"

As LGBTQ+ people, were we finally being accepted in this place that time seems to forget? Had there always been acceptance here? I suppose the irony is that within this quaint, time-forgotten place, our vibrant and hopeful event was slowly but surely starting to drag it screaming into the 21st century. There was certainly a lot of crowds supporting the day, mainly families with children, and I'm so glad to say, visually there were many allies, and I'm sure a lot were also families from the LGBTQ+ community.

Thinking back now, I know the feeling of nervousness was more to do with that dreaded feeling of exposure, of being outed, even though I was already out and proud, but the Isle of Wight did not represent being out and proud for me, quite the opposite.

It's sad in one way that I felt I had to leave this beautiful place that had been my home for the past seventeen years or so. But perhaps it was inevitable that I would end up living in a city. Life was tough in London at first, but there I gradually found myself again. Although I was 'out' on the Island, first with my family, and eventually with my work, I felt I could be 'out' and discover myself more within the anonymity of the big city. Strangely, I felt safer and more accepted living in London.

As a small community, the Island tends to feel cliquey and indifferent towards people who are different to the norm. I guess the norm is being straight and white. But, as part of my own history, I was a straight white male. So, yes, my history is chequered to say the least, and perhaps that's a story for another time? But strangely, in my previous life on the Island living as a straight man with two children, I never actually felt entirely accepted. It was like the other straight parents I befriended had sussed me out? I never felt entirely accepted or at ease with them. I stopped trying and despite my lovely family and dear friends, I felt more and more alienated.

So, moving back here from London was a daunting prospect, partly because I'd now be in an openly gay marriage living on the Island, I was especially scared that people who knew me in my former life would judge me as a fraud. So, to put that particular record 'straight', I wasn't a fraud, I was simply caught up in a life that was right for me at the time, a life that was born out of extreme fear of non-acceptance, of not fitting in. Fear was always with me, because this life journey had started away from the Island many years previous and fear was with me yet again. But this time, I had much more courage to be my authentic self, and this was only possible because of the support and love from my husband and my family. As we were planning to relocate back here, I recall feeling exposed as we viewed houses, and although I can't prove it, I'm sure that one of our house sales fell through because we were a gay couple.

Moving back has become a success for both of us, although it wasn't without its troubles. I have made new friends, reacquainted with old friends (who knew I was out) and settled into a job where nobody knew me before.

As a new member of staff, I always prefer to let people get to know me as a person before coming out to them. I don't expect them to come out as straight, so why should I come out as gay? Well, I suppose the coming out part happens organically through conversation, like "no, I don't have a wife, but me and my husband love gardening". So, needless to say, once you've had that conversation with one colleague, you don't need to have it with anyone else. I do feel very fortunate that all my colleagues have accepted me for who I am and don't have a problem with me being gay. I am totally out at work and feel comfortable with it. Perhaps as they got to know me as a friend, and I became a likeable character; they don't feel threatened by me.

I think for me, in terms of acceptance, it feels like the island has changed for the better, especially as I now know many people who are allies and who positively support the Isle of Wight Pride. However, there is still much more to be achieved. I feel there is a section of people who support our Pride event because the Island community does like a good street and beach party, it has to be said. One of my amusing memories of Pride night in 2019 was chatting to a straight couple at the bar in Bar 74, Union Street. I was waiting to be served, they were both drunk and in good spirits, they clearly realised I was part of the LGBTQ+ community, probably because of what I was wearing, so they asked me what LGBTQ+ stands for... when we got to the letter Q, I said it stood for queer. They both looked surprised and slightly horrified, because they thought the word queer was derogatory. I said it is derogatory if you call me it, but if I choose to refer to myself as queer, then it's me reclaiming that word. I could see that they didn't get it, and obviously, if we were in a different situation at a different time, I might have been able to explain it better for them. To change the subject slightly, I asked them what they thought of the parade, to which they replied, "well... it was a bit shit wasn't it?" I can only assume they were comparing it to Ryde carnival, or the previous year's Pride parade where we hosted UK Pride, which was bigger. I was attempting to explain to them that Pride isn't all about celebration and parades but also about struggle for equality, acceptance, acknowledgement of past inequalities and remembrance of past contributions to that struggle. They left the bar mid conversation, which was a bit rude, but I was happy that at least I'd tried to engage with them in a positive and constructive way. You can't win them all! We've come a long way, but our collective and personal struggles continue.

Charlotte's Story

What would that fifteen year old feel to see her older self attend her first Isle of Wight Pride with her wife and two children? Would she cry the tears of joy that the 35 year old did? Would she wonder why she was still on the Island? When that fifteen year old was desperate for escape. An escape from the isolation and the expectation of fulfilling the family script. Your sole purpose as a woman was to marry (a man of course) and have babies. Coming from a huge Island family where the number of children you had was prided on.

I struggled to accept who I was, I remember having a scrap piece of paper with the IW LGB switchboard number on and never quite having the confidence to ring… although I got to a phone booth once and let it ring twice!

Going to school in the shadow of Section 28, and dykes and poofs were sniggered at. We had one lesbian teacher and she scared me she was so butch to me. That was not who I saw myself as. Living on the isolated Island my perception was that lesbians were 'nearly men'.

I liked heels and make-up so how could I be gay? I needed to get off this island. Watching the soaps for ideas of another way of life, how I could be? But distraught at the homophobia, trying to gauge friends' and family's reactions but not too obviously, I hid behind the identity of a reborn Christian, finding some sense of containment there. I could hide saving myself for marriage amongst the young Christians of the Island.

I left to go to university wanting to escape this claustrophobic island. There is a truth in the joke that you wind your clock back twenty years when you go to the Island. The mainland eventually gave me the physical distance and the confidence to explore my sexuality, knowing I would be safe from gossip and amongst those who understand.

Eventually the secrecy and inauthentic life I presented with on the Island became too much. I came out. The family rejection I feared never came.

I stayed on the mainland and met my wife and it all made sense. I felt complete, I understood all the love songs and poems I had cynically dismissed. I understood I was living them. The Island didn't leave me alone here. We discovered that her father and my brother's father in law had worked together on the Island. Her dad had lived in East Cowes at the same time as mine and had even been at the same school. We married in church… or legally civil partnered as this was what the law allowed us to do at the time. Bringing my faith back to me. When a month later I was expecting our first child the Island called us home. Buoyed by family support and love. We have made our home in East Cowes. The rejection I had feared as a fifteen year old never came to be. The family we have made are treated as such although some curiosity occurs at times. Our daughter is now educating people in same sex marriage legalities at her church primary school! Now writing this in 'lock down' on the Island there is no place I would rather be.

Anna's Story

In October 1997, I walked into Karl's corner office at the Isle of Wight College to get a friend some condoms because she was too embarrassed to get some herself. I had not met Karl before but we hit it off straightaway. Over the next couple of months, I saw him a lot and he informed me of the World AIDS Day Disco at the Prince Consort in Ryde. Channel 4 had just released a wonderful new film, *Beautiful Thing*, a moving and sweet gay love story with a soundtrack made up almost entirely of Mamas and Papas songs. That soundtrack means just as much to me now as it did back then and the film is a big part of my story.

I was introduced to some other younger people, who were just starting to make an LGBT youth group on the Island. The first of its kind we believed. IGLYN (Island Gay and Lesbian Youth Network) was formed. Five members were the initial founder members, and as they all moved one by one, I was the only one left with the mobile phone (provided by Health Promotion).

With a bit of support, formal groups were held in the Pyle street clinic and then further along Pyle Street in the Cranstoun Drug Services building after hours. We had film nights, went ice-skating and mostly just provided a safe space for people to be themselves. It was a big secret, so many people feared losing their families, which became a reality, sadly for a lot of people. It all came to a halt when I moved off the Island for a couple of years, but eventually there was some funding and a professional group was started.

One of my best friend's parents was a devout Catholic. She couldn't accept that either of us was gay and would invite me round for dinner, in the hope that we could be together and get married. A lot of the people moved away, some committed suicide, not being accepted for who they were, and there was always a hush around it, the real reasons brushed under the carpet. It was this that, on reflection really, more than anything bonded us as a community that shared grief, and the understanding of how hard it was for a lot of people to be out. We created our own families of choice, where we could share in the heartbreak and grief for those we were losing, no matter the reason.

The switchboard, the newsletter, the social gatherings were a major lifeline, even for the most anti-social of us, because being around other gay people made you feel like home more than anything. It felt safe and although not without drama, it was a place to be yourself. I kept my membership card for the LGBT nights at the Plough and Barleycorn, and still have it today. You had to go in the back room and it wasn't fully private, but it was a haven for a lot of people.

It was a time where every little bit of visibility on TV was celebrated by all as if we had won the lottery, with people recording the programmes on VHS tape to watch over and over again. When Ellen came out, it was Channel 4 again who made a big thing of it, with a whole night of LGBT content in the build up to the episode, even if you'd never watched Ellen before, her coming out was a personal victory for us all. As the internet took off and *Bad Girls* hit the screens, chatrooms suddenly made the world smaller and the possibility of connecting with other gay people grew. I think it shifted people to some extent away from the social events, but other factors contributed to the changing landscape of the LGBT social community events on the Island.

Fast-forward to 2016 and the Pulse nightclub massacre in Orlando. It affected a lot of people worldwide, for its targeted hate towards the LGBT community and the significant death toll was striking. I wanted to do something, to make a statement about it and stand in solidarity with all those who were hurting and feeling this, to show love in the face of hate. After speaking to my employers and gaining their full support, I approached Hampshire Constabulary's LAGLO officers and with their support, the vigil was arranged. We did not know how many people would turn up, I thought, perhaps six or so of us, but it was the action that was more important to me than the numbers. With the murder of MP Jo Cox, just before the vigil, we made it about her too, because hate is not acceptable.

I had a couple of large Pride flags in the office and after some emails between a few agencies, it was agreed that the Pride flags could be raised – one on Newport police station and one at County Hall. I can still remember the calls and messages I got from people that day, one person who said they nearly crashed as they were coming onto Coppins Bridge roundabout from the dual carriageway when they saw the Pride flag. I know for me personally, to see the flags raised was the first time I had felt represented and seen by authorities here, and they were my flags!

As we were setting up in St Thomas' Square, outside Newport Minster, Peter Woodnutt approached me and introduced himself. He asked to read a poem he had written, called *Silent Love* which we welcomed with open arms. The crowd grew, it was spitting a little with rain at times and the wind made lighting candles pretty much impossible, but it didn't dampen the mood at what turned out to be a remarkable and historic event. To have so much visible police support was amazing. Speaking to a crowd of over 300 people, some who made signs and banners, others with Pride flags or their brightest clothes was humbling. When Peter read his poem it was beautiful, poignant and impactful. I can remember thinking of all those times I had been told that the Isle of Wight was not ready for a Pride event and I knew in that moment, we could make it happen.

Afterwards we were approached by Zoe Thompson from Ryde Business Association who had brought some young people from Ryde to support the event and she talked about the possibility of a Pride event. That was the beginnings of Pride on the Isle of Wight. Out of something so tragic and horrific, an act of hate several thousand miles away, the Isle of Wight responded with love and stepped up to the mark to celebrate diversity.

There will always be people who, sadly, don't feel able to attend Pride, or be visible, especially in our small Island community. However, Pride has become an important part of the Island's cultural calendar. It is, however, more than a once a year celebration, it is about creating change so that people are safe to be themselves and people are aware and respectful towards diversity. It's about funding services that meet the needs of a diverse population, not just the visible majority.

I am proud of the changes on the Island. I am extremely proud of all those who are finding their authentic selves and the strength and courage to live out and proud. To all the allies, businesses and organisations who realise the importance of being explicitly inclusive and who make the effort to be involved in Pride events and LGBT causes, thank you. You may never know when that rainbow flag saved someone's life, because they felt included and valued.

Trudy Howson

Stepping into our Destiny
Moving into the light
Proud to be L.G.B.T.
Here, on the Isle of Wight.

Honouring our Community,
And how our lives can be.
The courage and creativity,
Embedded in L.G.B.T.

Remembering our History.
Poets. Artists. Sailors.
Rooted in this island's rock,
Farmers. Fighters. Tailors.

Celebrating who we are,
Stylish, full of life.
Welcoming Love diversity
Its harmony and strife

On this day, we send a message
To our family worldwide.
Be yourself, you're beautiful
There is no need to hide.

Trudy Howson describes herself as a feminist and political activist. She works with NHS Trusts, Mind and many small grass root organisations. In 2016, Trudy was appointed the first LGBT Poet Laureate, a post devised by Camden LGBT Forum in London. Trudy has written the theme poem for Pride events across the UK including London and Isle of Wight Pride. During her research for the poem she says she fell in love with the extraordinarily varied internal and external landscapes of the Island. Previously, Trudy was an actor and loves performing, she has guested on Sky TV and also appeared in Coronation Street. She now runs a poetry event at which she also performs; Incite at The Phoenix, a theatre venue in London's West End.

GOING OUT

How or where would you meet other LGBTQ+ people on the Isle of Wight?

Alan Figueiredo-Stow

Whether you're out and proud as a peacock or straight-acting, shy and retiring, it's rewarding to have a social life, just to be with like-minded people, to have fun, relax or to meet a partner. We've looked at where the Isle of Wight's LGBTQ+ community has been going out over the last one hundred years in the days before social media, dating sites and mobile phones.

During these interviews we asked questions about going out and meeting other LGBTQ+ people. Where would you go? Which were the venues you frequented? How did you recognise and meet other LGBTQ+ people? What was the scene on the Island like?

We heard interviewees' wide-ranging experiences of being LGBTQ+ living on the Island. Their opinions can differ greatly according to what sort of life they have led, who they have met, etc.

Personally, I enjoy all kinds of socialising. I love going to the theatre, cinema, restaurants, bars, perhaps even someone's barbecue, or dinner party, but having said that, I can be painfully shy and sometimes feel I lack the confidence and presence to go out and make the proverbial effort. Sometimes it's easier to make an excuse and stay at home.

But like many LGBTQ+ folks, I need to feel safe and comfortable about where I'm going. Is it familiar to me? If it's new to me, then who will be there? Will I feel out of my depth? Do I feel up to it? Can I perform on a social level tonight? So, yes, I do suffer like many of us from a certain amount of social anxiety, but I suspect a little more than most. Having said that, perhaps I am a contradiction, because once I am in a particular social setting and feel safe and comfortable, I come out of my shell again and show my more extroverted side. And believe me, there is a very extroverted person inside waiting to be part of my tribe.

Perhaps the key to reduced social anxiety when going out is having a familiar place to go with familiar people, rather than coming out of your comfort zone. I am sure many people, however they identify, suffer from apathy and anxiety about going out. These barriers and anxieties relating to going out socially are far greater for the LGBTQ+ community who may not feel accepted or may face homophobia. I could argue that there are multiple reasons for this, which are certainly touched upon in these oral history interviews as our interviews show. I do feel however, that as a gay man living here, there has always been a lack of places to go and meet others who identify as LGBTQ+ on the Isle of Wight.

In my own experience after getting divorced and coming out (again) to my close friends and family, I suddenly found myself having to build a new social life. I had socialised with my work colleagues but I was rediscovering myself and all the old familiar fears which had left deep scars were resurfacing. Here I was, coming out for the second time in my life, and this time I was a grown man with a young daughter to consider, so of course along with these old shameful fears, there were new fears of failure and exposure to contend with.

In my earlier life, I was heavily influenced by my family and I wanted so badly to fit in and be like my brothers, so being gay and all the pain and suffering that came with it wasn't an option anymore for me. I slowly allowed myself to morph into a straight man, perhaps because it was easier and less painful, but also I knew that I wanted children. So, my life took that direction and off I happily walked into my sunset, believing it to be forever, only to discover years later my sunset led me straight back to my original rainbow.

Where do newly out gay men go on the Island in the mid noughties, especially young dads? Truthfully, at the time I did not have any other friends outside of work, and I certainly didn't know any other gay men to socialise with. There was nothing visible to me, I wasn't aware of any clubs or social groups. I can be a painfully shy person, and I'd still not learned how to deal with being out as a gay man to myself, let alone in public. Internalised homophobia can be a huge problem for those who identify as LGBTQ+, which often surprises our heterosexual counterparts who forget how destructive our own negative self-image can be. I was scared and full of self-doubt once again, the only thing that was accessible to me at the time was the internet, so I went online, found gay dating websites. I was convinced this was the only way to meet new friends and even a new partner, if I was brave enough.

Going out often falls into the trap of having to come out again. It is the same for all gay people, we all have the experiences of coming out every time we're introduced to a new friend, or a new group of colleagues, because they may assume that you are straight. But unless you've got it tattooed across your forehead, these wonderful straight folks will naturally assume you fit into their neat little 'normal' boxes.

For most LGBTQ+ people who decide to go out socially perhaps with their straight friends/colleagues, they will invariably go through this uncomfortable and sometimes embarrassing scenario. So, there is no wonder that the whole going out thing almost never ceases to be another new coming out experience.

Nowadays I am lucky in the sense that I have my own home, which I share with my husband, and one of the most comfortable choices is to invite people over to our home, which in some ways is easier with less anxiety (you would think!) Apart from stressing about what to cook, and is the house clean enough, and OMG, I must scrub the toilet for the hundredth time (!) and going into overdrive trying my best to make everyone feel relaxed and comfortable, is there enough food and drink? Okay, so throwing a social in your own home can be stressful, but at least I did not have to go out in public, right?

Our oral histories span a period of time from the '40s to the present day, so the range of places to go, and attitudes of the period, differ from story to story, including of course the different personalities who are telling their stories.

Some are extremely private individuals who are very fearful about coming out, and remain fearful all their lives, with others being quite extrovert and open about their sexuality, and why shouldn't they? However, this does not mean for an instant that the extrovert personalities have not had their struggles or faced public intolerance and homophobia throughout their lives.

The Isle of Wight, like many rural communities, has always lacked queer venues, so we can't compare going out here to going out in big cities. Going to queer venues in a metropolis like London or Manchester will have a certain appeal and anonymity, and can feel safer, even liberating for LGBTQ+ folk. However, we could argue that city bars and clubs don't always feel safe and relaxing for everyone, and there's something to be said for the regularity and familiarity of our own rural groups.

We found that during some periods there were organised groups with plenty of vibrant social events, especially around the mid to late 90s, a kind of heyday for the Island's LGBTQ+ community. We found notices for various LGBTQ+ events in *WightOUT News*, such as a Friday evening disco called 'Easter Bonnet' attended by over 50 people.[115] These groups were at times successful in finding local venues to support and host the events, but sadly we hear experiences where a lot of venues would eventually discourage regular LGBTQ+ evenings and events held on their premises. It is suggested in sections of the interviews that the reason for this was fear of being labelled as a 'gay bar'.[116] We can clearly see the amount of stigma around queer people, and it is sad that allies will also shy away because of this labelling and stigma. But despite this fear, some are still willing to lend or rent out a room or space, especially if it means making money during the quiet winter months.[117]

Although LGBTQ+ life on the Island is becoming more visible and perhaps it has started to be accepted by the wider public in recent years, it could be said that the visible turning point for this new found 'acceptance' came when, after some controversy, the Isle of Wight held its first Pride event. Suddenly there was a kind of tolerance from some members of the public, and a feeling that we did not have to hide from our collective shame. However, we cannot move away from the fact homophobia, biphobia and transphobia still exist, so for some the question around coming out, or even going out, is still extremely sensitive.

The Island does not have an exclusively gay venue; however, currently, we do have Bar 74 in Ryde that is an LGBTQ+ friendly bar. Is there a need for an exclusively LGBTQ+ venue on the Island?

We hear about other such experiences of gay men cottaging in Lind Street in Ryde, or at Coppins Bridge in Newport. In 1993, the police were reported to have made over 50 arrests for cottaging. Would that have happened if there had been a gay venue or even a gay sauna on the Island?

Why are LGBTQ+ spaces and venues even needed? Well, my first thought on this is that the simple act of going out socially, in whatever way, has always been a noticeably big part of the wider society and culture, everywhere. It helps enrich society, and when it includes the LGBTQ+ community, hopefully it encourages familiarity, leading to tolerance, breaking down preconceptions, stereotypes and greater acceptance, not only in the big cities but in coastal and rural places like the Isle of Wight.

I read an article recently in the *Guardian*, written by Alice Ross, entitled 'Out in the Country – rural hotspots found as gay population mapped' – Subheading: 'ONS finds that along with London boroughs, some bucolic counties are home to concentrations of LGBT people.'[118] In part of the research within the

---

[115]'Easter Bonnets at the Plough', *WightOUT News*, May 2003, 2

[116]Karl Stedman, interview by Franko Figueiredo, November 22, 2019

[117]Ibid.

[118]Alice Ross, 'Out in the Country – Rural Hotspots Found as Gay Population Mapped', *Guardian*. Guardian News and Media, April 19, 2017. https://www.theguardian.com/world/2017/apr/19/out-in-the-country-rural-hotspots-found-as-gay-population-mapped.

article, the Isle of Wight was one of the areas not mapped and simply labelled as no data. Mat Price, co-founder of Proud2Be, which organises the Totnes Pride festival, was quoted as saying:

> It might be that people are starting to feel like they can live in rural locations and not just in London, Brighton and Manchester, and maybe part of it is about feeling more confident to report it [hate crime]. In Totnes, we've had overwhelming support, but when the support becomes visible, you get the other side: when we do something that's visible like a procession, that tends to highlight some of the prejudice that still exists. There's still discrimination, there's still hate crime.[119]

Perhaps we have a similar feeling of being out and going out on our own Island. Yes, there's acceptance and tolerance, but scratch the surface and what will you find? What do queer people look for in a place when they are deciding which rural place to move to? Perhaps high on the list is a good work/life balance, but I would say high on the list would be how tolerant and open is the place they are moving too, what is the social scene?

In the following extracts taken from *WightOUT* in 2000, we get a flavour of the scene around the time and how the Island was perhaps viewed by visitors. It talks about how appealing it is for some people to move or retire here:

> People who have moved to the Island have found the local gay and lesbian communities friendly and supportive.[120]

We often assume the only LGBTQ+ people are either born here or have moved here for a new life; there are also many seasonal workers who come to the island for the summer season, a certain percentage of these seasonal workers would be LGBTQ+ and of course would have looked for gay venues and nights out:

> There are many gay seasonal workers visiting the Island during the summer months which brings a new dimension to the gay life on the Island. Local gay and lesbian groups are well established and support a variety of activities and social events.[121]

Here, we see considerations being made on visiting LGBTQ+ venues nearby on the mainland:

> There are gay bars just a few miles away in Southampton and Portsmouth which makes it worth considering living in the Ryde or the Cowes area, especially if you're going to be here for a while. This is

worth considering as ferry accessibility is not the best during the early hours of the morning, if you have to get home after a night out on the mainland.[122]

It's also interesting to see the views on why gay communities have been slow to develop:

> Life on the Island does go at a slower pace than on the mainland and sometimes it seems to take a long time before changes occur. Perhaps this is why it seems to have taken quite a while for the gay communities to develop. In fact, the Island is now moving forward at a good pace. But life here is not as dull as some people might make it out to be. Life here is what you and we make it together.[123]

Indeed, life is what we make it, but that assumption does come from a place of privilege. Is the Island moving forward at a good pace as it says here?

In an age of increasing intolerance, LGBTQ+ communities should have the courage to stand together in the face of prejudice and to report hate crime. This is the only way that we can move forward and become an Island and a world where it doesn't matter who you love and who you want to be.

[119]'Alice Ross, 'Out in the Country – Rural Hotspots Found as Gay Population Mapped', *Guardian*. Guardian News and Media, April 19, 2017

[120]WightOUT Helpline, 'Welcome to the Beautiful Isle of Wight', www.iowgayguide.org.uk via Internet Archive Wayback Machine, accessed July 15, 2020,
https://web.archive.org/web/20050307053351/http://www.iowgayguide.org.uk/.

[121]Ibid.

[122]WightOUT Helpline, 'Welcome to the Beautiful Isle of Wight', www.iowgayguide.org.uk via Internet Archive Wayback Machine, accessed July 15, 2020,
https://web.archive.org/web/20050307053351/http://www.iowgayguide.org.uk/.

[123]Ibid.

EXTRACTS FROM ORAL HISTORIES

Robin

It was Roy Jenkins who brought the law through in '66, the '66 government, yeah, that's right '67. I can remember there was a lesbian called George actually, she ran a pub on the Island, the Tiger Tavern it was at Sandown, it no longer exists. She was in London at the time, she was, "oh, I can remember when the Act was passed all the queers came out and danced in the streets", I thought, "oh, how wonderful".

There was the Isle of Wight Gay Group, they called it. Anyway, there was nobody there that I really fancied but, you know, we were all gay. I took on being the telephone contact for the Isle of Wight for the Island Gay Group and basically, I met lots of people and then came James and we clicked. We were actually talking and meeting and having parties and whatnot with other gay people. It was a mixed group, gay and lesbian, it was advertised in *Gay Times* and my number was given. I had so many people ringing up. I might add that some of them, I was very bloody innocent, I didn't realise until the end of it they were sometimes wanking off or something. I thought, how interesting. It became very obvious when it happened.

The local amateur dramatics, there I met a guy called Doug, my God, that set off. That went on for some while and actually that was the best sex I ever had! The only trouble is that he found someone he fancied more and that really did upset me, but there you are, it is the heartbreak sort of thing which features. There was a pub in Shanklin that had sort of a night, I don't even know if it is still open – The Plough and Barleycorn – is it still going?

This is back in whatever year it was in the 80s. It was via the Apollo Theatre that I met Doug and then I met all the others and there was sort of a gay group and eventually I took on the business of being the contact and they used to meet mostly at my house in Newport. Well, this is before the Gay Switchboard as such, this particular one, it was all really one telephone contact advertised in *Gay Times*.

I think it sort of followed on the tails of the various liberalisations. I mean, the truth is, I don't know how it is now I am completely out of touch. I'm afraid I prefer my slippers and a fire!

Robert

There were pubs, there was a ghastly old spit and sawdust pub called The Redan in Ryde which you have probably come across. It doesn't exist any more but people used to say, "that's a poofters pub, that is!" But I didn't go there because I'd seen some of them, you see, I mean what you got was elderly gentlemen in search of younger men and that's never an especially elevating picture. So, no, what I did I got in touch with people through other people basically and made relationships that way but I didn't go out to clubs and pubs. Even in those days that would have been a dangerous thing to do. Michael, to whom I referred earlier, got himself beaten up on regular occasions because he would pretend to be a doctor of massage and he really wasn't and what he wanted to massage wasn't always things he ought to massage! I was in the town one night and I heard a gang of youths say, "oh look, it's the Doctor of Massage", and they went after him. He ran like stink! I didn't want to be like that, I'd never wanted to be the kind of person people would say, "oh, he's always after kids" or whatever, young people, other people. It just wasn't me. I am far too conservative for that.

I don't think it [*The Isle of Wight Gay Guide*] was terribly useful but it existed, yes. I remember looking at it but, the trouble is, I did go to a group but it was all rather elderly gentlemen who were plainly looking for 'bedroom games' which, you know, "no thanks". And a few younger men but I only remember two of them; one was called Twiggy and the other one was Little Keith and Little Keith was as effeminate as Danny La Rue on steroids and that doesn't appeal to me. I tried, you know, I did try to join what there was but it was so shallow, it didn't lead into anything. So that was no fun at all really. I think it was in the wilds of Yarmouth or Newport or somewhere out there.

Ryde was very different, Ryde was a place where people sort of hunted in small packs but didn't really join in any kind of society because they kept these things quiet, not quiet, separate like quite watertight compartments: this is what I do in the evening or at night if I can get away with it, this is what I do in the day time and the two must not meet because if they do I am in trouble with my employers. That was a lot of the trouble.

I knew of people in Winchester, certainly, yes. Southampton, well, now there are one or two rent boys in Southampton and Portsmouth and Gosport whose profiles I have looked at. I am not going to do any more than look at them because, as I say, I mean, Christ! I'm 70, nearly, I mean, I am not going to do it. I wasn't aware of that but there's the internet now and you can look at these things and lust after them but, in those days, nothing. Personal column of *Gay*

Times, there was that. I did reply to a few of those with interesting results and got a few tolerable experiences out of that. This would be around about '85 to '86, I imagine. Local papers were useless, totally useless. There was an advert once which I found from one, 'Male masseur offers treatment to discerning gentlemen', something like that. He lasted one week and then you never saw it again. I think I know what sort of discerning gentleman he was after and what services he was offering but obviously the editor of the paper discovered the same thing. You wouldn't get that here. Not then. I doubt if you'd get it now either.

Karen

Obviously I knew Donna from work and she introduced me to a women's group at the time. I mean, on the Island in the 90s, it was a really big women's group. We used to go to parties over at Trish and somebody else's house and round different people's houses. We'd have nights out bowling but I got talking to other lesbians when I was there. It was a massive thing, there was something on every month and… there would be discos over at Westridge, I can't remember the name of the club upstairs, but they were always, once a month, really packed discos.

A big mix of gay men and gay women, there was a massive scene and I met a lot of people through that. Quite a lot of women went to that. I know they had funding from somewhere because there was a party because they received funding for something. But the issue was, it was always run by a couple of women and every time this couple of women had a falling out or broke up then the women's group… and I think the last couple Sharon and… I can't remember her name. They split up and then the whole women's group kind of crashed. But then I used to start hanging out with Joanne and there was a smaller group of us hanging out. And then it kind of all finished and to meet women was really difficult because there was no internet. There was the *Pink Paper* that you could send away for and then there was a local paper that had women's ads in it, so meeting women on the Island without a group and without the internet was really difficult.

The ones at Westridge were really, really good. There was a good mix of music and dancing and talking and there were always lots of poppers going off, that was always interesting. But there was no animosity, it was just really good fun and we all kind of got along. It was something to really look forward to and I really enjoyed them because it was only gay people there.

173

Then they moved them down to Patsy's nightclub in Ryde which was really funny because you used to have to knock on the door to be let in. I questioned why and he said, "in case there's trouble", and I just thought that was really funny, it's Ryde, no one is going to make trouble. But the disco in Patsy's wasn't so good because it was a big club and it was beginning to tail off by then. That has got to be about '95, 6, 7? Then we had some in the Prince Consort, they were always really packed as well. There was always something going on every month. Yes, the Prince Consort is down the bottom of Union Street, so that was where we had some, in the upstairs room.

In the olden days you had to use the telephone, there was no mobile phone, you used to ring people up. I think at one point there was a newsletter being sent out. But you just used to ring people up and find out that way. Sometimes they used to meet up in pubs in Cowes but they were starting to kind of tail off by then. I had gay friends and then I left the Island so then it kind of… I don't know what happened to the gay group. I've heard that it had crumbled and then Donna moved off the Island, and it all just kind of went a bit flat. I'd still see Joanne but it wasn't like it was.

I just carried on being gay. I met a few women through Diva. I had a couple of relationships but I've always been really comfortable and confident being gay. And then the gay scene on the Island had dropped off but I would see Joanne Brady and the women's group was beginning to pick up because we were having Friday nights at the Plough and Barleycorn in Shanklin, that was a new thing. We went there most Fridays and we had our own room and that was quite well attended so that was how the women's group kept going. But there were no other social evenings.

Between about '99 and 2002 it moved to a hotel in Sandown but I can't remember the name of the hotel, it's been flattened. It was run by a couple of gay women, Jean and Pam, they'd be running the group at one point. Jean was on her own she was trying to get this gay thing going in Sandown and she built it up like it was going to be a big thing and I went along and there was about ten people there. But they tried and I made some good friends there as well but then that kind of petered out as well and after that there was no more gay stuff.

I joined the football team to meet gay women and I was the only gay woman there, but I did meet other gay women later on. I started to play football on the mainland and there were quite a few lesbians on the mainland and we started to go over to Pompey. But in the Air Cadets I appeared to be the only lesbian apart from one other. I wasn't aware of huge amounts of gay people outside of the gay group.

It was just that you could ring up [the gay line] on a Friday between 8 and 10 p.m. and then on a Saturday; you could only be gay with a problem on a Friday or a Saturday night and then that was quite good. But then you'd listen and you'd think, "I know that person", because it is all very local and then there used to be one in Portsmouth I used to ring. Then the gay line on the Isle of Wight lost funding and shut down. I went to a few Gay Prides in London, that was quite awesome really, being part of a bigger thing, that was good.

And of course, the 'Out' thing at the Quay Arts, it was really good to see so many people and I saw women there that I thought, "oh, I know you". It was good to see that other women were out that you recognise but I think it would be good if you could build up to something bigger and be more integrated with the men like it used to be. I was thinking about this the other day, why the group isn't so big anymore, and I wonder if it is to do with social media and the internet now, that you can be in your home and you can be connected virtually rather than in person.

Karl L

So, if we think about the socialising that we did on the Island, we would have a monthly disco. A new group was started just after we arrived called The Isle of Wight Lesbian and Gay Group and that was started by people like John Reece and Tony Cutcher and there were other people involved in that as well who have now passed on in life. But they started those things, and a Lesbian and Gay Switchboard started because at that time we didn't have all this modern technology that everybody talks about in terms of smart phones and computers. I can remember being at college and I was one of two people in that entire college that had a computer. That's because I am dyslexic and so I spent my own money doing that, so when we came to the Island we had some skills that a lot of young people were just starting to enter. No smart phones. So we did communication by paper and I remember the magazine, I think it was called *WightOUT* that used to go around. If you missed your monthly *WightOUT*, you'd no idea where the next disco was or where people who were meeting and gathering were going to be.

So the first part of my experience, the first two years I worked for the Youth and Community Service here and then for the remaining six years I worked for health directly in a gay men's role that we started, the Island's Gay Men's Health Project. At that time there were some volunteers, in fact there was about eight or ten volunteers, and that continued up to more or less when I left, because things changed quite dramatically then because of the funding. The economic impacts of HIV then saw the money going away from prevention and into treatment.

Lots of things picked up in the 1990s but there had been some groups running before that. There was a men's group specifically which ran out of East Cowes. There were some quite funny things, or what we thought were quite funny things, about the Island. We remember going to the first disco. Well, actually we went across to the other side of the Island, we were invited, we heard through the grapevine because somebody was smiling at us in a bar and we were smiling at them. That was our only way into the Island's LGBT community at that point. That was the very first contact.

So, what I am really saying is that to access all of that, it had to be on that flirty type basis to start with because you had no idea who was gay and who wasn't gay. We were introduced to a couple of 'professional people' who were gay and then we went to a barbecue in the first ten or twelve weeks. We were wondering if we'd made the right decision and we went to this barbecue where we met several people, some people nearer to our age, and it all moved from that point outwards.

I always like to keep my social life very, very separate from my professional life, always have done, always will do. I put them into boxes and that's because, I guess, growing up as a young, gay man I was frightened. I did all of the things like almost getting married, all of those things that you were expected to do as a heterosexual.

It's a very different way of life now. If you look back to where we were then, we had very few communication systems which meant that you had to be close to other people to know what was going on. Now we have got technology which is evolving all the time, which enables people to have conversations and meet-ups and hook-ups and things without needing to have discos and community events. So when we first came to the Island we were a bit surprised when we did eventually enter the community.

Yes, there was a community here or, I should say, different communities which is really interesting in itself when you start digging underneath that because there was the 'Cowes set', we used a slightly different language. So, 'are you a member?' That's so we could talk in the streets without anybody hearing the word, 'gay, bisexual' and no touching, no hugging, no looking, make it discrete and that type of approach. Then you had a younger group who were much more, if you like, out, but there wasn't very much to be out to on the Island

Karl L

so the Island population would go off-Island as well as on-Island. You could count the number of young people under the age of 25 or even 30 on one hand in the entire community that I knew that I would describe as 'out'.

Now obviously, because of my work as a gay men's health worker, I came into a lot more contact with a lot more people and some of that work can't even be discussed really because of the confidentiality that was involved.

So we went to our first disco and we met one or two people and it was fun, we had a nice evening, but the men were predominantly out and you could count the number of women there on one hand. The women really weren't a part of the loop at that point and I would actually describe it, in those very early days of the 90s, there was a tension between the men and the women, very much so. There was a women's group that operated but they didn't really come together. But within that first couple of years there was a bit of an explosion of coming out, if you like, but not publicly, internally, because then we ended up with the Switchboard being created, and they became a bigger group. Again, this was all stimulated by HIV really and HIV funding as part of a way of trying to reach the community to deliver sexual health messages and messages of being well and keeping safe and so on. So that happened fairly quickly. So we had a Switchboard, then we had two LGBT groups; there was a women's group operating, and there is actually a Christian group which has been operating on the Island for at least 25 if not 30 years. It is still going today. That was operating then. Apart from that we had a naturist beach down at Blackgang Chine which still operates as a naturist beach today, but the important thing was that it was a place where people could go and meet, a meeting place, a contact place.

There was a West Wight group and I always think with great merriment, it makes me laugh really, the Leather Queens of Freshwater. It seemed that the Leather Queens from Freshwater were the only Leather Queens on the Island at that time although there obviously were others, and they used to arrive in their leather, complete with crash helmets, in a mini-bus. That used to make us giggle. A remnant of the '70s but really very much alive with some wonderful people.

Phaedra was the only 'transgenderist' person that we knew on the Island but, of course, there were lots of others who would go off-Island to the clubs of London, to stay in hotels which specialised in that. But they weren't out on the Island at all.

So funding was the driver of change on the Island and when that funding went then a lot of groups collapsed. It was all about individuals within the communities who were driving these things forward who were largely from the mainland. That had a big impact on the community because there were people who would want to meet me, and I had to meet them in parks and all sorts of things, away out of sight, just in case anybody identified me with them and so on. That's irrespective of what their health or position was.

So we'd lots of great things going on, we had lots of funds, we had lots of parties, all hidden away. I remember going to The Pugwash. The Pugwash was a barge. We never had the same destination for very long for our discos so we had, I can mention some of these names because that's okay. Tollgate Tim found us a place to go for our monthly discos which we went to for about eighteen months. The Crab Shack of all places, at Seaview. Miles from anywhere but we had regularly over hundred people turning up. Largely men, but turning up, of all ages.

But, of course, the LGBT community can be and is now more ageist than it was then because people don't have those social interactions now that they used to have then for all sorts of different reasons. Then we went to the Captain Pugwash and the Captain Pugwash was a barge on the river down here in East Cowes and we walked down this gangplank which was wobbly with all the leather queens screaming and crying. When you danced your hands would hit the end of the roof of the boat and it was freezing, I remember that. But we had two or three good parties there and then we moved on. The reason that we were moving on all the time is because the venue didn't want us because they didn't want the reputation of gay, bisexual, transgender being there and it was the same for some of the hotels and the venues that we went to. So we moved around a fair bit. We'd be there for several months and we would move on; there would be an excuse for moving us on, even in recent years.

I remember going to a place in Shanklin, I won't say its name, and they said, "oh that's fine". This is in recent years, "it is fine for you to come here in the winter but we don't want you in the summer". Now they didn't use those words but that was what came back through, because they didn't want the legacy of the label of LGBT attending, that is just how it was on the Island. So we never had a permanent place of our own.

When the money from HIV dried up, that then brought it to a stop and the socialising went down. I know why that happened because it is personality driven. Alan Martin was running the Lesbian and Gay Switchboard which started off as a big group and as time goes on people slip away and so on and times change. So eventually the National Lesbian and Gay Switchboard operated several days a week, operated one day a week or one day a month it might have been, from the Isle of Wight. That was then replaced by modern technology and, the internet, and iPhones and all those sorts of things. So there was no real reason; but what that does is it isolates, and so the Island became an isolated area.

So when I came back to the Island and I'd been here for maybe two years, settling in, working my way through, I actually went back into the same job that I left because of my contacts, briefly, to be an Isle of Wight LGBT worker this time mainly focusing on HIV prevention but a very different kind of HIV prevention. As part of that I had an idea which I discussed with some of my friends about starting an Isle of Wight Gay Men's Chorus and that is because I like male voice in terms of singing, with no skills whatsoever myself. He [David] is a little bit musical. So we decided that we would do this.

So that was the first thing that had really happened on the Island for a good number of years. We'd lost all of the *WightOUT* papers, because the communication was focusing more around Grindr and sex hook-ups, and I still think that it's sad that we have lost some of that communication. It is not really even happening now at this time. This project has brought some of that back.

So that ran for about eighteen months, but I had to leave that project within about six months because I then became ill with cancer so I had to drop out of that and I never returned. There were some internal political things that happened within it which also meant that I didn't want to be part of it. The Gay Men's Chorus then ended. In that same year then, the first Island Pride took place.

Melissa

So coming back to the Isle of Wight, I appreciate the Island a lot more as an adult. I love the Island as an adult like I didn't when I was a child and growing up here, but I am still aware that the Island as a whole is not, it still doesn't necessarily feel like a place for me. Since coming back I have been able to reach out to the queer, LGBT community in a way that I wasn't able to as a child because I am an adult now so I can access it. Bars and clubs and social media have also been a huge thing in how to find out about what's going on in our community on the Island.

So I have been able to reach out and feel a lot more connected to my own community on the Isle of Wight while still feeling that sense of, "oh, you'd better be careful". I think that is partly a sense that I have just existing in the world as a queer person. That's a consideration I have to make every day, when I start a new job, or when I go to a new doctor or anything like that. I do have to make that first initial weighing up of things where I see who people are and what they say when they don't know I'm queer before I decide whether it is going to be safe for me or whether I am going to be able to come out. And sometimes I'm not. Sometimes I find myself in quite a homophobic environment or transphobic environment and I don't feel safe and have to kind of re-closet myself.

I think safety is comfort. I don't know that you can be completely comfortable if you don't feel safe. As a queer person in the world I don't think I should have to sacrifice comfort for safety. I should be able to exist in the world and exist in all spaces comfortably in the sense that I should be able to not have to make that consideration of whether, if I come out they are going to find a reason to fire me, or if I come out with my doctor he is going to give me treatment that's not as effective, or whether they are going to just dismiss me and not treat me at all or whether if I come out to someone who has any level of authority over my life and my livelihood, whether coming out is going to affect me negatively. That's still a consideration that I have to make and it is a consideration that a lot of people have to make in a lot of different spheres.

Karl S

Yeah, people used to say, people said about a place in Shanklin, the Plough and Barleycorn pub which is at the end of Regent Street, that used to be, twenty years ago. It was never a gay venue, but it was certainly a place that was gay-friendly, it was known as somewhere that gay people could go to. But that's not the case any more.

There was a hotel on the clifftops that's been knocked down now and it's a block of flats, but they had a club down below in the basement that was, again, I don't know whether it was exclusively gay but it was certainly gay-friendly and older gay people on the Island have said that they met their partners there, or whatever. There seemed to be stuff going on 20, 30, 40 years ago but there isn't now. There have been a few places that have opened and then closed quite quickly. There were a couple of girls that had a hotel in Sandown, which again now has been knocked down and it's houses, when would that be? That would be about eight years ago or something like that. I think they were feeling that it wasn't going terribly well and that they would turn it into a gay venue. Now whether it was going to be a gay hotel as well I don't know, but they had an opening for a club/bar type thing. It was quite nice actually because it had a bar with a dance floor and then there was a separate room which had a bar in it and then you went into another sort of lounge. So I know a lot of people here say, "oh I don't want anything noisy, I don't want dancing and all that sort of stuff", and then other people say, "well, I don't really want a pub", but this seemed to have everything because it had a bar and a dance floor, it had a separate bar and it had a separate lounge. So it seemed to cater for everything and the first night it opened, we went the first night and they had a doorman and they had a coat check and all sorts of stuff and there were about 100 or so people there. It was fantastic, what a great night! It was really good and we thought, "yes, this is great! And we can walk home as well, it's only Sandown". And then a few weeks later and we were about the only people in there and we went to the bar and said, "can we have two pints of lager, please", and the guy said, "yes, of course!" And we noticed him go out the back door. We thought, "where's he going to?" Turned out he went to the corner shop and bought a couple of cans of Fosters, came back, poured them into our glasses and we paid the money and sat down and we said, "shall we have another drink?" "Okay". He did the same thing again, he hadn't even bought in bulk, he'd only bought a couple of cans! And we thought, "well, this isn't going to last", and it didn't and I don't know why because, as I say, so many people went the first night and everybody seemed upbeat about it and it seemed to have something for everybody.

A few years ago a guy, I think he was a policeman, yes he was, a young guy, he was a policeman and he set up a gay night at one of the hotels on the front at Shanklin [The Shoreside] and we thought, "well, this is great, this really is walking distance, this is fantastic!" We went about four or five times I think, it was during the winter and I think it was every Friday and there were roughly about 70 people there each time we went and they weren't the same people. That's always good. Although people were quite in their little cliques, because it can be quite cliquey here, after a few of the sessions barriers started to come down and people were smiling and saying hello when you came in, that sort of thing. Then the owners of the place said, "well, this has been great hasn't it? But, thank you very much, the season is about to start and we really don't want to have a gay night because we think that that will put our straight punters off and so we are going to stop it", and they did and we went along the next week just to see how many people were there and there was nobody there! Now why would a venue that's got 70 people in it drinking all night say, "stop, we don't want... Our straight customers would?" And to be honest, I don't think, I think if a straight customer had come in they wouldn't have really noticed that it was a gay, I mean, there weren't a load of screaming queens, there was just guys sitting having a drink, they probably wouldn't even have noticed that it was gay. If they had, well, so what? So we were rather chuffed that actually they didn't have any punters in there at all, they weren't making any money. Things like that have happened in the last couple of years, the last few years, but nothing has stayed.

We don't have a huge social life here. We were clubbers and bar people, but there aren't the places here to go to so we don't do that at all. We are fairly self-contained really and I think a lot of people that come to the Island are and I think that's one of the problems. Well, it is not a problem; if you're self-contained then you're self-contained.

It's difficult, I don't know that gay people are particularly friendly over here. I know they are quite cliquey. I don't know whether they are [with] people that they work with or people that they spend a lot of time with, maybe they were at school together or maybe they met. I know some people, when we were in Brighton, there were some people that we met there that came from the Island and they were friends with other people that went to Brighton. I don't know, it's difficult, people can be quite standoffish. I think it's a problem here with generations as well, that there are older gay people and when I say older I mean people in their 60s and 70s and such who, they tend to be the dinner party type of people and they go on the cruises and they are probably quite good at meeting up every so often and things. There are the young people, the teenagers and a bit older who haven't gone off the Island yet but probably will at some time and maybe they meet up but the people from sort of 20 to 45 or so, I don't know how they meet up, if they do even. Maybe if you join an amateur dramatic society or something like that, you know, I know that's clichéd, isn't it? But maybe they get a sort of social life from that. I don't know how people meet up on the Island nowadays.

Joanne

There was an LGBT group, it was called The Social Group that was advertised in the *County Press* and they held a meeting and I went along to this meeting, where was it? I can't even remember where it was? The George, I think it might have been. And there was just a group of you sitting there and you'd be all, do you know what I mean? You wouldn't say anything, and then I went to the party and met Midge who I was with for twenty years. And we had gone to different houses but you wouldn't tell anyone, do you know what I mean? It was all hush-hush cause it was frowned upon, you know what I mean? Back then, it was. People did think we were disgusting, you know? But I didn't care by that stage quite honestly and I sort of, I was, I liked to shock people, so I would say it just to get a reaction.

There'd be an ad in the County Press saying LGBT, there was a nightclub in Newport that was called Glitz – have you been on the Island a long time? No, it was before your time then. You know where Man in the Moon is? Upstairs used to be a nightclub but you know where there is lane way beside, that was the entrance, and they used to do a gay night but you were too scared to go because people would know you were gay. It was weird, very surreal, so you didn't go because you'd get stuff, like there'd be people outside waiting and that. And you just used to sort of talk to each other and we'd go around to each other's house. The Social it was called. Then when it got bigger, we'd hire a hotel or something and have a disco. In the Vectis Club we used to have discos upstairs, that was going further now, and the Crab Shack which was in Shanklin [Seaview]. So we did, and do you know what? We had great times. There was quite a big group of us and that's how, how you would meet. I think it is harder now, quite honestly for people to meet up. It seems more open, I think we felt safer maybe. I don't know. We knew we were all together and we were all the same and we were the odd ones, and we had a great time. Yeah. It was, it was just word of mouth and going out and getting drunk, that was it really.

Well it was literally through the *County Press* and the social group, that is the only way and that got bigger and then a friend would tell a friend and they would come along so there was quite a big amount of us but we're all close. Like if you could live in Ventnor, George actually, he was in Ventnor and he was, back then he was probably about 65 or 70 but he looked a lot older so from that age down to, I was only eighteen, do you know what I mean? And we were all from all over the Island, but it was literally through the *County Press* and word of mouth that's how we did it back then. Yeah, it was literally, or we'd go off to Drummond's. Like, I've got a friend that I met in Portsmouth and we are still friends now, I was 21 and she was 42 and she'd come over and she said, "oh I feel ever so sorry for you". My ex was a bugger, she was always going off. She said, "I feel really sorry for you sitting there by yourself", and we are still friends to this day. So yeah, just sort of, I'd talk to anyone, the more the merrier, I am quite a social butterfly.

Michelle

It's a different community to Yarmouth but my knowledge of the Yarmouth community was 25 years earlier. So it was difficult, people then, I was comparatively young and people were comparatively old in that community and I hadn't come out. I think people used to say, "you come to live on the Isle of Wight and you live in a time warp fifty years prior". I would say now you live in a time warp which is 25 years prior but it is still a bit of a time warp and there are more younger people because the folk who lived on the Island when I was first working here were a much older group. So I decided during my research that there was a more accommodating atmosphere to transgender. But by then I had fully transitioned and I was old enough to… I think there is some jargon which talks about 'passing', when you get to my age you don't worry about things like that and I found on the whole that I have been accepted for who I am but there is, I suspect, a latent difficulty with getting to know me better so you become lonely, lonelier, and that is more or less where I am now. Well, I am isolated except that I am a mentor for The Prince's Trust so I have mentees who I see but at the moment I haven't got any because they have all moved on. I wouldn't say I feel isolated. My family, my three girls all live abroad, two of them live in Italy, one lives in Canada, but my son lives in the north of London and I see my son from time to time. So, I don't feel isolated but I would prefer some more contact and that is when I met you two. I hadn't realised there was this book club so I have only been twice now but I think it has got a nice sense of acceptance there.

I go there [Time for T] from time to time when I can. But you see, Anna was part of our group but I think Anna felt very much the way that I did, that it was more of a talking shop so she wanted to set up something which was more supportive which she has done and for a while, Jo, as long as she was working was doing a first class job but now she has gone back to work in Portsmouth so I am, well, we'll see. Time for T is doing its thing and it is wonderful the way that it has grown and I found it so interesting to meet mothers whose young children were not necessarily coming out but considering gender transition or coming out as gay or whatever it may be, and I thought that was very interesting because those discussions really were not available two or three decades earlier. So, I've enjoyed that.

Anonymous

Now and then there was an Isle of Wight LGBT Youth Group and I went to that and the first time I went to that, that's when I became close to one of my friends who was also in the SHAG group, because when I went to that for the first time, so it must have been after that whole SHAG group experience, because when I went to the Isle of Wight LGBT group for the first time it was quite awkward. I mean, it was in this kind of centre and the guy running it was called Tony, I think his name was Tony, and I was the first one to turn up and I was sitting there with my body hunched over, really shy, and this guy comes in, an older guy and I think he said something like, "I'll need 200 packets of lube" or something like this, which scared me even more and I was like, "oh my God! This is terrifying!" But then the girl that I became friends with, who I had seen several times in college and who had sort of said, was always friendly to me but I think she later said to me, "as soon as I saw you I knew you were gay", she sort of came in and she looked at me and she went, "hello, you!" Knowingly, you know, that I was eventually going to turn up at this LGBT Youth Group. That was the only thing, I think it was run once a week, the LGBT Youth Group. I met a really good friend from there.

Well we sort of did, I guess we met up and talked really, talked about different things. But there were no pubs on the Island. Once or twice you'd have a gay night in Ryde or Sandown and then I think once they opened a gay pub in Sandown or Shanklin and it was like a back door room of a pub and you had to go to the back door and they had a little slit in the door, in the top of the door, where the owner opened the door and said, "you know this is a gay night?", and closed the slit, and you'd say, "yes, I'm gay", and then he'd close the slit and you'd go in the door and you'd play pool and stuff like that and there was only about five or six people in there. I later heard, I don't think it lasted, I later heard it got a brick through its window and closed down.

Well, I'd just go out with my straight friends I suppose and we'd go to places like The Balcony in Ryde or sometimes Sandown, Colonel Bogey's, and I'd hang out with my friend who I met at that group and we'd go out just driving. I mean there was not a lot, if you are young on the Island there's not much to do, I think that's why I hated it so much! There's a place, I was also studying media at one point and we got to take cameras out and do footage with cameras and lights and stuff and go round, so that was quite fun and there were some haunted places you'd go to and things like that, we would take drugs there. But gay nightlife and gay life on the Island? It was non-existent really.

The first gay pub I ever went to I went to Southampton, I took a boat to

Southampton with some others and we went to The Edge I think it was and another bar. I was just terrified, it was just very kind of new to me and different and not like being, I mean, in those days as well, you got your kind of, I remember going to The Edge and I had my butt patted a couple of times which doesn't really happen now. You don't really have that because there's so much sexual awareness now, you know. You don't touch other people and things like that and it was just very, kind of like, terrifying.

Sydney

From about sort of the age of fifteen, sixteen is when we started going out drinking. We used to hang out in cemeteries and drink Jack Daniels and smoke Marlboro Red. You had to drink Jack Daniels and smoke Marlboro Reds because that's what rock stars, that's what metal guys drank and smoked like Slash from Guns and Roses or whatever. It was all very artful and very conscious and stuff and then we would kind of hang out in a place in Ryde, the Squaddie, The Royal Squadron, they used to have a back room and local bands used to play there and the bouncers used to have a pretty tolerant, they didn't really care how old people were, you know? Eventually that got the place shut down, just serving booze to underage people essentially, serially. It was a real scummy sort of dive of a place. When that shut down we always used to sit and drink on the seafront on Friday nights. That was what we did, and sometimes we went to Portsmouth or Southampton to go to concerts and things like that. It felt like there was… that was the kind of culture I was a part of, that sort of rocker, subculture, alternative kind of thing and there was a little more freedom of gender expression and things like that, it was not entirely open, there was boys that wore make up and did their hair and all sorts of thing. It was the closest thing there was to any kind of queer culture on the Isle of Wight. Certainly at the time.

Jude

Well it grew. At first it was just the Island Lesbian and Gay Social Group and we met in about seven peoples houses once a fortnight or whatever it was, it might even have been each week. Then there was a hotel in Shanklin called… oh God! It was just up from where my son's cafe was. It begins with E I think. They used to have gay social evenings there. Somewhere I've got photos of Halloween parties, Christmas parties there with people really dragged up, some just in stunning outfits. There were a couple of guys who used to look absolutely gorgeous and then there were others who came along, kind of, there was a lovely guy who worked at the college, I can't remember his name. He went off to the mainland. He would come either in some really frumpy or some evening gown for a middle-aged old woman.

One guy, little Keith who lived in East Cowes above a bakery, he's since went to the mainland and I am not sure I may have heard that he died at some point. His flat, that was brilliant, you know, the only difference I didn't provide any alcohol. If they wanted to bring wine, beer or whatever they could. There was a chap in Newport who was quite well known, dignitary, he used to have them at his house and his house was like a museum and everything, I mean, I used to be going, "oh my God, you can see your face in this door knob!" Everything was sparkling. I still know him. I am trying to think who was the woman who, the original woman, Jane her name was, she upset me. She's dead. So there was hers. Mine we used to have a party, Keith's we used to have a party, and the others we'd just sit around and chat and play a bit of music and some of us would take some records along.

It really was a good social group. I mean it was great. We used to have a newsletter and somewhere, I had it in my hand a few months back, I've got an early Island Lesbian and Gay Social Group newsletter which interestingly enough has an article from Karl Love who had come back to the Island and was doing the loo watch thing, handing out condoms to blokes going into particular loos. We used to advertise in and again, I just remembered, when we had the Island Lesbian and Gay Social Group, the newspaper, the *County Press*, wouldn't accept an advert that said lesbian or gay.

I researched a bit and found KENRIC.[124] Maybe. I think that could have been it. KENRIC then had a KENRIC mothers' group which was really, every month when the newsletter came through, my son would be there, he'd get it first and he'd open it up and he'd get the KENRIC mothers' group, that was a couple of sheets, and he'd go down and go, "oh, look Mum! This woman has got two girls my age, and this one's got…", I'd ask, "what are you trying to do?"

---

[124]"KENRIC was founded in 1965 by lesbians in the Kensington and Richmond areas of London and are now the UK's longest-running lesbian social group. KENRIC organises a variety of social events aimed at providing opportunities for lesbians to meet, socialise and just be themselves.

Jude

So the kids were all, I mean they grew up going to Prides like I say, on the mainland. Whenever my sons, if we were out and my sons, bearing in mind my sons, most of them had long hair and were quite slight built, and if they wanted the loo, they would go in the ladies because they didn't feel safe going in the men's loos. And I mean that was until they were about fourteen. Dan's 37 and he was like two when I came out. So that was 35 years ago. No, I remember, yes, it was 35 years ago.

I was the Isle of Wight contact for KENRIC, and we had quite a good social group going but there were a couple of women who would come along and get pissed, well, we would meet in the pub, the place that used to be the old cinema in the High Street in Newport; there's two pubs very close to each other, but they're pub-restaurants. We would meet on whatever day it was and it was quite good because there was a good mix of people but then when you got a couple of people who would've got there already having drunk a couple of bottles of wine or half a bottle of whisky or whatever and one in particular was very loud and very aggressive and the more she drank the more aggressive and horrible she got. So a lot of people just walked away from it which was a shame but you see that had changed so much that we had gone from, like there was a little place in Ryde down near the seafront that was like a basement, mould and water running down the walls. I think I probably went there twice but it was kind of out of the way and a bit secret and then not that long on. When you come down the main road you've got the roundabout that takes you round to the esplanade, it was up that way instead of round. I mean I don't think it's… I don't even know if it's a building still, but if it is it has probably been turned into luxury flats or something. Like I say, I didn't really go, apart from anything else I travelled on buses because I didn't drive. The Plough and Barleycorn at Shanklin, that was another place and that was interesting because we went there once a month, the ordinary Isle of Wight drinkers also used that pub and there was like an odd little cross-over between them and us.

Lucy

It was only the… I started going to… they have these things called Dressing Services. You heard of them? I started going to them a couple of times a year. It was mainly in London. Yes. I would just make the excuse and say that I was going to go into London and do some shopping or something and I used to visit the Dressing Service a couple of times a year. [I felt] not loved, but approval and I was normal. They were nice people. That was later on, that was when I was in my forties. Yeah. Pretty much until I was in my early forties at least, I just didn't do anything. It was pretty much usually one-on-one, a one-on-one experience. I used to go to this one in particular, a trans lady who used to do them, it was in her house so it was just a one-on-one experience.

We have a club that meets once a month. It's called 'Time for T'. Through a very nice lady called Anna Murray, I don't know if you know her, she works for Age Concern, plus she also does a lot of LGBT stuff and domestic abuse stuff in her work. And also the Island's LAGLO Officer, the police, it is [a] police officer who specialises in lesbian and gay, her name is Lisa Paul she's … her and Anna set up this group for us, there's about 70 members. I mean, they're not all trans, quite a few of them are trans, but a lot of them are parents because some young trans go there. We just get together and just have something to eat. I've met, I've just met people and I've just got some fantastic, some wonderful friends now.

Callum

I didn't really know much about the LGBT+ on the Isle of Wight. It was very, apart from the occasional looking on Grindr to see people nearby, I felt at that point in time, I still almost feel that the, actually no, less so now because of the events and more openness, the community, more so on the Island than before. Before I went to university I just didn't know where to go. Looking back maybe further, at school we had sex ed classes about relationships and LGBT people.

Social life was a lot of beach parties. I didn't have any really gay friends or lesbian friends or anyone like that growing up. I kind of knew people who were, who identified as gay or whatever but at that point in time I didn't really know myself, that's how I felt, so it was always a kind of bit of denial and so I kind of stuck with people who I'd grown up with and in my friendship groups we don't, we would go clubbing but more like beach parties or house parties.

I think partly, it is probably living on the Isle of Wight, you have this kind of sheltered, this bubble in a way. It probably sounds… I said one thing and it kind of goes against the other, but I think you kind of stick to your tribe, you kind of know the places where you go because you feel comfortable. I mean, at university for me it was a very liberal environment so naturally you are going to get people from all walks of life. Generally, people that go to university are people that, you know, this may be a far-speaking comment, I think [a] certain type of people go to university especially now tuition fees are so high, they want to do well and they want to get on with life and they want to get a good job and buy a place or whatever their ambition is in life. So you are going to go there and you are going to embrace that mentality and so for me, being gay at university, there was no homophobia in fact the university embraced differences.

I think, moving back, and obviously since I have been going out with my boyfriend for two years, you meet people through them and obviously you get to know them very well and I made close friends through him. You find places that you enjoy going, there are different places we enjoy going, not gay bars but they are very gay-friendly. You meet people there and you probably get to know them. I think the community on the Island is growing, I think it's evolving. It is certainly bigger than it was when I left the Island, people are more open and more out. I still think there's a long way for people to go and some of the challenges I still feel face young people on the Island. I think things are very different now, people are more understanding and people are more educated. But I stick to the places I know because I feel comfortable there. If I go out in the evening I want to go somewhere that I feel comfortable and enjoy.

Bar 74. The places where we go are very supportive but then there's also venues that are also very supportive that I don't go because, like Coburgs in Ryde, they support LGBT+ events but I don't go there because I don't like the venue, it's a club. I am not into… I feel like my clubbing days are far behind me in that sense.

Rosa

Well I came to the Island in 2003 with my partner and one of the first things I did when I came to the Island was I tried to find out where all the lesbian and gays and LGBT community was and there was a Lesbian and Gay Switchboard at the time so I volunteered and worked on that. I was also on the committee for it. So we used to get quite a lot of phone calls, people ringing up for things,

events, what's happening? Do you know if there's any clubs open? People that were visiting the Island as well. A lot of the time they would say, "oh, where's the best place to go on a Friday night?" So we had all that information there and we would give it out to people. At other times people would ring up for other things like they were having difficulties with whatever.

One of the things we did was, we had things on a website which advertised a lot of things and every now and again we would check the website just to

Callum

see if it was okay and a lot of the time it was blank. It was all taken off. I used to go down to Shanklin library and type in 'lesbian and gay events on the Island', and there would be nothing there. So I brought it up at one of the meetings, I said, "look, all the stuff that we're advertising, it doesn't appear to be on the computers in the library, it's all been blocked, it's blanked". So the chairman at the time, I won't mention his name because he might not want to be mentioned, he went to the council and tried to find out what was happening and why was all our information not on the computers in the libraries, not available for anybody coming, visiting, who can go into the library, type in 'gay and lesbian events', and find information. That was not there although we had put it forward, we put that information out. So, we found out that they had filters on the computers so any words that were considered to be not acceptable, say, 'paedophile', 'gay' was also on it. So we tried to get that changed, the information went back on the computer again. A few weeks later, I went back to Shanklin library, checked it, and it was all taken off again. So we had this battle going on constantly with trying to get our information out to the Island, basically, and also because people who were visiting the Island, their first main port of call would be the library to type in any events to find out what was happening.

So, we found out that we were being discriminated against in a really insidious way because when we challenged it they had no recourse but to put it back but as soon as our backs were turned, it was taken off again. So, that was really quite difficult and eventually the Lesbian and Gay Switchboard lost the funding so we no longer had that. I don't know why that happened; maybe we made too much of a fuss, I don't know. But anyway, we were disbanded. From then on it did seem to be a lot more difficult to get in contact with other lesbian and gay groups on the Island. In fact, we ended up going to Portsmouth to go for a disco, they used to have a disco over in Portsmouth once a week and we ended up going there because all the places on the Island gradually slowed down and were just closed and there didn't seem to be any reason for that.

When I first came to the Island there was a place round the corner from here called the Plough and Barleycorn where they used to have a lesbian and gay night every Friday and we used to go because it was nice. There were quite a few clubs in Ryde but gradually bit by bit they just seemed to disappear, and I don't know whether, you see, I could be suspicious and think well perhaps the council squeezed them out, I don't know, but I do know that the amount of places for lesbian and gay people and people of the LGBT group have been reduced considerably from when I first came to the Island in 2003.

I know a bunch of us get together in the summertime sometimes and go camping but that's for a different reason – we go camping and meet there in memory of somebody who died. She was a lovely lady and she got cancer, she was a lesbian and a very good friend and she died a few years ago and so what we do once a year now is all her friends get together for a weekend once a year and just camp because that is something that Sara liked to do, she liked camping, and so it is a way of remembering her and honouring her memory and just meeting up, all her friends meeting up for a weekend and just remembering her and the lovely, lovely person that she was.

She was the first person that really befriended me when I came to the Island because I remember I'd been taken to the Plough and Barleycorn by Jean, she was the contact for the women, and she left me in there and she introduced me to everybody and they were all sat around and they all knew each other, I didn't know anybody so I was feeling a little bit kind of, not anxious, but I was feeling a little bit out of it because I didn't know anyone and they were all chatting. They weren't being horrible or anything, they weren't leaving me out for any particular reasons it's just that they didn't know me. I had been dumped there by Jean, you know! Anyway, I was sitting in the Plough and Barleycorn thinking, "how can I leave without being...?" You know, I wanted to leave basically, sort of make my excuses and go. Then Sara came in. I didn't know her name then but she came into the Plough and Barleycorn, she looked across at the group of us that were sitting there and she looked at me and she said, "ah, a new face!" And she marched straight over to me, sat down next to me and started chatting and I thought, "what a lovely person you are". You know, she just saw a new face and came in and started chatting to me and that was my first introduction to Sara. God rest her soul.

We used to go across to Portsmouth [to socialise], Farsi's was one club and there was a women's disco once a week over there. Because I came to the Island with a partner as well, that's the other thing. I came here with a partner so we kind of had our own little life and group of friends that we made and most of them were couples so we kind of, in a way, had a bit of an insulated, maybe false existence because we all met around each others' houses and we had meals out or went to the theatre and stuff like that.

This year my partner and I broke up, well, she broke up with me, well it was mutual but it was her idea. I went along with it but it wasn't my decision and since then I've kind of noticed how isolated you can be as a lesbian on the Island without having a partner. It's a lot more difficult and I almost feel like I need to start from scratch again, I need to start from the beginning and make new friends because the friends I had, there's nothing wrong with the friends I had but they were our mutual friends and so none of them have contacted me, which I am not complaining about, they probably don't want to take sides or don't want to get involved. I don't know. So I just feel like I need to start all over again, re-invent myself, recreate myself, recreate a network for myself so I am kind of in the process of doing that at the moment.

They've [LGBT Women's group] been very welcoming, they have been lovely, they have made me feel like I fit just right in there, it's been lovely. They've been kind, they've been welcoming, invited me out to stuff so I feel like I've got some kind of a place where I feel welcome, I can meet new people, have a chat, not feel so isolated. It just makes you feel a bit more like you're connected. So yeah, I'm doing that at the moment.

I went recently, at Christmas, to a dance over at the Riverside, it was organised, a lesbian and gay event. Nothing wrong with it, the music was nice, it was all Christmas music, lots of people came, they all knew each other, I didn't know anybody so I thought, "well, as I'm here and as the music's nice", I do like dancing so I just got up and danced and I danced by myself and I had a nice time but I was beginning to think, "am I invisible, does anybody actually see me?" I mean, the guy at the bar was very chatty and he was very kind and made me a cup of tea because I was driving so I didn't want to take any alcohol, so that was fine but I just felt a little bit like, "I'm sure they know I'm here alone, because I am obviously dancing on my own".

Anyway, it was about halfway through the evening, there were two guys sitting on a table near the door and one of them sort of waved to me and I thought he was waving to somebody behind me and I looked around to see if there was anybody behind me and there wasn't so I pointed, "are you waving at me?" He said,"'yes, yes". So I went over and he introduced himself, very nice, two guys, and they said, "we noticed that you're on your own", I said, "thank God, because I was beginning to think I was invisible. It's a lovely venue here and everything but I don't know anybody". So they said, "yeah, it can be a bit like that sometimes", and they were chatting to me for a little while and they were very, very friendly and I felt more relaxed and I felt like I belonged somewhere in this little corner with these two guys which was very sweet of them, to notice that I was on my own and it would have been nice for somebody to invite me to join them. But you can't invite yourself, you know, you can look sad and lonely but you can't invite yourself to people's tables and introduce yourself and say, "may I join you?". I wouldn't do that but it was very nice of those two guys to actually invite me over so that was nice.

But that kind of thing doesn't happen in London. When you go to London, it doesn't matter who you are, if you walk in on your own or you walk in with a crowd, I always feel welcome. People always say, "oh, hello! Haven't seen you before!" and they seem to be happy to introduce themselves and converse with you and whatever it is you are there for, whatever activity, to involve you in it. Whereas here on the Island it is a little bit more reserved, I'd say, a little bit more conservative. I use the small 'c' for conservative not capital 'C', the small 'c', but it can be a little bit more conservative, a little bit more reserved and so, yeah, you're right, it may be something to do with the fact that it is a beautiful Island but it's very rural. I don't want to be prejudiced against rural places because they are beautiful but maybe the attitudes are different? I don't know. Maybe there is less diversity so there's less awareness, I don't know.

WRITTEN HISTORIES

On Dating

An anonymous story

I have done my best to avoid dating other women on the Isle of Wight. There are too many complications in such a small place, where everyone knows everybody and it's hard to exist without everyone knowing what you are doing. One day, on the wings in Parkhurst I was walking with a colleague, new to the Island. Her boyfriend was still in Wales and he would visit at the weekend. As we walked into the wing office, one of the officers said "problems with your boyfriend?" Puzzled my colleague said "pardon?" another office piped up "oh, you were seen at the beach over the weekend with your boyfriend and you weren't holding hands". She couldn't believe it, and had never experienced anything like it in her life. I told her that this was Island life and that there would be many more incidents like this happen.

For me, I have never been able to hide who I am. I am a big, short haired woman, who wears masculine clothes and has a keychain from her pocket. In a lot of people's eyes I look like a stereotypical lesbian. If I am not being misgendered, I am constantly being watched by others. Even as a child, I would always be called a boy, or told I wanted to be one. I just wanted to be me.

The truth is, I am physically uncomfortable in women's clothes (as illogical as that is as clothes have no gender), and only slightly more comfortable in my biological body. I have spent most of my life explaining, apologising or running away from the comments and abuse that I've experienced just for being my authentic self. In nursery school, there was a short dividing wall between the girls' and the boys' sides. One day, as I made my way to go to the toilet two boys grabbed hold of me by the neck of my T-shirt. "You aren't a girl, you're a boy, go to the boys toilets", no matter what I said, they did not believe me and I was forced into the boys' side where they waited outside the door until I had been to the toilet in there.

It was the start of a long list of challenges I've experienced in my life, just trying to access the toilet, or go about my daily business. I've had security guards, police, and men challenge me, some in nicer ways than others. I've had mothers cover their kids' faces so they didn't have to look at me when I walked into the women's toilet. 'Nicer' comments include telling me that I am in the wrong toilet, directing me to where the men's toilets are and also telling me that I should be dressing more like a woman. When you look at the traditional picture representation that indicates a toilet is for women, I have never fitted that picture, and I never will. Some days I was able to challenge, but mostly I did not have the energy to challenge others when they reacted to me that way.

Due to me fitting the stereotype, and people's prejudice, be it overt or otherwise, I live in a constant state of alertness. Many friends and colleagues have been fascinated to see others' reactions to me, or just how much of a walking, talking sex act I am. That is all most people understand about LGBTQI+ people – we are walking talking sex acts, not real people, not decent people. The amount of times I've been accused of having an affair with a woman, or sleeping with a woman, just because I was seen talking in the street, or heaven forbid, shopping together in a store. Unless you've been there, or seen it first hand, it's hard to acknowledge it even happens, or even validate my experiences. I've had malicious and false allegations made against me, even at work because people are quick to jump to conclusions or have issues with my sexuality.

For me, dating on this Island doesn't feel right. It's just too under the microscope. A couple of years ago, I was blessed to go to Brighton as part of a secret wedding party. There were four of us, the two women getting married, myself and a straight friend. In an ironic twist, the only person who had ever been to a gay wedding before was the straight woman. As we walked around the seafront, post wedding, it really hit me just how free I felt. The contrast from living on the Island is great, and it saddens me. I would love to feel that free here, but I don't. Even being out and one of the most visible out people on the Island, I don't feel free.

So many people I know have lived straight lives on the Island and lived for the weekends in towns and cities where they can be free, or who have left the Island completely because of their gender or sexual identity. You may say, if you are so unhappy, if you feel like that then why stay? I stay to make things better, to educate and inform, to be visible and out, to be proud of my authentic self and support others in being their authentic self too. I stay to challenge the inequalities and discrimination, to change services for the better and support families to be more accepting. To make the future more positive, because there is so much change that still needs to happen.

I have lived and worked on the Island for most of my life. I have seen how the secrets have harmed people, and how people have taken their own lives rather than be out to their family, because of the reactions. Kids, as young as ten, rejected by their family for who they are. I have seen people struggle with dependency issues, mental health problems and more, people who never lived authentically for far too many different reasons, but the majority linked to how society has treated them.

I've seen loving partners denied access to their loved ones when they become ill, or lose their property, their lives they created with the person they loved because their relationship could not be recognised in law, or because of the hatred within biological families. If people really knew of the stories and the hardships, I think a lot of attitudes would change. Most people think they are inclusive and embrace diversity but for the most part, they lack any real depth of knowledge and understanding about any of it and most have no interest to learn more.

There are many people that I might be the only person who knows their real name, who has seen their authentic self, or shared the struggles they have faced. It is an honour and a privilege to be trusted with such a beautiful gift. There is nothing more beautiful than being your authentic self. Recently, a beautiful young soul came out to me as being bi. I want her future to be different, for her to be free and accepted as she is, for her to have a bright future where services are accessible and you don't have to go back into the closet to access them. The Isle of Wight is a beautiful place, and it's time that LGBTQI+ matters are embraced and embedded within the community, where diversity is celebrated and seen for the richness it brings to the world, not as some scary entity. When all is said and done, I want to have peace in my heart that I have done my bit to make that happen and to help others live authentically.

OVERCOMING CRIMINALISATION

Bronwyn Hamilton-Brown
and Franko Figueiredo-Stow

LGBTQ+ history is a history of overcoming criminalisation, which stems from the Middle Assyrian Law Codes (1075 BC)[125], the first to condemn the act of same sex intercourse. These codes became the primary historical justification for penalising sodomy and continued with the Judeo-Christian valorisation of sex within the context of procreative marriage. Under Roman Catholic natural law and Protestant (Puritan) fundamentalism, fornication, adultery, and same sex sodomy are sins because by definition they occur outside the context of marriage; contraception, abortion, masturbation, and all kinds of sodomy are sins because they are by definition non-procreative".[126]

In the UK, religious objections to same sex attraction have existed since at least the Middle Ages[127] and were first endorsed in law in England in the 1533 Act of Henry VIII, also known as the Buggery Act, which classified sodomy as an illegal act between man and woman, man and man, or man and beast.[128] This law, which was re-enacted in 1563, was the basis for all male homosexual convictions until 1885, when the Criminal Assessment Act extended the legal sanction to any sexual contact between males.[129]

From the days of the Buggery Act to the cruel treatment of Oscar Wilde and his peers, our LGBTQ+ history is infused with many dark moments, too many to list here and some are very recent. We arrive in 2020 with relative enlightenment. Changes in the law, although hard fought and slow, have been dramatic for the LGBTQ+ community.

Today, it seems archaic and shocking that to love, demonstrate attraction or have relations with a member of the same sex can still be punishable by death in some countries. The knock-on effects of criminalisation, homophobia or even mild disapproval of an individual's sexuality have led to feelings of isolation and poor mental health and even suicide as borne out in our interviews. It is not easy to be fully out, and though societal acceptance has improved, things aren't perfect, and persecution and prosecution of LGBTQ+ folk has not gone away.

Progress in the UK has not been linear. In 1772 we had the first public debate about homosexuality where a more progressive attitute was demonstrated during the trial of Captain Robert Jones who was convicted of sodomy and was eventaully pardoned; also, in 1785, the English utilitarian philosopher and advocate of law reform Jeremy Bentham led a public campaign for the decriminalisation of sodomy in England. Bentham believed that 'hostility to sodomy and to sodomites was rooted in religious asceticism and in the associated fear of sexual pleasure' and argued that 'homosexual acts did not weaken men, nor threaten population or marriage.'[130] This was followed, however, by a period of rife persecution, with many cases making newspaper headlines, such as the case brought against Oscar Wilde. In 2019, Matthew Sturgies gave a talk at the Isle of Wight Literary Festival examining the contradictions and confusions of Wilde's life. And here, Wilde illustrates the unjust punishments endured at the end of the nineteenth century. This letter, to his lover, Lord Douglas, documents the trials and pain inflicted by a legal system which reflected the beliefs of society in that era:

> All trials are trials for one's life, just as all sentences are sentences of death; and three times have I been tried. The first time I left the box to be arrested, the second time to be led back to the house of detention, the third time to pass into a prison for two years. Society, as we have constituted it, will have no place for me, has none to offer; but Nature, whose sweet rains fall on unjust and just alike, will have clefts in the

[125]*Internet History Sourcebooks*. Accessed July 23, 2020, https://sourcebooks.fordham.edu/ancient/1075assyriancode.asp.

[126]William N. Eskridge. *Gaylaw: Challenging the Apartheid of the Closet*. Cambridge, MA: Harvard University Press, 1999, 161.

[127]Richard Davenport-Hines, Sex, Death and Punishment. Attitudes to Sex and Sexuality in Britain since the Renaissance, London, Collins 1990, XV + 439 Pp. Nuncius 5, no. 2 (1990): pp. 377-379, https://doi.org/10.1163/182539190x00589.

[128]Jeffrey Weeks. *Coming Out: Homosexual Politics in Britain from the Nineteenth Century to the Present*. London: Quartet Books, 1991.

[129]Ibid.

[130]Bryne R.S. Fone. 'A cry for reform', in *Homophobia: A History*. New York: Picador, 2001, 254-256.

rocks where I may hide, and secret valleys in whose silence I may weep undisturbed.[131]

Our research uncovered a circular letter from 1913 where the Admiralty had deemed there to be sufficient cause to dismiss sailors for infection and unnatural offences.

Dr Clifford Williams' research revealed that:

> In the summer of 1921 two men appeared at court charged with gross indecency. They were seen at 10 p.m. on Monday 13 June by Sergeant Morrison in Appley Rise Road, near Ryde, in a state of embrace and with loosened clothes. They were charged with gross indecency and appeared at Ryde Magistrates Court the following day. The two men; Cecil Howard Minter Tarrant, a 31 year old single man and hairdresser from Ryde, and Frederick Clark, a 35 year old married man and clerk of Seaview, were bailed to reappear a week later.[132] Both were subsequently committed to the Hampshire Assizes and appeared at court in Winchester the following month. At the Assizes both pleaded not guilty. Clark said he was drunk while Tarrant said Clark was the instigator. The jury found both guilty. Clark was sentenced to three months hard labour. Tarrant was sent to a home for mental defectives.[133]

After the Second World War, a large number of arrests and prosecutions took place; some of these were high profile and famous individuals, Alan Turing and Lord Montagu of Beaulieu, amongst them. This led to the Conservative government setting up a departmental committee to consider homosexual offences and prosecutions, under Sir John Wolfenden. Between 1957 and 1967, various organisations repeatedly petitioned the Home Office to try and effect changes in the law. The Campaign for Homosexual Equality (CHE) and the Homosexual Law Reform Society (HLRS) both put pressure on the government. The HLRS was founded on 12 May 1958, directly in response to the recommendations of the Wolfenden Report, to campaign for decriminalisation. The CHE was founded in 1964 by Allan Horsfall and others as the North Western Committee for Homosexual Law Reform.[134] The Bill received royal assent on 27 July 1967 after an intense late-night debate in the House of Commons, ironically the same week as The Beatles' *All You Need is Love* was at the top of the charts in the UK.

This was a hugely significant moment in the history of liberation for gay and bisexual men. However, the reform was deeply limited. The 1967 Sexual

Offences Act:

- set a higher age of consent for homosexual sex acts than that for heterosexual ones;
- only applied to England and Wales; it did not apply to Scotland, Northern Ireland, or the Channel Islands;
- did not apply to the Armed Forces or Merchant Navy;
- had an 'in private' clause that was different from heterosexual couples.[135]

On the Island, Nikki Dorakis founded the Isle of Wight CHE group in the early 70s and was a key figure in the Gay Rights movement as one of many pressure groups and activists, both visible and invisible, who would continue to work tirelessly for equality.[136] Our research also uncovered records of local support for the CHE from straight allies such as the leader of the Liberal Party Mr David Steel, and we also found letters from local islanders to newspapers making appeals on behalf of the LGBTQ+ community. Not surprisingly, there are also many records of opposition from Conservative members, including the Church of England.[137]

These forces opposing the CHE took any opportunity to reverse even the smallest achievements; the Conservative government's Section 28 in 1988 is one example, which dictated that local authorities:

shall not intentionally promote homosexuality or publish material with the intention of promoting homosexuality … or promote the teaching in any maintained school of the acceptability of homosexuality as a pretended family relationship.[138]

[131]Oscar Wilde. *De Profundis*. Amsterdam: Meulenhoff, 1971. 33.

[132]*Isle of Wight Observer*, 18 Jun 1921

[133]Ibid, 16 Jul 1921.

[134]Vicky Iglikowski-Broad, 'The Passing of the 1967 Sexual Offences Act', *The National Archives blog*. The National Archives, July 24, 2017, https://blog.nationalarchives.gov.uk/sexual-offences-act/.

[135]Ibid.

[136]'Nikki Dorakis'. Amazon.co.uk: Nikki Dorakis, accessed September 30, 2020.

[137]Timothy Hopkins, 'I Was Surprised', *The Isle of Wight County Press*, August 28, 1976, sec. Letters to the editor, 14

[138]'Local Government Bill', Local Government Bill. *Hansard*, 11 January 1988, accessed February 22, 2021, https://api.parliament.uk/historic-hansard/lords/1988/jan/11/local-government-bill#column 965.

Added to this we had the societal fears manifested in the AIDS and HIV epidemic, thus further hindering progress. In recent memory, we found records of homophobic attacks[139] outside some of the Island's LGBTQ+-friendly venues such as Patsys.[140] Years of progress could, arguably, be said to be partially undone.

Bringing about changes in the law is a wonderful achievement, but how long will it take for the customary law to change? An Act of Parliament will not change people's perceptions overnight. Prejudice, fear, misinformation, scapegoating, ignorance, as well as active aggression and violence towards the LGBTQ+ community would further stall equality for those not belonging to a heterosexual world. Governments would, arguably, encourage homophobia which in turn promoted division. The sexual education of children in the 80s up until very recently was absolutely deficient; children would have been taught that loving relationships precluded same-sex relationships, thus missing out significant aspects of their communities and perhaps their own family dynamics – a proactive blotting out of LGBTQ+ life, as if some people didn't matter, or that some people were too damaging to be acknowledged.[141]

It may feel, from the earliest time, that the axe fell heaviest on men, that the criminality, the prejudice and the pain have been felt almost entirely by the gay male community. One might think that lesbians were luckier, possibly because their 'crime' was seen as a lesser 'crime', the impact of their relationships was seen as less damaging, less debauched perhaps?

---

[139]'Ryde Waiter Might Be Jailed for Attack on Gay Man', *Isle of Wight County Press*, October 20, 2000, sec. Local News, 14.

[140]'Compensation Order over Attack', *Isle of Wight County Press*, February 1, 208AD, sec. Local News, 6.

[141]Read more about the impact of Section 28 in the chapter here entitled 'Section 28: Politics, Intent, Spin, Impact and Aftermath. A Very Political Act' by David Bennett.

[142]Brian P. Levack. *The Witch-Hunt in Early Modern Europe*. London: Routledge, 2016, 129.

[143]Steven T. Katz. *The Holocaust in Historical Context*. New York: Oxford University Press, 1994, 468-469.

[144]Alyssa A. Samek, 'Violence and Identity Politics: 1970s Lesbian-Feminist Discourse and Robin Morgan's 1973 West Coast Lesbian Conference Keynote Address', *Communication and Critical/Cultural Studies*, 13:3, 232-249. https://doi.org/10.1080/14791420.2015.1127400

[145]British Newspaper Archives. 2013. 'The Obscenity Trial of Miss Radclyffe Hall's novel, 'The Well of Loneliness'' – 16 November 1928 in Headlines from History. https://blog.britishnewspaperarchive. co.uk/2013/11/15/the-obscenity-trial-of-miss-radclyffe-halls-novel-the-well-of-loneliness-16-november-1928/?ds_ kid=39700045269534934&gclid=Cj0KCQjw6uT4BRD5ARIsADwJQ1--vw-hwcuz2SQFOccos1mS4qgp6x9Kxh REzI5Hqu_poP8xvYFjUn8aAolSEALw_wcB&gclsrc=aw.ds accessed 23 July 2020

[146]Great Britain. UK Government. John Frederick Wolfenden Wolfenden of Westcott, introduction by Karl A. Menninger. 'The Wolfenden Report: Report of the Committee on Homosexual Offences and Prostitution'. New York: Stein and Day, 1963

The truth is that women had already been condemned to the cages of patriarchy from time without beginning, shackled by the chains of a system which placed the female sex in a precarious, powerless position. Some researchers estimate that nine million Wicca (witches or wise women) were burned to death during the Middle Ages and 'many scholars have argued that it was the women who seemed most independent from patriarchal norms, living outside the parameters of the patriarchal family, who were most vulnerable to accusations of witchcraft'.[142] 'The reason for this strong correlation seems clear,' writes Katz: 'these women had never given birth and comprised the female group most difficult to assimilate, to comprehend within the regulative late medieval social matrix, organised, as it was, around the family unit.'[143] Women had to fight for their own liberation first, before they could go on a fight for intersectional equality. As Robin Morgan explains 'It is awfully hard to be a lesbian without being a woman first'.[144]

Undeniably, records of criminal acts could only be found for males as it has never been unlawful for women to participate in same-sex sexual acts, though guilty of the same 'crimes'. Most public records and references are of notable female couples in alleged same-sex relationships, often found in high-society 'gossip' columns.

The fact is, our research didn't reveal any records of female prosecutions. The closest to it was when Radclyffe Hall's lesbian novel, *The Well of Loneliness*, found itself in the dock on a charge of obscenity. The powers-that-be had decided that they did not like the novel's 'unnatural offences', hence the decision to prosecute. The magistrate eventually decided that the book was obscene and ordered that it be destroyed.[145]

References to female homosexuality tend to include those who enjoyed a more affluent or creative lifestyle such as the wealthy Joe Carstairs, Virginia Woolf and Vita Sackville-West. Female couples were seen as companions; relationships were masked as friendships. Queen Victoria's attitude led and reflected how society viewed gay women, or inverts, as they were coined. Prosecutions of 'offending' women had failed for this very reason, as, seemingly, there was no case to answer.

For the male, intimacy, transgression from the 'norm' and subsequent conviction could span all class boundaries, though typically the media would, understandably and predominantly, focus on the newsworthy rich and famous. Wolfenden, in his 1957 Report, states: 'There must remain a realm of private morality and immorality which is, in brief and crude terms, not the law's business'.[146]

Whilst the Sexual Offences Act 1967 made it legal for relations to take place between consenting males in private, sexual acts taking place in public places were specifically outlawed. Men could be charged, fined, conditionally discharged or imprisoned for gross indecency.

Prosecutions, particularly between 1981 and 1993 on the Isle of Wight, in common with the mainland, were generally for importuning in public toilets.[147] The implications of prosecution could be catastrophic, and no doubt this is why some of those caught denied being homosexual, or claimed to have been in the wrong place at the wrong time. Hampshire Constabulary introduced Lesbian and Gay Liaison Officers (LAGLO) in 1996 and there are now LAGLOs in every part of the force and they work for safer LGBT+ communities.[148]

Similarly, those in the armed forces faced much discrimination. Former Ryde High School pupil Royal Navy Lieutenant-Commander Duncan Lustig-Prean was discharged in 1994 when his sexuality became known following a blackmail threat.[149] Elaine Chambers, Isle of Wight resident, recounts in her autobiographical book *This Queer Angel* the struggles of having joined the Army in 1982 as a student nurse, later a junior sister, in the rank of Lieutenant, only to be forced to resign when her sexuality was contested by colleagues.[150] Elaine, together with Robert Ely, formed Rank Outsiders, a group campaigning for gay men and lesbians to be allowed to serve in the British armed forces. Ex-Royal Navy Lieutenant-Commander Duncan Lustig-Prean and three other ex-servicemen, took their case to the European Court after it was rejected by the Appeal Court in London. The judges 'declared unanimously that such a bar on entry into the army, navy and air force was illegal under the European Convention on Human Rights, which safeguards an individual's right to privacy'.[151]

---

[147]Read more in the chapter here entitled 'Morality, Hypocrisy and Public Sex on the Isle of Wight' by Mark Woolford

[148]Troman, Kristen. 'Two decades Plus of Safer LGBT+ Communities in Hampshire and the Isle of Wight', *Fyne Times*. https://www.fyne.co.uk/two-decades-plus-of-safer-lgbt-communities-in-hampshire-and-the-isle-of-wight/ accessed 5 Aug 2020

[149]'Big Costs for Ex-Officer in Gay Test Case', *Isle of Wight County Press*, June 9, 1995, 25.

[150]Elaine Chambers. *This Queer Angel*. London: Unbound, 2018, 193-197.

[151]'UK Military Gay Ban Illegal', *BBC News*, September 27, 1999, http://news.bbc.co.uk/1/hi/uk/458625.stm.

The long-standing ban on homosexuals in the armed forces was finally lifted in 2000 in an historic move forced on the government by the European Court of Human Rights.[152]

From 2000 to the present day, there have been great strides in the LGBTQ+ fight for equality and decriminalisation and Section 28 was repealed in 2003.

In December 2002, the Lord Chancellor's office published a Government Policy Concerning Transsexual People document that categorically states that transsexualism 'is not a mental illness'.[153] And Since 4 April 2005, the Gender Recognition Act 2004 has made it possible for transgender people to change their legal gender in the UK, allowing them to acquire a new birth certificate, affording them full recognition of their acquired sex in law for all purposes.[154]

The Marriage (Same Sex Couples) Act 2013, which allows same-sex marriage in England and Wales, was passed by the UK Parliament in July 2013 and came into force on 13 March 2014. For many LGBTQ+ people, this fundamental change in law has made the most enormous difference to their lives.

It can easily feel as if we have finally reached the peak of equality, at least legally. And yet, in 2017, Isle of Wight MP Andrew Turner[155] was forced to step down after an outcry over alleged comments made by Mr Turner during an A Level politics class, in which students of Christ the King College said he called homosexuality 'dangerous to society' and 'wrong'.[156]

[152]Richard Norton-Taylor, 'Forces Ban on Gays Is Lifted', *Guardian*, Guardian News and Media, January 13, 2000, https://www.theguardian.com/uk/2000/jan/13/richardnortontaylor.https://www.theguardian.com/uk/2000/jan/13/richardnortontaylor accessed 23 July 2020

[153]Department for Constitutional Affairs Online Archives. Transsexual people in People's rights. https://web.archive.org/web/20080511211217/http://www.dca.gov.uk/constitution/transsex/policy.htm accessed 23 July 2020

[154]The National Archives. Gender Recognition Act 2004. https://www.legislation.gov.uk/ukpga/2004/7/contents accessed 23 July 2020

[155]Steven Swinford, 'Tory MP stands down after allegedly telling students that homosexuality is "wrong and dangerous to society"', *Daily Telegraph*, April 28, 2017

[156]'Andrew Turner Steps down as Isle of Wight MP after Outcry over Alleged Homosexuality Comments', *Isle of Wight County Press*, March 22, 2018), https://www.countypress.co.uk/news/16107600.andrew-turner-steps-down-as-isle-of-wight-mp-after-outcry-over-alleged-homosexuality-comments/.

In the same year, Stonewall published a report on LGBT hate crime, revealing: 'Anti-LGBT abuse extends far beyond acts of hate and violence on our streets'.[157] In 2019 there were 410 hate crimes in Hampshire and the Isle of Wight targeting someone's sexual orientation, and 98 targeting someone's gender identity. Stonewall reported that 'many LGBTQ+ people, locally and nationally, still endure poor treatment while using public services and going about their lives, whether in their local shop, gym, school or place of worship'.[158]

In September 2020, relationships and sex education (RSE) has, at long last, become statutory in all secondary schools in England and relationships education has become statutory in all primary schools in England.

As I write this article, hate crime reporting centres on the Island are being depleted of funding, many have stopped taking reports, and there are major delays in information sharing for those who are supporting hate crime on the Island within Hampshire Constabulary.

On 14th June 2020, the *Sunday Times* reported that the UK Government intends to scrap the Gender Recognition Act reform and roll back the hard-won rights of trans and non-binary people.[159] This announcement led to a few protests around the country, including the Isle of Wight.[160]

These most recent events are clear evidence that we must remain vigilant to ensure our hard-won rights are not taken away. In a recent article, Peter Tatchell advocated for the need to transform society rather than just seek equal rights within the flawed hetero-dominated status quo. He says:

> As well as changing laws and institutional practice, it is also essential to change attitudes, values and institutions, to win public opinion in favour of accepting equal rights for all. If ignorant and intolerant attitudes linger, then prejudice, ostracism, hostility and informal discrimination will continue – and damage people's lives.[161]

The *Out On An Island* project has demonstrated that we need to guard these rights, and improve on them; we need to promote further social and educational programmes until LGBTQ+ folk can live fully comfortably and are free to express who they are, to be seen and welcomed into all spaces, without fear. We need to ensure that LGBTQ+ people of any sexuality and gender can visit and/or live on our Island and those born here can remain without fear of persecution and without feeling that their quality of life will improve if they migrate across to the mainland.

[157]Kristen Troman, 'Two Decades plus of Safer LGBT+ Communities in Hampshire and the Isle of Wight', *Fyne Times*, May 20, 2019. https://www.fyne.co.uk/two-decades-plus-of-safer-lgbt-communities-in-hampshire-and-the-isle-of-wight/.

[158]Chaka L. Bachmann Chaka and Beccca Gooch. 'LGBT in Britain Hate and Crime Discrimination', Stonewall (2013). https://www.stonewall.org.uk/system/files/lgbt_in_britain_hate_crime.pdf accessed 23 July 2020

[159]Tim Shipman, 'Boris Johnson Scraps Plan to Make Gender Change Easier', *Sunday Times*, June 14, 2020, https://www.thetimes.co.uk/article/boris-johnson-scraps-plan-to-make-gender-change-easier-zs6lqfls0.

[160]Yve White, 'Passionate Speeches at Protest for Trans and Non-Binary Rights', Isle of Wight News from *On The Wight*, July 16, 2020, https://onthewight.com/passionate-speeches-at-protest-for-trans-and-non-binary-rights/.

[161]Peter Tatchell, 'Beyond Equality: Why Equal Rights Are Not Enough', Peter Tatchell Foundation, January 9, 2018, https://www.petertatchellfoundation.org/beyond-equality-why-equal-rights-are-not-enough/.

MORALITY, HYPOCRISY AND PUBLIC SEX ON THE ISLE OF WIGHT

Mark Woolford

A number of the oral history interviews carried out revealed public sex and criminalisation to be a particular issue for gay men on the Isle of Wight.

Further research also revealed many documented cases of islanders partaking in the practice of cottaging on the Island, with many making the local newspaper, *The Isle of Wight County Press*. These cases have involved local councillors, head teachers, local businessmen and tourists.

Although this is a complex subject and still very much taboo, we cannot ignore its impact on the local LGBTQ+ community and its history.

Simon Button explains, in an article for *Attitude*, that cottaging has links

> 'dating back to at least the 17th century, with the first recorded instance of entrapment being the 1698 case of Captain Edward Rigby, who was lured to a private room in a London tavern by a man on the payroll of the Society for the Reformation of Manners, a group which aimed to suppress what it saw as profanity and immorality by bringing private prosecutions!'[162]

Whilst the Sexual Offences Act 1967 permitted sex between consenting men over 21 years of age when conducted in private, the act specifically excluded public lavatories from being 'private'. 'The Sexual Offences Act 2003 replaced this aspect with the offence of "Sexual activity in a public lavatory" which includes solo masturbation'.[163]

Possible penalties for being caught having sex in a public convenience include:[164]

- A prison sentence on summary conviction of up to six months and/or a fine.
- A caution. If you accept a caution as an alternative to prosecution, this forms part of your criminal record and can be used as evidence of bad character if you're prosecuted for another crime. Unless a conviction is a certainty, therefore, don't accept a caution.
- A ban from specified premises. If you're found cottaging in, for example, a shopping centre by security staff, they could ban you from the premises in future.

- Your name could be added to the Sex Offenders Register in some circumstances if you are cautioned or convicted under the Sexual Offences Act 2003.[165]

Where prosecution has been successful, a small fine is often levied as it is felt the shame of being in the local newspapers can be enough of a deterrent to prevent further offences occurring.

The act of cottaging is generally an underground, secretive activity but on occasion the practice can get into the news and thus the wider public consciousness. Actor John Gielgud, Record Producer Joe Meek, MP Louis Eaks and, more recently and perhaps most famously, pop star George Michael was arrested twice for the offence, once in LA and again in London. He later released a single 'Outside' accompanied by a humorous video clearly based on the episode, which provoked the seemingly sensitive cop whom it depicted to sue him for damages, a case the courts dismissed.

Research carried out by Dr Clifford Williams found that *Gay News* often reported on police activities in gay meeting places on the Island, he writes:

> Sometimes the reports were written with a touch of humour. For example, in *Gay News* issue 47 of 1974 we read of a man from Cowes who, when offered a penis through a hole in a toilet cubicle, 'took off his belt, fixed it round the offending part, and tied the other end to the downpipe of the cistern'.[166] The person on the other end of the belt shouted 'Ease it off'. Whereupon the witness who had tied the belt replied that he would have to wait until he had called the police. The police arrived to find the 40 year old defendant 'strung up helpless in the East Cowes Town Hall toilets'. On arrival at the police station he had to be treated by a doctor for minor injuries caused by the belt. At court the defendant pleaded guilty to trying to procure an act of gross indecency. Sentence was deferred. The *Gay News* reporter put it 'that was presumably to satisfy the magistrates that the accused (who is

[162]Simon Button, 'Why Do so Many Gay Men Still Go Cruising and Cottaging?', *Attitude*, October 5, 2018, https://www.attitude.co.uk/article/why-do-so-many-gay-men-still-go-cruising-and-cottaging/15681/

[163]Sexual Offences Act 2003, https://www.legislation.gov.uk/ukpga/2003/42/contents, accessed July 20, 2020

[164]Lucy Trevelyan, 'The Legal Status of "Cottaging" in the UK", InBrief.co.uk. https://www.inbrief.co.uk/offences/cottaging/ accessed March 21, 2017,

[165]Ibid.

[166]'Caught by the Short and Curlys', *Gay News* issue 47, 1974

named in the article) has no further hang ups!'. It is somewhat amusing that one of the few gay pubs listed for the island in *Gay News* at that time was called 'The Hole In the Wall' in Market Street, Ventnor.[167]

Dr Williams continues:

> Issue 50 of *Gay News* in Jul 1974 was more typical of reporting on legal matters. It warned holiday makers to the island to be wary because there were informers on gays about. Under the heading "Billet-doux" (love letter) a court case involving folded notes being passed in a Ryde toilet is reported. A man in the cubicle where the notes landed took them to the police officers who, conveniently for him, were standing nearby outside the toilets. A 29 year old man in the cubicles was subsequently arrested. Although a handwriting expert could not ascertain with certainty that the man had written the notes, there was nevertheless sufficient evidence to convict. The case was taken on appeal to the Crown Court at Newport. The judge dismissed the appeal.[168]

One such case occurred on the Isle of Wight on the 15 and 16 November 1993, when twenty four men were arrested and twenty one of them were charged after being caught by police in a public convenience in Newport. The police mounted a surveillance operation after they had received complaints about activities taking place in the men's toilets at Coppin's Bridge in Newport. The police hid two officers in the roof of the building whilst a third waited outside, in radio contact with the other two and keeping a note of what was happening. Nine men were tried in the first hearings, five of the men were fined £120 and the other four were fined £200 and all had to pay costs. They were fined different amounts based on their financial situation. All of the men had their names, the street and town where they lived and, if relevant, their current occupation made public. The defence lawyers tried to argue that the acts had effectively been in private due to the way the cubicles had been constructed. The only way the police could observe the activities was by hiding on the roof looking through the skylights. As a result of these prosecutions one of the men was immediately suspended from his job as a care assistant after informing his

---

[167]'Paper chase', *Gay News*, issue 54, 1974

[168]'Billet-doux', *Gay News*, issue 50, 1974

[169]'9 Fined for Acts of Gross Indecency', *Isle of Wight County Press*, December 10, 1993, 3.

employer and also had a new contract that he was about to take up withdrawn, thus leaving him unemployed.[169]

Another story that made the local newspaper occurred in East Cowes where a local man was caught with another man with a long history of sexual offences in public conveniences on Ryde Esplanade. The man, married with three children, claimed that his behaviour was not typical and it had happened because he had drunk a large amount of alcohol. He went on to say that he hated homosexuals after being assaulted by one earlier in his life and he normally would enter a public convenience with the aim of taking any homosexuals he encountered outside to "beat them up".[170]

Other documented cases in the local papers include the story of a local man caught passing sex notes to a police officer who was sitting in another cubicle. The man was prosecuted for the offence but argued that he was merely carrying out research into the behaviour of transvestites and transsexuals and he himself was neither of these, nor was he a homosexual.[171] Similarly, also reported by the *Isle of Wight County Press*, an Isle of Wight Conservative councillor was found guilty of engaging in sexual activity in a public toilet in Carisbrooke. He was charged back in August 2010 and the same day issued a statement to 'Ventnor Blog' saying, 'he is physically incapable of performing the alleged acts' due to a heart condition.[172]

A further incident involved a head teacher of a local school. Once again caught by the police, the man in question strenuously denied being there for the purposes of having sex. Instead he claimed he was simply unable to urinate. He was charged £200 plus £500 in legal fees. In passing the sentence, the judge stated 'You have brought on yourself and your family far more suffering than any penalty this court will enforce!' He went on to say 'I take into account your good character and I hope you will in the future serve the community as you have done in the past. Other people have found themselves in the same position and have picked up the pieces and the continued support from your family will be of enormous value.'[173]

---

[170]'9 Fined for Acts of Gross Indecency', *Isle of Wight County Press*, December 10, 1993, 3

[171]'Freshwater Man Found Passing Sex Notes Under Door in Toilets', *Isle of Wight County Press*, February 28, 1992, 9.

[172]Simon Perry, 'Cllr David Whittaker Found Guilty Of Sex Charge', Isle of Wight News from *OnTheWight*, January 11, 2011, https://onthewight.com/cllr-david-whittaker-found-guilty-of-sex-charge/.

[173]'Head Found Guilty of Importuning in Toilets', *Isle of Wight County Press*, September 11,1992, 1.

One theme running through these cases is the way the defendants denied that they had been cottaging. *In White Tiles. Trickling Water. A Man!* Johan Andersson and Ben Campkin argue that 'at least since 1726, when the *London Journal* ran a front-page editorial listing 'markets' and 'bog-houses' where men met 'to commit Sodomy, the British media have reinforced a link between male homosexuality and public conveniences. Despite a general liberalisation of attitudes towards gay sex and relationships in recent years, certain parts of the media remain obsessively preoccupied with this association!'[174]

They go on to suggest 'the stigma attached to these places contributed to the exclusion of homosexual men from identification with normal lives'. This is supported by Houlbrook's detailed historical analysis of the legal response to cottaging in London:

> In 1917, 81 percent of homosexual incidents resulting in proceedings at Bow Street Police Court were detected in locations positively identifiable as public conveniences. Arrested primarily in urinals, the homosexual was constructed in the image of that place. Harold Sturge, Old Street magistrate, made explicit the connection between the dirt and defecation of the lavatory and the homosexual. Homosexual acts were, he argued, 'morally wrong, physically dirty and progressively degrading'.[175]

Accounts such as these can show how, historically, the legal establishment set out to portray an image of homosexual men as being dirty and contaminating by closely associating them with the act of cottaging in public conveniences.

Over the years many people have been prosecuted for this offence. Gay rights campaigner Peter Tatchell has estimated that between the trial of Oscar Wilde in 1895 and the 2003 Sexual Offences Act, somewhere between 50,000 and 100,000 gay or bisexual men were convicted for cottaging offences.[176]

Whilst in some instances, getting caught in the act of cottaging does not seem to have had too much of a detrimental effect on someone's life, in other cases it can be a devastating and life-changing experience. In the UK, it used to be the case that if you were 'cottaging' you were running the risk of physical assault,

---

[174]R. Norton. *Mother Clap's Molly House: The Gay Subculture in England 1700–1830.* London: GMP Publishers, 1992, 66

[175]Matt Houlbrook. *Queer London: Perils and Pleasures in the Sexual Metropolis, 1918-1957.* Chicago: University of Chicago Press, 2020, 62

[176]Graham Kirby. 'Cottaging: How Having Gay Sex in Public Toilets Changed My Life', *Vice*, accessed June 16, 2020, https://www.vice.com/en_uk/article/av9zjg/gay-britain-uk-cottaging-sex-in-public-toilets-696.

blackmail, entrapment, arrest and imprisonment. If you were convicted, you stood to lose everything – your job, your reputation, your family. But still, undeterred, gay men went cruising for sex.[177] With the risk of being fined, prosecuted and publicly shamed if caught cottaging, it is worth considering why gay men would risk participating in the act of cottaging.

Looking back at the changes in the law regarding gay rights, it is possible to see how the activity originated. Before the gay liberation movement, many, if not most, gay and bisexual men at the time were closeted and there were almost no public gay social groups for those under legal drinking age. As such, cottages were among the few places where men too young to get into gay bars could meet others whom they knew to be gay.[178]

One reason why cottaging has, despite changes in legislation and the advent of digital dating, remained popular with some people is because it can still offer a discreet way for gay men to meet up with sexual partners, develop friendships or even find potential life partners. Before homosexuality was partially decriminalised in the UK, in 1967, this was one of the only ways that members of the community could meet other people of the same sexual orientation and even today remains one way for gay men to meet other gay men, especially in rural communities without dedicated gay bars and clubs. Even in places where there are such venues, there is still a stigma attached to being gay that many people find hard to overcome, and the idea of being spotted going into or coming out of a gay venue can prove to be an obstacle that can take a long time to manage. Derek Jarman writes:

> Outside London it was this or nothing. Most towns had, at best, a dreary pub. This is still the case if you live in a small town or village. The 'cottage' is the foundation of our historical lives. It was here that we were condemned by Heterosexual Society – which fought the opening of the bars, their minds, and anything that might suggest we live normal lives.[179]

In an article on cottaging and cruising in *Attitude* magazine, one of the contributors, Bernard Greaves thinks cottaging, at least in Leicester where he

---

[177]Gareth Johnson, 'What Are the Laws about Cruising for Sex?', *Means Happy*, January 21, 2021, https://meanshappy.com/what-are-the-laws-about-cruising-for-sex-in-the-uk/.

[178]Bruce Galloway. *Prejudice and Pride Discrimination against Gay People in Modern Britain*. London: Routledge, 1983, 43

[179]Derek Jarman and Michael Christie. *At Your Own Risk: A Saint's Testament*. Woodstock, NY: Overlook Press, 1994, 60

lives, for some people remains a necessity:

> There are lots of people who are still in the closet. Using Leicester
> as a case in point, the idea of being openly gay in ethnic minority
> communities, or for that matter in Eastern European communities, is
> still appallingly difficult and lots of them are using cruising areas and
> saunas.[180]

In the same article another interviewee, Zia X, goes on to explain why saunas that are often used in a similar way to cottages also remain popular in today's world, when there are other more high-tech ways of contacting potential sexual partners. It is a reminder that gay sex is still furtive for many people, even if they've taken it indoors. 'Living in quite a queer world, I assume everyone is out but going to saunas it's like: "Oh wow, there's a swathe of people who are in straight marriages, with kids, who aren't out"', Zia says. 'There are still lots of people who haven't found that place to express their desires openly so they use these more secretive places to do so. It's a part of queer life that is still very much with us.'[181]

GMFA - the gay men's health project, posed the question: 'Who still has sex in public toilets?' and the answer given was 'quite a lot of people!'[182] The article went on to point out that under the Sexual Offences Act 2003 it is 'illegal to procure or engage in sex in a public toilet and it is against the law for both gay and straight people. You can risk being arrested for cottaging regardless of whether you are being discreet or not. For example, having sex in a cubicle behind closed doors is still illegal!'[183]

What is interesting about the last paragraph is that it mentions that straight people having sex in public toilets is also illegal. George Michael, after his infamous arrest, remembered something else about the policing of toilets. 'In Liverpool Street I used to see endless girls pissed out of their brains and disappearing into cubicles with men. In the gents. And nothing was done about them. They don't get prosecuted.'[184]

In an article in the *Metro* entitled 'Straight Men Share Why They Love Having Sex In Public Toilets!' published on Tuesday 10 April 2018, straight men share their accounts of having sex with women in public conveniences. The article presents the activity in a fairly positive light. At the end of the article there is some advice for any reader contemplating taking part in the activity. 'If you are in a long-term relationship, anything you can do to spice things up is going to have some benefit. In this case, you could talk about it first or else it may seem out of character. If you are both in agreement, the excitement of doing something a bit naughty could work wonders.' Lastly, and perhaps most importantly, Preece adds: 'Whatever you do, just remember to wash your hands afterwards!' There is no mention in the article that the activity is against the law and that you could get a criminal record if prosecuted. Instead it is presented as a saucy way to spice up a couple's sex life![185]

Before homosexuality was partially decriminalised in the UK, this was one of the only ways that members of the community could meet other people of the same sexual orientation and even today remains one way for gay men to meet other gay men, especially in rural communities without dedicated gay bars and clubs.

On the Isle of Wight, as I write this, there are still no dedicated gay pubs or clubs, just one that describes itself as 'gay friendly'. With the gradual acceptance of homosexual lifestyles and culture into mainstream society and the advancement of dating sites and apps, the need for gay people to seek out furtive sexual encounters has impacted on the amount of cottaging and cruising that takes place nowadays.

There is also the view that straight society has about cottaging. For example, in an article in *GQ Magazine*, Justin Myers contemplates the way gay sex in general and activities like cottaging are presented in the media: 'If you were to believe the papers, you'd think gay sex was seedy, thrilling, and dirty!' He continues 'it seems off that the tabloids can plaster the wobbly bits of female celebrities and pruriently broadcast their personal lives and nobody bats an eyelid, but when there's a whiff of same-sex action, all of a sudden everyone is thirteen again and either pulling up their chair to hear more, or choking in disgust!'

So cottaging and cruising could possibly be seen as the last taboo in the eyes of the mainstream straight society.

---

[180]Simon Button, 'Why Do so Many Gay Men Still Go Cruising and Cottaging?', *Attitude*, October 5, 2018, https://www.attitude.co.uk/article/why-do-so-many-gay-men-still-go-cruising-and-cottaging/15681/.

[181]Ibid.

[182]Gareth Johnson, 'A Modern Guy's Guide to Cruising', *GMFA Gay Men's Health Project*, accessed July 2, 2019 https://www.gmfa.org.uk/fs148-a-modern-guys-guide-to-cruising

[183]Justin Myers/ The Guyliner, 'You've Probably Had Chemsex and You Didn't Even Know It', *British GQ*, accessed July 2, 2019. https://www.gq-magazine.co.uk/article/chemsex-cruising-bareback

[184]Patrick Strudwick, 'This Is Why Men Meet For Sex In Public Toilets', *BuzzFeed*, accessed August 12, 2017, https://www.buzzfeed.com/patrickstrudwick/men-are-still-meeting-for-sex-in-public-toilets-and-the.

[185]Samantha Rea, 'Straight Men Share Why They Love Having Sex in Public Loos', *Metro*, accessed December 12, 2019), https://metro.co.uk/2018/04/10/straight-men-share-love-sex-public-toilets-7454131/.

EXTRACTS FROM ORAL HISTORIES

Karl L

It was very difficult then because, particularly for a lot of… it's a generational thing as well. I was on the Island when there were lots of arrests at Coppins Bridge at that time and this was about 1993, maybe 1994.

The arrests were for cottaging; public sex offences. It was quite a significant number and talking to people afterwards, you know, the police officers, it was clearly a challenge as to how many they could arrest; the bigger the number, the better and it was a game.

At that time, the vice squad would come over from Southampton, and a lot of people were arrested. That caused great upset and distress on the Island to a lot of people which effectively pushed people back into the closet. People were of the opinion, the population of the Island, "it was a disgusting and lewd public act", but then you have to look at the history and say to yourself, "well if there was no other way that people could meet, there was no communication systems, people were frightened of being identified", and cottaging carried on[on] the Island in a more prolonged way than it did on the mainland because it still happens today, but to a lesser degree.

It was more important for Island people because one, it could allow bisexual men to meet, two, it could allow some of those closeted Isle of Wight gay men to meet. But then they had to risk imprisonment and so on. It has been going on for hundreds of years on the Island, it is no different here than it was anywhere else, it is just that an Island culture hung on and on and on because we didn't have… because of the fear of being identified. People would have lost their jobs here.

You've got to remember that it was also isolated in a large car park out on its own so there was a certain amount of activity that went on around there after dark and so on. It doesn't happen now like it used to do because people have got social media and other things, but generational-wide.

So there were things that were happening here that always brought negativity to the community and there was very, very little in the press. We weren't getting any press support whatsoever in those early days apart from negative images. So my job as a professional was to try to address that.

Jude

We used to have a newsletter and somewhere, I had it in my hand a few months back, I've got an early Island Lesbian and Gay Social Group newsletter which interestingly enough has an article from Karl Love who had come back to the Island and was doing the loo watch thing, handing out condoms to blokes going into particular loos. Well, he… I can't remember how it was decided, but at one point I was going to go as well but then they decided that that might freak out blokes so it was always two blokes went to certain loos that were known as cottages. They would approach; they could tell the guys who were just caught short and wanted a wee and the others. I believe they used to hand out free condoms, they used to just chat to the guys first. I don't know what they did but it was really to keep these guys as safe as possible. I know at one point… the building was single storey with an apex roof and apparently two coppers, two male coppers, were laid as far as I know, this is what it was… were laid in there. I think there were probably holes in the roof so they could see down, see where people were, two of them going into a cubicle.

Robert

When I moved out, I moved into Ryde which is a town in which there is a lively community of all sorts of… yes, one could say perverts if one wanted to! I took full advantage of that, I rather plunged in. At the same time I still had to be careful to whom I revealed anything. There were places in Ryde you could go and I went there. Well, there were the Lind Street lavatories which were notorious.

It was bloody difficult [meeting other gay men]! You just had to rely on your own inbuilt radar, which fortunately never let me down, to the point at which I got my nose broken, but did occasionally. I'm not the kind of person to put my hand on someone's knee, you know, they would just say, "no, not me, no, sorry". On the other hand there was one that said, "no, not me, hang on, though, how much?" That worked as well. So I have entertained myself, as it were.

The police were always quite active around the public lavatories as well and were not averse to hiding in the roof space to spy on people. I thought that pretty contemptible but I suppose it put their arrest rate up. I can't remember them specifically now but I do remember them. The magistrates courts records, if they exist, will certainly show you a few cases where gross indecency was the usual charge or exposure in a public place or soliciting for sex. They never caught me because I was probably too careful but they caught friends of mine.

You would have police officers, quite deliberately trying to look as seductive as possible until the moment they arrested someone, that was the trouble.

I suppose if they got caught it was people like Gielgud who got caught in London, cottaging in London. He was terrified at the time of being booed on stage, but he was dragged on stage and applauded. Well, people were more understanding of individuals who got caught in the sense that they would say, "well, he was lonely wasn't he?" Lonely, that's what it is, not gay, not homosexual, no, no, no, just lonely, he was looking for company. All sorts of excuses were made for people which, of course, to which they concurred because they wouldn't want to admit it, they wouldn't want to admit that they, really, were homosexual. They'd just been unlucky.

David

When I was a young man working in London… I arrived on my first day I was moving in, because I had the basement flat because it was a four-storey town house in Hampstead. They said, "right, okay, now you're here we are going away for two weeks to do this job" (they were interior designers). "There's a new kitchen being fitted in here, everything is in the dining room and I shall ring you every day to see how they are getting on. I want to know if they arrive on time. Oh, and we've got a dog, a puppy, which will need walking every day". I said, "that's fine", beautiful Boxer, he was absolutely fabulous… anyway… I used to take it for a walk. Now, I'd never heard of places like Hampstead Heath and whatever and they were a stone's throw. So I thought, "oh, it's a park, I could take you walkies there", and there's all these men walking about with dogs! All looking each other up and down and I thought, "oh", and then one came over to talk to me and he was talking about the dog and whatever and before I knew it I was inviting him back for tea! [Laughs].

And so it went from there, I found out I was gay and it was almost like I had gone on a rampage, I had been denied it for 27 years. But it was against the law still so you were still sort of walking on eggshells when you went out at night, you had to be very careful because the police would send in and around Hyde Park, there were police officers walking and they were holding their helmets behind their back. So it was an entrapment thing which, I mean, you wouldn't get away with now.

Working on the Island Health Project… I was very proud that I had a letter from a Chief Constable which said that I was out working for the Health Authority, and he was aware of the work that I was doing, and if any officer

David

stopped me they had to have good reason for it and let me carry on with whatever I was doing. You see, in those days there was a lot of homophobia in the police force … But the Hampshire Constabulary in those days from the Chief Constable back then, I can't think who he was now, we had so much support from them that they were voted by Stonewall the best police authority in the country because of the level of support. But we still had one or two police officers who… and I had one in Newport stopped me and he really became nasty until I produced this letter and then it was, he messed his pants and he went. I said, "no, but you have to read your notice boards to see what's going on". John, who was our support officer in those days, he was so nice and it was quite funny because his wife was a sergeant in the same force.

We had our good times and there was times when you thought you were making an effort even though in the end there probably wouldn't impress on people to be safe. In those days when this AIDS thing started it was nasty and people were frightened to death of it. We had to tread carefully even to try to reassure them – as long as you are safe sexually and take proper care of your health you will be okay. And we were getting through to them. I thought we were getting through to a lot of… you had the diehards that wouldn't take any notice of anybody.

But as I say, in the police, we did get a lot of support from our Chief Constable, which really is very important. I had a phone call… I had a direct number to the Vice Squad in Portsmouth, this is after Karl had gone, and if they were going to raid a public loo on the Isle of Wight – if they got so many complaints about it, they would do a raid – they would ring me and give me two weeks' notice to try to clear it up and if I could clear it up in those two weeks they wouldn't come over. So I used to stake out whichever loo they had told me and when I saw what was going on I would warn people that the Vice Squad were coming. Whether they moved somewhere else or they were being more discreet or whatever, I don't know. We didn't get raided while I was doing that so I did get it through to a lot of them

SECTION 28: POLITICS, INTENT, SPIN, IMPACT AND AFTERMATH

A Very Political Act

David E. Bennett

Gay rights became a political battleground during the 1987 general election. The Conservative Party successfully leveraged rising levels of homophobia during the 1980s,[186] fuelled by the AIDS pandemic[187] and lurid claims in the right-wing tabloid press.[188]

Gay rights groups had achieved influence within a Labour Party that had recently begun to differentiate itself from the Conservatives on social as well as economic values. Some Labour councils had begun to include selected books in libraries and teachers' resource centres.[189] The Conservative Party had found two of the things they hated most combined in one target: homosexuality and the Labour Party.

The Conservative Party successfully used claims that the Labour Party was intent on introducing promotional gay literature in primary schools, calling for Conservative votes to 'keep politics out of the classroom', implying that an exclusively heteronormative curriculum is somehow politically neutral.[190] Once re-elected, the Conservatives made good on this promise with the introduction of Section 28 of the Local Government Act 1988, which ruled that local government 'shall not intentionally promote homosexuality or publish material with the intention of promoting homosexuality' or 'promote the teaching in any maintained school of the acceptability of homosexuality as a pretended family relationship'.

---

[186]Alison Park and Rebecca Rhead, 'Homosexuality', NatCen, accessed February 22, 2021, https://www.bsa.natcen.ac.uk/latest-report/british-social-attitudes-30/personal-relationships/homosexuality.aspx.

[187]M. Clark, M. Gosnell, and D. Witherspoon, 'AIDS - Special Report', *Newsweek*, August 12, 1985, 20-27.

[188]Sue Sanders and Gill Spraggs, 'Section 28 and Education', schools-out.org.uk, 1989, 11 http://www.schools-out.org.uk/wp-content/uploads/2013/11/Section-28-and-Education-Sue-Sanders-Gillian-Spragg-1989.pdf.

[189]Janine Booth, 'The Story of Section 28', *Workers' Liberty*, January 2004, https://www.workersliberty.org/node/1531.

[190]Sue Sanders and Gill Spraggs, 'Section 28 and Education' schools-out.org.uk, 1989, 4-5, 11 http://www.schools-out.org.uk/wp-content/uploads/2013/11/Section-28-and-Education-Sue-Sanders-Gillian-Spragg-1989.pdf.

The breadth of activities legally covered by the word 'promote' ensured that Section 28 became a 'wholesale prohibition, potentially affecting the whole range of activities funded by local authorities', effectively making reliable information on sexual diversity unavailable, rendering homosexuals invisible in municipal organisations, and fostering the growing atmosphere of intolerance.[191]

Intent to harm

Section 28 was anticipated by a private members' bill introduced by Earl Halsbury in 1986. Earl Halsbury made no pretence in the House of Lords about his intention to discriminate. As he told the House of Lords:

> One of the characteristics of our time is that we have for several decades past been emancipating minorities who claimed that they were disadvantaged. Are they grateful? Not a bit. We emancipated races and got inverted racism. We emancipate homosexuals and they condemn heterosexism as chauvinist sexism, male oppression and so on. They will push us off the pavement if we give them a chance.[192]

Spin

Both the Halsbury Bill, and later Section 28, were presented not as an attack on the liberties of LGB people, but to curb alleged 'abuses' in local government.[193]

Jill Knight MP, who introduced Section 28, claimed that 'little children as young as five and six' were being taught about homosexuality using books where 'brightly coloured pictures of little stick men showed all about homosexuality and how it was done', and that 'explicitly described homosexual intercourse and, indeed, glorified it, encouraging youngsters to believe that it was better than any other sexual way of life'.[194] This sounds appalling but we

[191]Sue Sanders and Gill Spraggs, 'Section 28 and Education' schools-out.org.uk, 1989, 4-5, 11 http://www.schools-out.org.uk/wp-content/uploads/2013/11/Section-28-and-Education-Sue-Sanders-Gillian-Spragg-1989.pdf.

[192]Local Government Act 1986 (Amendment) Bill. *Hansard*, 18 December 1986, 310. accessed February 22, 2021,https://api.parliament.uk/historic-hansard/lords/1986/dec/18/local-government-act-1986-amendment-bill#column_

[193]Sue Sanders and Gill Spraggs, 'Section 28 and Education'. schools-out.org.uk, 1989, 6 http://www.schools-out.org.uk/wp-content/uploads/2013/11/Section-28-and-Education-Sue-Sanders-Gillian-Spragg-1989.pdf.

[194]Local Government Bill, *Hansard*, 6 December 1999, accessed February 22, 2021, https://api.parliament.uk/historic-hansard/lords/1999/dec/06/local-government-bill-hl-1#column_1102.

Councillors 'bigots' over Section 28

should not accept this frenzied interpretation at face value. If the above description was accurate, how did such a children's book ever escape censorship?

We should also use the reaction of other Conservative MPs at this time as a benchmark. Elaine Kellett-Bowman MP went on record supporting the arson attack on the *Capital Gay* newspaper office in December 1987 because it was 'quite right that there should be an intolerance of evil'.[195] Harry Greenaway MP denounced Ealing Council for suggesting schools display notices about the Lesbian and Gay Switchboard, proclaiming them to be 'an incitement to children'.[196] Presumably he feared that factual and emotional support might 'incite' LGB children to better tolerate bullying and avoid committing suicide. None of these MPs seem to have seen anything connected to homosexuality clearly or proportionately.

Justifying her position years later, Knight gave her fear of the influence of the Gay Liberation Front's radical queer rhetoric on Labour policy as further reason for introducing Section 28:

> Why did I bother to go on with it and run such a dangerous gauntlet? ... I was contacted by parents who strongly objected to their children at school being encouraged into homosexuality and being taught that a normal family with mummy and daddy was outdated. To add insult to their injury, they were infuriated that it was their money, paid over as council tax, which was being used for this. This all happened after pressure from the Gay Liberation Front. At that time I took the trouble to refer to their manifesto, which clearly stated: 'We fight for something more than reform. We must aim for the abolition of the family.' That was the motivation for what was going on, and was precisely what Section 28 stopped.[197]

---

[195]'Prohibition On Promoting Homoxexuality by Teaching of by Publishing Material', *Hansard*, 15 December 1987, accessed February 22, 2021. https://api.parliament.uk/historic-hansard/commons/1987/dec/15/prohibition-on-promoting-homosexuality#S6CV0124P0_19871215_HOC_423.

[196]Janine Booth, 'The Story of Section 28', *Workers' Liberty*, January 2004, https://www.workersliberty.org/node/1531.

[197]Local Government Bill, *Hansard*, 6 December 1999, accessed February 22, 2021, https://api.parliament.uk/historic-hansard/lords/1999/dec/06/local-government-bill-hl-1#column_1102.

Opposition from the Church of England

Despite 'frequent lip-service given by the Bill's supporters to "Christian" moral values',[198] the Church of England opposed Section 28. The Bishop of Manchester warned of 'the terrible dangers of encouraging prejudice'[199] and the Archbishop of York attacked Section 28 as 'dangerous and unnecessary', adding that: 'If a small group of local authorities sometimes goes over the top in pressing the claims of minorities, it is ... a far lesser evil than to introduce the principle of government interference.'[200]

Repeal

Section 28 lasted for twelve years in Scotland, until it was repealed by the newly formed Scottish Parliament on 21 June 2000. Three years and several attempts later, it was finally repealed in the rest of the UK by the Local Government Act 2003.

Impact: growing up gay under Section 28

Section 28 deliberately isolated and denied freedom of expression to young lesbian, gay and bi people and denied the fundamental truth that homosexuals are normal people, many of whom form families and live productive lives for decades to come.

Growing up under the shadow of the Act from age seven to twenty-two, I still resent its impact on my generation. As a librarian, I condemn the collaborators dressed as librarians from my youth. Librarians have a creed: 'no religion, no politics, no morals'. Libraries are supposedly committed to preserve information and make it, however controversial, available to anyone who wants it without fear nor favour. They instead chose to collaborate with a homophobic government, cowed by the threat of funding cuts.

Despite legal reassurances that providing information, such as the addresses of local LGBTQI organisations was not prohibited under Section 28, many local authorities still chose to stop their services for LGBTQI people, withdrawing works on sexual diversity and growing up gay and ceasing to stock LGBTQI newspapers and magazines.[201] In some cases LGBTQ+ materials were reclassified under 'mental illness' and removed to the adult collection where they could not be borrowed by anyone under eighteen, only read without privacy in the library. I remember my mother trying to find reliable information on homosexuality when I was a child, a decade before the internet, and finding only books that told her I was mentally ill and at risk from sexual predators.

LGBT support groups were reduced to lacklustre affairs maintained under the auspices of sexual health promotion, Section 28 having long since done away with lesbian, gay and bisexual student support groups in schools and colleges.[202]

The only fond memory I have of growing up gay is of a school teacher and ordained minister who continued to teach about homosexuality and sexual diversity in clear breach of the legislation.[203] I am still awed at his courage, generosity, thoughtfulness and integrity.

[198]Sue Sanders and Gill Spraggs, 'Section 28 and Education', schools-out.org.uk, 1989, 19 http://www.schools-out.org.uk/wp-content/uploads/2013/11/Section-28-and-Education-Sue-Sanders-Gillian-Spragg-1989.pdf.

[199]Local Government Bill, *Hansard*, 11 January 1988, accessed February 22, 2021, https://api.parliament.uk/historic-hansard/lords/1988/jan/11/local-government-bill#column_965.

[200]Local Government Bill, *Hansard*, 2 February 1988, accessed February 22, 2021, https://api.parliament.uk/historic-hansard/lords/1988/feb/02/local-government-bill#column_999.

[201]John Vincent, 'Why Do We Need to Bother?: Public Library Services for LGBTQI People'. *Library Trends* 64, no. 2 (2015): 288, https://doi.org/10.1353/lib.2015.0050.

[202]Knitting Circle. *Knitting Circle: Law, 1989 Section 28 Gleanings*, accessed February 22, 2021, https://web.archive.org/web/20070818063344/http://www.knittingcircle.org.uk/gleanings2889.html.

[203]Sue Sanders and Gill Spraggs, 'Section 28 and Education', schools-out.org.uk, 1989, 25 http://www.schools-out.org.uk/wp-content/uploads/2013/11/Section-28-and-Education-Sue-Sanders-Gillian-Spragg-1989.pdf.

Andrew Turner steps down as Isle of Wight MP after outcry over alleged homosexuality comments

Aftermath

Section 28 continues to throw a long and enduring shadow.

Visible support for LGBT people in schools has never recovered, school LGBT societies have not reopened, school and public library LGBT collections remain vanishingly small and poorly signposted, and schools in general remain silent on LGBT rights and issues, ignoring the institutionalised oppression of minorities.[204]

Public library LGBT collections remain extremely limited, most libraries making only minimal efforts to acquire the most mainstream LGBT authors.[205] A survey found librarianship graduates insisted a 'one size fits all approach' designed to serve a heterosexual, white majority to be 'liberal and fair', expecting anyone seeking LGBTQ+ literature to submit, and pay for, interlibrary loan requests.[206]

Lessons learned by the gay rights movement

The gay rights movement has evolved from attacking its opponents to fostering empathy and mutual understanding, and demonstrating how supporting the rights of different social groups protects all groups. The overt support from Stonewall for civil partnerships between opposite-sex couples in particular demonstrated how the campaign for sexual and gender equality seeks to empower and protect everyone, and not simply to advance the agenda of minority groups.

---

[204] Janine Walker and Jo Bates, 'Developments in LGBTQ Provision in Secondary School Library Services since the Abolition of Section 28', *Journal of Librarianship and Information Science* 48, no. 3 (October 2016): pp. 269-283, https://doi.org/10.1177/0961000614566340.

[205] Elizabeth L. Chapman, 'No More Controversial than a Gardening Display?: Provision of LGBT-Related Fiction to Children and Young People in U.K. Public Libraries', *Library Trends* 61, no. 3 (2013): 549, 553, https://doi.org/10.1353/lib.2013.0010.

[206] Jacqueline D. Goldthorp, 'Can Scottish Public Library Services Claim They Are Socially Inclusive of All Minority Groups When Lesbian Fiction Is Still so Inaccessible?', *Journal of Librarianship and Information Science* 39, no. 4 (2007): 240, https://doi.org/10.1177/0961000607083215.

EXTRACTS FROM ORAL HISTORIES

Robin

I can remember, once at school there was a very big thing actually. Section 28 was brought in in all schools, certainly all secondary schools were required to formulate a policy. So we had this awful film, instructional film, and I was put on this group anyway to discuss things and how we would implement this bloody Act and it talked about one in ten and all the rest of it. I said, I can remember, I can feel it now, my breath, and I said, "well, as one of the one in ten…", and I don't know if they were shocked, I don't know, what I do know is that dear Ann Witcherly drove me home especially and I had a pounding headache and it was so nerve-wracking as you can imagine because you could literally – I don't know if you know this – you literally could have been sacked for being gay as a teacher and people were and some things went to appeal. Now I don't know when that was repealed, it was in the Blair government, they repealed it but I know of one or two cases, not personally, but they were in the papers, the very fact that somebody was queer was considered sufficient grounds for dismissal for a teacher. I have to say my colleagues were wonderfully nice about it, you know, I encountered no prejudice at all, they were intelligent people after all.

Julian

I think that the Isle of Wight is a very conservative area, I mean conservative socially and politically as well, because remember the things Andrew Turner said a few years ago. But in the last couple of years I think Pride has been massive on the Island and really well appreciated and very well supported. So I think that the Isle of Wight – most people think that the Isle of Wight is twenty years behind the rest of the country, but people here are just starting to talk and starting to be a bit more open about things. I think it's the new Archdeacon, Arch-canon of the Church of England is a married gay man now on the Island, so things here are changing.

When I lived in Bognor I used to go to Brighton a lot and I think Brighton was a lot more open – that's ten years ago – but I think the Isle of Wight is starting to catch up now, keeping an open dialogue and not judging people and allowing people to dress and express themselves in the manner that they need to.

Before there would be people like that doctor who was very, very judgemental and mocking and, as I said, my school counsellor and things at school were… I think I said this before about Section 28, but that was a generational thing, that was for the whole country.

Do you know what? I'd say people are not a lot more informed and educated because I think most of the teachers who are teaching now were educated under Section 28. I think that they've still got Section 28 influence even now because they would have been at school and they would have probably entered training during the time that Section 28 was in action.

I think that there's still a legacy of it. Nobody was taught anything about relationships or respect and most of the sex education came from… it was part of your biology or science course work and I left school believing a lot of things about human biology and human sexuality when really it was about animals. There was always the thing about the chicken and the egg and things like flowers being pollinated and the stuff that was actually about human sex ed was always about the horrors of pregnancy. I think at that time they were just trying to use this stuff to frighten. I think that they had a belief that there was a lot of what they used to call, 'gymslip mothers', and teenage pregnancies and they used a lot of sex education to frighten kids out of having sex rather than teaching respect and consent. They just tried to use the fear factor.

A lot of this stuff about campus rape culture and that comes from the problem that they've never really taught respect and they've never really taught consent. If you just sort of treat things as being animalistic and biological, there is not any respect or consent in it because people aren't taught about relationships, they are just taught about sex and what bit goes into what bit and how you make babies.

Anonymous

You know, they used to call me 'gay' and things like that and it's quite difficult talking about this part actually, being gay and queer and things like that. I mean I didn't have it as bad as some other kids but I think they picked up that I was going that way. I usually shrugged it off. I got bullied for a lot of other things, but you couldn't be an out gay student back then, as a kid, it was just impossible because you would be… you would just be… Also you had Section 28. Section 28 was quite difficult. Even if I'd realised I was gay I wouldn't have been able to speak to a teacher about it because the teacher would be very, "I can't help you at all here". So, it was very difficult and I was talking to a friend about this recently, about Section 28 and how there are a number of gay men, in the '80s I think it is, that have grown up during this period where they haven't been able to talk about it. There's this kind of shame that's grown up with them because they haven't been able to deal with anything. But it was a bit like that. It wasn't until I went to the Isle of Wight College, because I went to the Isle of Wight College after school, that was when I sort of really woke up and realised that I was gay.

WRITTEN HISTORIES

Robin's Story

You may not have heard of Section 28 and you are the better for it. But it is necessary LGBTQ+ people know their history because it can always gain new life – look at the abortion scandal in the USA where decades of progress are being rolled back by right-wing fundamentalists and the Republican Party. Section 28 was an open attack on the queer community by the Thatcher government and its aim was to deny knowledge of homosexuality to schoolchildren, leaving them in ignorance. It particularly affected secondary schools and it was a threat against any school and any teacher who mentioned the subject in a favourable or even neutral way, hostility was acceptable.

I was a secondary teacher at the time and remember the fact that working parties were set up in the school to discuss how the policy would be implemented. Really there was no choice – comply or else. For me it had a fortunate side – I came out to the ten members of my group and they were all kind and supportive as, I suspect, most teachers throughout the country would have been. I guess it was an open secret but in those days the fact that I was queer could have lost me my job and there were cases elsewhere which led to dismissals for being gay that were upheld in tribunals. Apparently queer teachers were threats to their students, i.e. paedophiles, and other such gross slanders. This was the time of the AIDS epidemic and if you weren't born then, think yourself lucky in this case.

As a teacher I always was on edge at this time. Apparently many of my students 'knew' it. How naïve I was to think otherwise, especially on the Island, but when scribbles on desks informed the reader that 'Mr Ford is gay' and, more alarmingly, 'Mr Ford has AIDS' I got a bit jittery. This was the sort of thing that parents might pick up and all hell would be let loose. But I must pay tribute to Cowes High students – apart from these incidents there was no trouble and indeed, when I was ill once, a whole troupe of sixth formers came round to visit me and found me with my then (and now) partner, they didn't turn a hair and nothing was ever said or attitudes altered. So what, you may say – but it was a different world then.

I am an old man now but grew up in a world utterly hostile to LGBTQ+ people. It was not until I was 24 when the law permitted any sort of queer activity. Before then you could be jailed for two years if found out, plus innumerable other social sanctions. Above all I grew up in utter ignorance of what my identity really was and even – disastrously – got married, as many gay men did at that time, in search of a 'cure'. And this was what was really evil about this application of Thatcher's Victorian values – the sponsoring of ignorance for no doubt thousands of teenage boys and girls about realising their identities and the sponsoring of ignorance, which leads to bigotry, in millions more over the years.

I'm not really in touch with schools now – I retired over twenty years ago. I only hope that young LGBTQ+ students grow up in a much more enlightened world.

Robin

HISTORICAL LGBTQ+ PEOPLE ON THE ISLE OF WIGHT

Franko Figueiredo-Stow

Set foot on the Isle of Wight and you will find yourself surrounded by castles, monuments, manor houses, royal residences, well-manicured gardens and rich landscapes. It is an island full of contrasts, with exclusive second homes only streets away from areas of social housing in Ryde, Newport and villages like St Helens and Bembridge – an island rich in heritage and teeming with stories. Everyone who has lived in or contributed to these special places has left their footprint, either in their collections, the buildings themselves or their gardens and landscapes. Some stories are more visible than others.

In the early days when I was dating my husband, we went to visit Dimbola Lodge in Freshwater. We knew that Virginia Woolf's aunt had lived there, and that Virginia was a regular visitor and had written a play entitled *Freshwater*, but little else. As we toured Dimbola Lodge, I was thrilled to learn of its strong queer connections. To tour Dimbola Lodge without acknowledging that many of the people that contributed to its history were folks like Virginia, herself bisexual or gay, would have felt frustrating to say the least. It was and it is life-affirming to be able to appreciate the true audaciousness, the artistic and political dissent of the bohemian people for which the place served as a haven, providing queer artists with the freedom to flourish as themselves. To know that our queer predecessors were here some hundred years ago really enhanced our visit.

LGBTQ+ identities have existed as long as humans have, but history books tend to either barely mention, completely ignore or deliberately erase LGBTQ+ people's existence and contributions. These days we can be a bit braver about exploring and enjoying the UK's rich LGBTQ+

heritage and I'd reason that without the awareness of LGBTQ+ heritage, our experience of certain historical places is incomplete. Indeed, to acknowledge the potential of queer stories from the past is to open a space for their recovery, and to build a fuller more fascinating picture of how our historical places have been used and shaped by their owners and occupants.

It is a challenging job, unearthing all these stories, for various reasons, for instance many queer people, or their family members, would have destroyed personal letters or diaries either because it was illegal, or shameful. However, if you dig deep, you will find that some of those stories have been preserved and important materials and artefacts have survived. Difficult as it may be, we have a crucial role in educating people, young and old, about the real history of how people lived, embracing historical figures in their entirety, including the parts of their lives which are not so clear-cut or easy to interpret from a modern standpoint.

In-depth exploration of how LGBTQ+ communities describe the meaning and significance of their shared interests, hobbies and pursuits suggests there is 'a lot to learn' with LGBTQ+ communities, and their representatives must be fully acknowledged for their contributions. In doing so, we are a step closer to erasing the shame that has been connected to queer lives.

The material we found and the stories we uncovered provide us with fair, accurate, inclusive and respectful representations of LGBTQ+ people and their contributions to our community.

In this chapter, we celebrate and appreciate some of the inspiring LGBTQ+ notable figures who were born, grew up or lived on the Isle of Wight.

OSCAR WILDE AND LORD ALFRED DOUGLAS

Dr Clifford Williams

References to the Isle of Wight pop up in the letters and journals of a number of notable people, often in connection with a holiday.

A visit to the archives of Magdalen College, Oxford principally to look at material relating to Oscar Wilde and his young friend Bosie (Lord Alfred Douglas, 1870–1945), both of whom were undergraduates at the college (at different times), revealed a letter to Bosie from a man called Ivor Goring. In the letter Ivor refers to sailing across Fishbourne Creek on the Isle of Wight, and the contents suggest Bosie and Ivor have visited places on the Island before. There is no date on the letter. Notes with the letter say it was 'from Ivor Goring, the boy who inspired the sonnet, Limpsfield 1927'.[207] I

JABEZ HUGHES & MULLINS,   REGINA HOUSE, RYDE, I.W.
PHOTOGRAPHERS THE QUEEN AND THE ROYAL FAMILY.

Oscar Wilde Λ
photographed by Jabez Hughes and Mullins Studios, Ryde, Isle of Wight, 1884. Courtesy of British Library.

couldn't find out more about the time the two may have spent on the Island. I am told Ivor Goring went to the USA and worked as an actor. Goring said of himself that he was the reincarnation of Dorian Gray.[208]

Poet and playwright Oscar Wilde (1854–1900) visited the island. A fine photograph of him taken on the Island features in Richard Ellmann's 1987 biography.[209] It is dated in the book 1885, but research by Daniel Novak suggests it was more likely taken in 1884 when Wilde was in Ryde to deliver a lecture in the Town Hall.[210] Wilde was lecturing in Ryde in October 1884 and had some photos taken by Cornelius Jabez Hughes and Gustav Mullins. Hughes died in 1884 but Mullins retained the name for commercial reasons.[211]

According to the *Isle of Wight Observer* of 11 Oct 1884, many came to see the spectacle that was Wilde and to scoff and laugh at him, but he was warmly applauded at the conclusion of his lecture on 'Dress'.

> ...many in the audience came with the intention of having a good laugh at the apostle of aestheticism. Whatever eccentricities Mr Oscar Wilde may have been guilty of in the past, his appearance did not offer much food for mirth... and the rather long hair which he still affects was rather becoming than otherwise.[212]

Wilde spoke of female and male fashions and dress. He was 'unsparing in his ridicule of the corset, tight lacing, small wrists and small feet'. At the conclusion of his talk he was 'warmly applauded'.[213] The following year Parliament passed legislation on gross indecency between males. This was before Wilde had met Bosie (Lord Alfred Douglas). They were introduced to each other in 1891. They had a rather tempestuous affair. Wilde indulged Bosie.

In 1895 Wilde became a prisoner following conviction for gross indecency. He was sentenced to two years hard labour in prison. He served most of his sentence in Reading Gaol. Upon his release from prison, in May 1897, he sailed for France, never to return to the UK again.

---

[207]Letter to Lord Alfred Douglas from Grosvenor Crescent, London SW1, no date. Magdalen College Oxford Archives Ref MC.P204/1/13c/20.

[208]Douglas Murray. *Bosie: A Biography of Lord Alfred Douglas*. New York: Hyperion, 2000, 266-269.

[209]Richard Ellmann. *Oscar Wilde*. London: Penguin, 1997, 211.

[210]Daniel Novak, 'A Wilde Ryde: Oscar Wilde in the Isle of Wight', *The Wildean*, January 12, 1998.

[211]Geoff Dibb. *Oscar Wilde a Vagabond with a Mission; the Story of Oscar Wilde's Lecture Tours of Britain and Ireland*. London: The Oscar Wilde Society, 2013, 147-148

[212]Daniel Novak, 'A Wilde Ryde: Oscar Wilde in the Isle of Wight', *The Wildean*, January 12, 1998.

[213]'The Dress of the period', *Isle of Wight Observer*, October 11, 1884. 5

ALFRED, LORD TENNYSON

Dr Clifford Williams

Tennyson lived on the Island for much of his later life. He rented Farringford House, near Freshwater in 1853 and then bought it in 1856. But he felt pestered by tourists and so moved to Sussex in 1869. However he retained the house and spent winters there right up until his death in 1892.

Tennyson was an 'Apostle' at Cambridge where he met his beloved friend Arthur Henry Hallam in 1829. Few relationships between men in the nineteenth century have been more subject to sexual speculation than that between Alfred Tennyson and his close friend Arthur Henry Hallam.[214] Hallam met and fell in love with Tennyson's eighteen-year-old sister, Emily. Hallam died suddenly in Vienna aged 22 in 1833. Grief struck, Tennyson wrote 'In Memoriam A.H.H.' as a requiem. According to Plummer, the poem provoked censure from the *Times*.[215] The poem was completed in 1849 and Tennyson named his eldest son Hallam.[216] If you are interested to learn more about their relationship I recommend *Alfred and Arthur: An Historic Friendship* by Gareth Jones.

Alfred, Lord Tennyson ∧
photographed by Margaret Cameron, 1869. Courtesy of Dimbola Lodge.

---

[214]Jack Kolb, 'Hallam, Tennyson, Homosexuality and the Critics'. The Free Library, accessed March 2, 2021, https://www.thefreelibrary.com/Hallam%2c+Tennyson%2c+homosexuality+and+the+critics.-a084841799.

[215]Douglas Plummer, Queer People ; the Truth about Homosexuals (New York: The Citadel Press, 1965), 31

[216]Jack Kolb, 'Hallam, Tennyson, Homosexuality and the Critics'. The Free Library, accessed March 2, 2021, https://www.thefreelibrary.com/Hallam%2c+Tennyson%2c+homosexuality+and+the+critics.-a084841799.

One of the most quoted lines in Tennyson's poem has a certain resonance for many LGBT people:

> I hold it true, whate'er befall;
> I feel it when I sorrow most;
> 'Tis better to have loved and lost
> Than never to have loved at all.[217]

Even if I cannot know how they themselves thought of their relationship and interactions, we are including Tennyson here because of the intimate language and behaviour he employed towards Hallam. In keeping with the aims of this project, I am embracing historical figures in their entirety, including the parts of their lives which are not so clear-cut or easy to interpret from a modern standpoint.

ROBERT NICHOLS

Franko Figueiredo-Stow

> Other loves I have, men rough, but men who stir
> More grief, more joy, than love of thee and thine[218]

The *Penguin Book of Homosexual Verse* lists Nichols' poem 'The Burial in Flanders' as 'one of the century's greatest gay poems to men who are wholly untroubled by gender'.[219]

This listing intrigued me and prompted me to research more about Nichols, and here's what I found out. Robert Malise Bowyer Nichols was born on the Island, at East Mount, Shanklin, on 6 September 1893. Brief notices of the birth of a son to Mrs Bowyer Nichols appeared in various newspapers.[220] In the early 1890s East Mount was leased by Robert's paternal grandparents from Mary Nunn Harvey of The Cliff, Shanklin.[221] Nichols was baptised at St Saviour on the Cliff, Shanklin on 25 November 1893.[222]

---

[217] Alfred Tennyson. *In Memoriam*. London: Macmillan and C0., 1904.

[218] Edward Marsh. *Georgian Poetry 1916-1917*. London: The Poetry Bookshop, 1918, 62.

[219] Stephen Coote. *The Penguin Book of Homosexual Verse*. Harmondsworth, London: Penguin Books, 1986, 46, 305.

[220] Helen Thomas, Secretary, Shanklin & District History Society [S&DHS], email message to author, August 15, 2020.

[221] 'East Mount and the Nichols' in 'The Story of The Shanklin Hotel', S&DHS Newsletter No 37, January 2019. 3

[222] Ancestry: Genealogy, Family Trees & Family History Records, accessed August 20, 2020, https://www.ancestry.co.uk/.

Nichols was the eldest son of John Bowyer Buchanan Nichols (1859–1939) of Lawford Hall, Essex, artist and author and a descendant of John Nichols, the eighteenth-century antiquary.[223]

The outbreak of the First World War cut short Nichols' university career and in October 1914 he became a second lieutenant in the Royal Field Artillery. Ill health meant that he only served in France between late June and early August 1916, after which time he was declared permanently unfit for general or home service and spent several months in hospital.

Having begun to write verse at school, Nichols became one of the soldier poets of the First World War; his 'Invocation' (1915) and 'Ardours and Endurances' (1917) were widely read and quoted, and established him as one of the most highly acclaimed younger poets of the day. He was regarded as a sort of new Rupert Brooke, and in E. B. Osborn's noted collection *The Muse in Arms* (1917), there were more poems by Nichols than any other writer. Nichols wrote graphic records of the battlefield, but his poetry was inherently more idealistic than that of his friends and fellow war poets Siegfried Sassoon and Robert Graves.

The First World War poets did not write as a collective, homogenous group though Robert Graves, Robert Nichols, Isaac Rosenberg, and Siegfried Sassoon were often seen in the same circles and their work appears as a collection in Edward Marsh's *Georgian Poetry, 1916–1917*.[224] I can imagine how the trenches, an all-male environment, could have provided, for many, their first close encounter with homosexuality. A new community where the classes cooperated closely and forged passionate alliances could easily give some officers an unexpected glimpse of love amidst the horrors of a war. For the most part, the bonds formed between officers and men, although intense, are often documented as paternalistic and platonic. However, for young homosexuals like Wilfred Owen, Robert Graves, Siegfried Sassoon and others, these relationships were tinged with the erotic.

In the diaries and correspondence Nichols, Graves and Sassoon kept, one finds the young men's admittance to a 'vague sexual element' in 'our war-harnessed relationship'.[225] They all seem to end up being torn emotionally by a succession of disappointing homosexual relationships. Sassoon, though, is the only one to write about it in his private diaries,[226] which until 2013 had been kept secret by his son.[227] We must remember that any evidence of homosexual acts on active service would result in a court-martial, and the consequences were greater if the relationship was between an officer and a private soldier. In fact, during the Great War, 22 British officers and 270 soldiers were court-martialled for homosexual acts.[228] Deep and close bonds

240

might be safest if expressed in the romantic language of the love poem. In his poem 'Casualty', Robert Nichols wishes:

> My comrade that you could rest
> Your tired body on mine, that your head might be laid
> Fallen and heavy – upon this my breast

In the *Oxford Dictionary* Graves, Nichols and Sasson are described as 'idealistic homosexuals', though they all end up in unhappy marriages. In 1922, Nichols married Norah, daughter of Frederick Anthony Denny, of Horwood House, Winslow, Buckinghamshire, and niece of the composer Roger Quilter. When he was engaged to marry her, he wrote with shocking brutality to her parents: 'I shall certainly chuck Norah if she comes between me and my work'.[229] Their relationship was fraught to say the least and ended in divorce. They had no children.

Nichols and Graves had a very close relationship; at one point when Nichols was about to have an operation for appendicitis, he asked his father, in the event of his death, to transfer part of his allowance to Graves. Their relationship also deteriorated over that time, particularly as Nichols grew incredibly condescending about Graves' work and personal relationships. Graves became quite offended by Nichols, who insisted in referring to Graves' wife as 'the lady' and the letters they exchanged on this matter have tinges of jealousy.[230]

[223]'Nichols, Robert Malise Bowyer (1893–1944), Poet and Playwright', *Oxford Dictionary of National Biography*, accessed August 13, 2020, https://www.oxforddnb.com/view/10.1093/ref:odnb/9780198614128.001.0001/odnb-9780198614128-e-35223

[224]Edward Marsh, *Georgian Poetry, 1916-1917*. London: Poetry Bookshop, 1918.

[225]*Siegfried Sassoon Letters*, 1917-30, Oxford University: Bodleian Library, Special Collection

[226]*Siegfried Sassoon Diaries* [1915–25], ed. R. Hart-Davis, 3 vols. (1983–5)

[227]Jonathan Thompson, 'New Diaries Reveal the "Dark Secrets of Siegfried Sassoon's Swooning"', *Independent*, July 18, 2013, https://www.independent.co.uk/news/uk/this-britain/new-diaries-reveal-the-dark-secrets-of-siegfried-sassoon-s-swooning-affair-321646.html.

[228]'Homosexuality and the First World War', Exploring Surrey's Past, accessed February 18, 2021, https://www.exploringsurreyspast.org.uk/themes/subjects/diversity/lgbt-history/fwwhomosexuality/.

[229]Anne Charlton and William Charlton. *Putting Poetry First: a Life of Robert Nichols, 1893-1944*. Wilby, Norwich: Russell, 2003, 256

[230]Ibid., 176

Anne Charlton, in *Putting Poetry First*, Nichols' biography, reveals a volatile, troubled soul, a personality that swung between wild, infectious enthusiasm and maddening self-pity. Sassoon writes: 'He was at his best today; and when he is at his best one forgives him everything.'[231]

Blunden and Sayoni describe Nichols as 'tall, thin, and impulsive in movement, with a face in which the wit and the poet found expression by turns. His talk was rapid and humorous, but tending towards the defence of the lofty Romantic attitude of which he saw himself as protagonist.'[232]

In 1920, Nichols stayed at Quarr Abbey on the Island. He was attracted by the community's Gregorian chant and was also collecting material for his play *Guilty Souls*.[233] Anne Charlton's biography fails to delve deeper into Nichols' personal relationships. The author explained that 'many important letters have not come down to us... Norah may have done some censoring; certainly there is a notable absence of correspondence...'[234] I cannot help but feel even more curious to know what the content of these letters was, and why Norah chose to keep them from the public. Nichols had a number of affairs, notably with Vivienne Wilkinson, to whom he would leave the income of his estate.[235]

In 1924, Nichols went to Hollywood, where he acted as adviser to Douglas Fairbanks senior in his film-making. The more we read, the more we understand that Nichols' life had been a turbulent one with alternating moods of infectious elation and deep unhappiness and indecision. Further research produced some contradictory historical accounts of Nichols', some suggesting that 'Nichols regarded himself as a writer of plays' and others 'He believed he was born to write poetry and for him that always came first'. Similarly, we found accounts of a very successful career in Hollywood, and others describing it a flop.[236]

---

[231] *Siegfried Sassoon Diaries* [1915–25], ed. R. Hart-Davis, 3 vols. (1983–5), 114

[232] Blunden, Edmund, and Sayoni Basu. 'Nichols, Robert Malise Bowyer (1893–1944), poet and playwright', *Oxford Dictionary of National Biography*. Oxford University Press. accessed August 13, 2020, <https://www.oxforddnb.com/view/10.1093/ref:odnb/9780198614128.001.0001/odnb-9780198614128-e-35223/version/1>

[233] Anne Charlton and William Charlton. *Putting Poetry First: a Life of Robert Nichols, 1893-1944*. Wilby, Norwich: Russell, 2003, 108

[234] Ibid., vii

[235] Ibid., 254

[236] Ibid., 255

Anne Charlton paints him as an irrational, unreasonable man, who was at his best with his literary friends: 'Living in lodgings, separated from his possession, without a wife or child and forgotten, as he felt, by the public, he accumulated great reservoirs of self-pity'.[237]

Robert died on 17 December 1944 of acute heart failure resulting from coronary disease. His name is now at Poets' Corner, Westminster Abbey.

ALGERNON CHARLES SWINBURNE

Melissa Gilmore

Algernon Charles Swinburne was an English poet, playwright and novelist. He was born in London on 5 April 1837 to Admiral Charles Henry Swinburne and Lady Jane Henrietta. Swinburne spent his childhood largely at East Dene in Bonchurch on the Island. In 1848, Swinburne went to live with Reverend Foster Fenwick at Brooke Rectory in West Wight, where he was to be prepared for Eton.

Swinburne attended Eton from 1849 to 1853 where he won prizes in French and Italian. It was during his time at Eton that he first began to write poetry. It has been posited by biographers that it was Eton's tradition of corporal punishment that gave Swinburne a taste for sexual masochism later in life.[238] He went on to attend Oxford University at Balliol College, from 1856 to 1860, though he never received a degree.

Swinburne cultivated a collection of literary friends and acquaintances, including Dante Gabriel Rossetti and William Bell Scott. His own literary contributions leaned towards the controversial, with topics including lesbianism and sado-masochism alongside themes of the ocean, death and

[237]Ibid., 256

[238]T. V. Moore. 'A Study In Sadism: The Life Of Algernon Charles Swinburne', *Journal of Personality* 6, no. 1 (1937), 5. https://doi.org/10.1111/j.1467-6494.1937.tb02235.x

time. Critic Robert Buchanan referred to both Swinburne and Rossetti's poetry as 'the Fleshly School of Poetry', due to their sexually explicit content. Swinburne enjoyed his rather debauched reputation, going so far as to spread the rumour that he had had sexual relations with a chimpanzee which he then ate.[239] Oscar Wilde said of Swinburne: 'a braggart in matters of vice, who had done everything he could to convince his fellow citizens of his homosexuality and bestiality without being in the slightest degree a homosexual or a bestialiser'.[240]

Swinburne lived for a period with Rossetti after the death of Rossetti's wife, Elizabeth Siddal, a good friend of Swinburne's. A commonly told tale from this time is that: 'Dante once had to leave the studio where he was working in order to ask Swinburne to keep the noise down, and found him and a boyfriend sliding naked down the bannister.'[241]

Another story goes that Rossetti attempted to give Swinburne his first experience with a woman by persuading a friend of his sister's, Adah Menken, to seduce him. Menken reportedly had to abandon the attempt, telling Rossetti, 'I can't make him understand that biting's no good!'[242]

In his later years, Swinburne's social activities began to catch up with him. In 1879, his poor health and alcoholism led to his friend Theodore Watts-Dunton taking Swinburne into his care at The Pines in Putney, where he died in 1909. He is buried in Bonchurch on the Isle of Wight.

---

[239]Robert Williams Buchanan and Thomas Bird Mosher. *The Fleshly School of Poetry, and Other Phenomena of the Day.* London: Strahan, 1872, 334.

[240]Glenn Everett, 'A. C. Swinburne: Biography', Victorianweb.org, accessed October 20, 2020, http://www.victorianweb.org/authors/swinburne/acsbio1.html.

[241]Ciaran Conliffe, 'Algernon Swinburne, Dissolute Poet', Headstuff.org, December 19, 2016, https://www.headstuff.org/culture/history/terrible-people-from-history/algernon-swinburne-dissolute-poet/.

[242]Ibid.

VIRGINIA WOOLF

Franko Figueiredo-Stow

In 1923, Virginia Woolf wrote her only play, *Freshwater*, a comedy in three acts, about her great aunt, the pioneering photographer Julia Margaret Cameron (1815–79). The play is set amidst the Victorian bohemia of Dimbola Lodge, in the small West Wight town of Freshwater, where Virginia Woolf's parents first met.

Julia Cameron first visited the Isle of Wight as a guest of Tennyson before buying two adjacent cottages, later linking them with a gothic tower to create Dimbola Lodge. She was one of many Victorian A-listers who chose to make the Island their home, or enjoyed visits with creative company and inspiration whilst taking in the sea air, including Lewis Carroll, Charles Dickens and Virginia Woolf. Dimbola Lodge became something of a creative hub.

The plot of *Freshwater* revolves around the attempts by the young actress Ellen Terry to escape from her marriage; the play is a satire on Victorian conventions, which Woolf and the Bloomsbury group had fought to escape.[243]

Woolf often struggled with and criticised the conventional expectations of young women.

> Society in those days was a perfectly competent, perfectly complacent, ruthless machine. A girl had no chance against its fangs. No other desires – say to paint, or to write – could be taken seriously.[245]

She delivered lectures on the need for both a literal and figurative space for women writers within a literary tradition dominated by men, later published as *A Room of One's Own*.

Woolf had researched the life of her great-aunt, publishing her findings in an essay, and in an introduction to her 1926 edition of Cameron's photographs.

---

[243]Masami Usui. 2007. 'Julia Margaret Cameron as a Feminist Precursor of Virginia Woolf'. Doshisha.repo.nii.ac.jp. info:doi/10.14988/pa.2017.0000011068

[244]Virginia Woolf. *The Complete Works*. Musaicum Press, 2017.

[245]Virginia Woolf. *A Room of One's Own*. Orlando: Harcourt, 1991.

She had begun work on the play based on an episode in Cameron's life in 1923, but abandoned it. Instead, encouraged by Vita Sackville-West, Woolf concentrated on working on her novels *To The Lighthouse* and *Orlando*.

In 1928, Woolf finished *Orlando*, an imagined biography, which she dedicated to Sackville-West. Orlando is a queer hero whose life spans three centuries and who changes gender halfway through their journey, experiencing the world both as a male and a female. It was published in October, shortly after Sackville-West and Woolf spent time travelling together in France that September. Theirs was a very public affair. Nigel Nicolson, Sackville-West's son, wrote:

> The effect of Vita on Virginia is all contained in *Orlando*, the longest and most charming love letter in literature, in which she explores Vita, weaves her in and out of the centuries, tosses her from one sex to the other, plays with her, dresses her in furs, lace and emeralds, teases her, flirts with her, drops a veil of mist around her.[246]

Woolf directed a production of *Freshwater*, which was performed in 1935 at her sister Vanessa's studio in Fitzroy Street in London. The cast were mainly members of the Bloomsbury Group.

Under the play's comedic elements, there is an exploration of both generational change and artistic freedom. Both Cameron and Woolf fought against the class and gender dynamics of Victorianism and the play shows links to *Mrs Dalloway*, *To The Lighthouse* and the feminist lectures she would later deliver at Cambridge.

Today Dimbola Lodge runs as a museum showcasing Cameron's life and work, with a gallery which hosts visiting exhibitions and a tearoom; it also pays homage to the 1970 Isle of Wight Festival with a life-size statue of Jimi Hendrix in the gardens.

---

[246]Harry Blamires. *A Guide to Twentieth Century Literature in English*. London: Methuen, 1983.

FERGUSON'S GANG

Charlotte Reynolds

Passionate about the historic and natural environment, a group of young women formed Ferguson's Gang in 1927. Inspired by the book *England and the Octopus,* by Clough Williams-Ellis, they wanted to help protect rural England from rapidly spreading urbanisation. They made many generous donations to the National Trust, and supported the growth of the organisation in their pursuit of conservation. This included saving Newtown Old Town Hall on the Isle of Wight.

The Gang adopted pseudonyms, remaining anonymous during their lifetimes. The six core members were known as Bill Stickers, Sister Agatha, Red Biddy/White Biddy, The Lord Beershop of the Gladstone Islands and Mercator's Projection, Kate O'Brien the Nark and Shot Biddy. They enjoyed dressing up, and adopting disguises, including masks. The Gang's leader, Bill Stickers, was the only one who formally revealed herself, as Peggy Pollard (née Gladstone), in a letter sent on her instruction to *The Times*, after her death in 1996, aged 92. It is only recently that the identities of the others have been revealed. Their stories were researched and compiled by Polly Bagnall and Sally Beck, in the book *Ferguson's Gang*, published in 2015.

Having taught herself Sanskrit at the age of sixteen, Peggy won a scholarship to the University of Cambridge in1921, aged seventeen, becoming the first female student to gain a Double First in Oriental Languages there. She completed further research at university in London, writing a book for which she was later awarded a PhD (but not until 1952, as women weren't allowed to be awarded full degrees or PhDs at the time she undertook them). They were impressive achievements, particularly for a woman in the 1920s, when few had the opportunity to undertake academic studies or enter professional careers.

Peggy caused quite a stir during her time at Cambridge, being known for wearing masculine outfits and having bobbed hair. It was fashionable to blur gender boundaries at the time, with some women wearing trousers when skirts were the norm. One night, she was stopped by university staff for not wearing the proper academic dress required by men, only to have a friend point out that Peggy was a woman and so subject to a different dress code, much to their embarrassment. She had a number of flirtations and two 'very brief affairs'[247] with women – Sally Keigwin, 'a fat girl with a blonde bob and a South African background, reading History in which she got a Double First; and Polly Falcon, a tall slender beauty with red hair'.[248] An art fraud scheme including 'mildly pornographic sketches'[249] got her involved with a group of lesbians, amongst them 'three rich, notable lesbians, Sheila Stoney-Archer, Prascovia Shoubersky and the Countess Vanuuci-Pompei, who reputedly kept a bottle of Vermouth hidden under her bed'.[250]

She took part in a masque produced by the openly gay Dennis Arundell,[251] and kept company with a number of other gay men. Her masculine appearance attracted the attention of Arthur Elton, which amused Peggy to begin with. She accepted an unexpected proposal from Elton, on the grounds that he seemed a good prospect of whom her family would approve, before Frank Pollard, a friend with whom she had edited the student magazine, also proposed. Eventually the novelty wore off with Elton, with his expectations for her to be more masculine, whilst he would have preferred a more feminine role in the relationship. After many years as a bachelor he did eventually marry a woman some twenty years later. It was Pollard that Peggy became engaged to after leaving Cambridge in 1924. He had said he liked her for being 'so unlike a woman'.[252] Despite Peggy's flirtations with women, and having an independent spirit, there was still an expectation that women of her class should marry, and they wed in 1928, although his lack of status didn't meet her family's expectations for her. Much to Peggy's disappointment, the marriage was not consummated. He seemed to have little interest in sex despite Peggy discovering no evidence of him being gay, nor having a mistress, and they lived as companions.

Whilst living in Cornwall Peggy had a passionate affair with a woman named Pauline Tweedy, in which Peggy finally felt she was treated like a woman. She later also had her first sexual experience with a man, a Russian guitarist, whilst Pollard was away on an adventure on his yacht, but it didn't go well and wasn't repeated. She returned to her affair with Pauline, but Pauline's fiancé Jimmy wanted an end to it and put down an ultimatum. This was devastating to Peggy, who had finally found physical as well as emotional fulfillment in their relationship. Things continued for a while longer, but eventually Jimmy won, although his marriage to Pauline did not last.

Aged 70, Peggy unintentionally broke a world record when she embroidered 1330 feet (405.38 meters) of cloth with scenes from the Narnia story – typical of Gang members' undaunted approach to projects. All the members had a great sense of fun, and were quite unconventional for their time. Some others were also lesbian or bisexual. They loved fine food, having Fortnum & Mason deliver hampers for meetings and excursions. They were open to subscribing members, to help their funds and causes, with a diverse mix of people involved.

The Gang secured the future for places such as Shalford Mill in Surrey, where a room was used for Gang meetings, as well as Newtown Old Town Hall on the Isle of Wight. They also funded the purchase of stretches of the coastline of Cornwall, Priory Cottages at Steventon in Oxfordshire, and supported appeals for money to purchase land in Derbyshire, the Lake District, Devon and Wiltshire for the National Trust. Whilst the Gang did not initially set out to seek press attention, they attracted a lot of publicity through their unusual acts of donation. They found they could use this to their advantage to further their causes. On one headline-grabbing occasion they triggered a bomb scare, when dressed in capes and masks they deposited a metal pineapple at a National Trust AGM, which in fact enclosed one hundred pounds.

Anne Gladstone, the mother of Bill Stickers/Peggy Pollard, moved to the Isle of Wight in 1922, following the death of her husband, John Gladstone (nephew of the former Prime Minister). She lived at The Briary in Freshwater, which had been the home built in 1873 for the artist G.F. Watts, at the suggestion of poet Alfred, Lord Tennyson, and was where the Watts and Prinseps (the photographer, Julia Margaret Cameron's family) had stayed. Cameron's great-niece was Virginia Woolf, part of the Bloomsbury Group of writers and artists, many of whom had liberal views towards sex, with various complex relationships amongst the group.

In February 1927, one of Anne's close neighbours, the second Lord Tennyson, presented 155 acres of land, now known as Tennyson Down, to the National Trust in memory of his father. Seeing at close hand how the countryside could be protected by the Trust may have provided some

---

[247] Polly Bagnall and Sally Beck. *Ferguson's Gang*. London: National Trust, 2015, 19.

[248] Ibid., 18.

[249] Ibid., 19.

[250] Ibid., 18.

[251] Dennis Arundell was an actor and opera scholar. Dennis was openly gay and his boyfriend was Cecil Beaton, later celebrated photographer and designer

[252] Polly Bagnall and Sally Beck. *Ferguson's Gang*. London: National Trust, 2015, 21.

inspiration to Anne and Peggy for their future contributions. It was during a stay at The Briary that Peggy/Bill first became aware of Newtown, after her mother had asked at a dinner party, 'When is someone going to save the Old Town Hall at Newtown?'[253] The next day she cycled the eight miles to Newtown to inspect it.

Newtown had been a significant port in medieval times, with an official building on the site of the Town Hall since around the thirteenth century. In 1699, the Town Hall had been substantially rebuilt, with further eighteenth century alterations. After steady decline in the area, by the 1930s the building was in a very poor condition in what was now a very small village. It had previously been known as a rotten borough[254] for many years.

Ferguson's Gang, ∧ *1935. Courtesy of Polly Bagnall and National Trust.*

The dilapidated hall had captured Peggy's imagination, and at a meeting in March 1933, it was suggested as the Gang's second building project, after Shalford Mill. It was purchased from Sir John Simeon for £5, and the neighbouring field for £100, but would take over £1,000 to repair the hall, a considerable cost at the time. The Gang visited on 17 March 1934 to inspect works, with a typically lavish picnic and eccentric rituals to bless the place.

The gang concluded the Town Hall should have a use following its repair. They agreed with the National Trust that the Youth Hostel Association (YHA) would make use of it, provided the Gang may still occasionally visit,

[253]Polly Bagnall and Sally Beck. *Ferguson's Gang*. London: National Trust, 2015, 87.

[254]Rotten borough is a borough that is able to elect an MP despite having very few voters, the choice of MP typically being in the hands of one person or family.

[255]Polly Bagnall and Sally Beck. *Ferguson's Gang*. London: National Trust, 2015, 93

without becoming members themselves.

In December 1934, a payment for the Hall was delivered to the National Trust, along with a 'bottle of poison' – sloe gin.[255] The Town Hall was used as a Youth Hostel between 1935 and 1939, until the outbreak of war. George Macauly Trevelyan was a member of the Gang, known as Poolcat, and had been responsible for establishing the YHA in Great Britain in 1931. Newtown was therefore a fairly early Youth Hostel, and shows the Gang's fondness for supporting and promoting organisations which helped people to enjoy and preserve the countryside. In the Old Town Hall women slept upstairs, with the Council Chamber used as a common room, and the men slept downstairs, where remnants of the old kitchen and washrooms still survive.

Without the young women of the Ferguson's Gang, it is unlikely that Newtown Old Town Hall would still be standing today. Beyond the saving of this building, significant in the Island's history, they also made important contributions to the growth of the National Trust, and other organisations, helping people to experience, enjoy and conserve the historic and natural environment of the UK.

It was for this contribution that I nominated them as Isle of Wight Hidden Heroes, as part of a collaboration between Island museums and heritage sites, which saw a range of exhibitions across the Island in 2018 to 19. As a volunteer at the time at Carisbrooke Castle Museum I contributed the text for the website and museum exhibition on the Gang. A previous small exhibition at the museum about the Island's first Pride had drawn a mixed reaction from volunteers and visitors. There were a few homophobic comments, and questions as to why the Pride event was historic and worthy of a display, so I knew that Ferguson's Gang could potentially be a contentious choice, given some members were lesbians or bisexual.

I was also a volunteer and then a member of the National Trust staff the following season at Newtown Old Town Hall, where the stories of these remarkable women captured my imagination. I was privileged to visit Shalford Mill, the Gang's first project, near Guildford in Surrey, for an event where Polly Bagnall, author of the *Ferguson's Gang* book of 2015, was leading tours of the mill. Her mother had grown up there following its repair led by her architect father John Macgregor, also know as The Artichoke. She still lived in the mill, and although rather elderly, had memories of the mysterious Gang visiting when she was a child.

Inspired by my trip, I was keen to share the stories of the Gang further at Newtown. The National Trust in recent years has had themes for exhibitions each year. During 2017, my first year at Newtown, the theme was Prejudice and Pride. Some mainland properties encountered objections from volunteers and visitors about this LGBTQ+ theme, particularly where it was felt someone was being 'outed' in a way which may not have been acceptable in their own lifetime. The Trust on the Island didn't promote any LGBTQ+ stories, so our only visible involvement was some of us wearing rainbow-coloured National Trust oak leaf badges.

In 2018, the theme was Women and Power, marking a century of some women being given the vote by exploring remarkable women's connections with Trust properties. I was given the opportunity to prepare and present a number of tours of the Old Town Hall, which explored the Ferguson's Gang's significant contribution to Newtown. I remember showing my draft script to one of our volunteers, who pointed at the sentence which said 'some of the Gang members were lesbians or bisexual', and they asked "Do people need to know that?" Although there are clearly still challenges around sharing LGBTQ+ stories at museums and heritage sites, which I have experienced first hand, fortunately all the tour members seemed as fascinated by these women as I am.

JOHN SEELY AND PAUL PAGET

Margaret Montgomerie

Mottistone Manor embodies all my fantasies about the quintessential English home (fantasies where I am wealthy without being obnoxiously privileged). It sits between the sea and the downs, combining the adventure of the ocean with the deceptive tranquillity of the lush green countryside. The manor house nestles against the hillside which engulfed the west wing for more than 200 years after a landslip in 1703. The house is large but not ostentatious, one can easily imagine oneself living there (I do every week, often confusing visitors to the gardens). It is built of local materials and its soft grey and buff coloured walls indicate the long history of the building along with the mullioned windows and gently twisted panes of glass. The porch indicates that it dates back to 1567 when Thomas Cheke added the northwest wing.

If visiting the house in April or May and approaching from Brightstone, you will see it beyond the glorious wisteria which covers the boundary wall of the lower garden, a breathtaking sight. Once you enter the grounds you encounter the monocot borders with palms, grasses and exotic lilies, bamboos and a wide range of colourful perennials which surround the large lawn featuring a mulberry and a tulip tree. Walking up the slope you see the wonderful blue and orange borders which face the house and lead the way to the tea garden and 'The Shack' (more of this later). Opposite you can enter the yew-hedged gardens and find the rose gardens featuring the heavenly scented Roseraie de L'Hay and the glorious double borders. Up another slope there is the organic kitchen garden, the orchards, the olive groves, a wild area, the gully and woodland walks.

In my previous life as a university lecturer teaching Media, Gender and Identity, I had got through the interminable meetings, which always spawned more meetings, by allowing myself to imagine I was working in a sun-dappled garden (highly reminiscent of the work of Gertrude Jekyll) attached to a romantic stately home.[256] Haddon Hall in Derbyshire was my recurring daydream. In 2016, I had the opportunity to make my dreams a reality. My partner, Anne, got a new job in Portsmouth and I found I

---

[256]Gertrude Jekyll (1843-1932) created some 400 gardens in the UK, Europe and America. Her influence on garden design has been pervasive to this day.

could take early retirement the following year. We decided that after living and working in large cities in the centre of the country including Sheffield, Manchester, Derby, Stoke-on-Trent, Birmingham and Leicester, we would take the plunge and move to the Isle of Wight. We envisaged ourselves strolling on the beaches, kayaking, and rambling on the downs, revelling in the fact that the Island does not have a city or a motorway.

However, I had niggling doubts. I had grown up in rural Hampshire and had enjoyed the liberation that cities offer when I left home to go to Sheffield Polytechnic. I had always missed the sea and the countryside but was worried that the Isle of Wight would prove too straight and narrow for two queer women who had experienced and been shaped by the vibrant LGBTQ+ communities of Sheffield (Sheffield Women's Cultural Club, Climax, Liquid, the Hiking Dykes), Manchester (Follies, Dusty's) and Leicester (Rubyfruit and L-Fest). I had my first relationship with a woman in Sheffield as a LOL (late onset lesbian). This only seemed possible because I lived in Meersbrook where it was often commented 'there was something in the water' which accounted for the vast number of lesbian women. Anne had left a small town in East Germany (GDR) and experienced her coming out in Leipzig as a student at the university. We both knew that small communities could be restrictive. Just after we found the house we would buy on the Island, the local MP was compromised for allegedly making homophobic comments and resigned. We worried that this could be indicative of local attitudes. Before we moved to the Island we joined the first Pride march in Ryde, out of a sense of necessity rather than celebration.

Little did I suspect that Mottistone Manor Gardens would not only allow me to live out my fantasy of working in the beautiful gardens of a heritage house but would also introduce me to the tantalising tale of Paul Paget and John Seely, who definitely had a homo-social if not a homosexual relationship. Their story reminded me that 'queer', non-normative people are part of our history, that we have contributed to the culture and fabric of society although we have often been seen as the enemy and have had to hide our relationships, desires and interests. 'The Shack' offers the Mottistone clue to Paget and Seely's relationship, which started in their twenties at Cambridge and lasted until Seely's death in 1963. It provided a country retreat where they could be together without compromising their families. Paul Paget's father was the Bishop of Chester and John Seely's father was General 'Jack' Seely, the first Lord Mottistone. Both families were very well connected and regularly met with the great and the good of the era. Churchill, J.B. Priestley, John Betjeman and the Courtaulds all visited the restored Mottistone.

Seely and Paget built 'The Shack' to be externally in keeping with its historic surroundings. It was made of state-of-the-art materials to be sited in the grounds of Mottistone Manor which they renovated as their first commission as architects. The two men had met at Cambridge where Seely studied architecture and Paget was remembered as an extrovert and entertainer rather than for his studies. In an interview with Clive Aslet (1987) Paul Paget noted of his relationship to John Seely 'it was just the marriage of two minds, I mean we virtually became one person' and 'we lived a completely common life together.'[257] They referred to each other as 'the partner' and it seems family and friends referred to them as 'the partners'. The extent of their interconnectedness becomes evident when Paul reveals that he wrote all of John's letters, both business and personal. He paints a picture of 'the partner's father' General Jack as a dashing and forward-looking man with a keen interest in the latest trends in architecture who introduced them to both Le Corbusier and Lutyens. Although General Jack Lord Mottistone and the Bishop of Chester were clearly respected establishment figures they did not seem to question the closeness of their sons. Rather, they did everything they could to establish their reputation as preeminent architects in the inter-war period. General Jack gave them their first commission, although with the proviso that Lutyens should vet the plans. This meant that they had the Lutyens' seal of approval, combined with an article in *Country Life* in 1929 about their renovation of Mottistone, which must have smoothed their path.

Paul Paget commented that, 'I can't emphasise enough the extent to which it was the age of privilege.[258] This privilege meant that he and John Seely were introduced to the right people. Gladys Cooper and J.B. Priestley were amongst the first to commission them for domestic work, while their grandest and best-known commission was Eltham Palace for Stephen and Virginia Courtauld. Through Paul Paget's father they also became established as church restorers and designers. By the 1960s they had completed restorations of Lambeth Palace, Eton College and Fulham Palace and many more prestigious buildings. This led to John Paget becoming the Surveyor of the Fabric of St Paul's Cathedral. This substantial portfolio of work made the partners wealthy.

---

[257]Clive Aslet and Paul Paget. 'An Interview with the Late Paul Paget 1901-1985', *The Thirties Society Journal*, no. 6 (1987): 16-25, accessed October 30, 2020. http://www.jstor.org.arts.idm.oclc.org/stable/41859261.

[258] Ibid.

When 'the partners' started out they had borrowed money to buy a house in Cloth Fair Street, Smithfield. As their careers developed, they bought the whole street and moved in with their friends and family. Descriptions of the house and Paget's account of entertaining at Cloth Fair Street evokes Evelyn Waugh or E.F. Benson's versions of the 1920s and 30s. They also bought the house opposite them and bricked up a window, covering it with a mural so that they could have their breakfast in privacy. Their bathroom featured twin 'moderne' baths so that they could bathe together in comfort. An article in *Country Life* features their manservant cleaning the baths. The same manservant was sent out to buy lace to cover the heads of their female dinner guests so that they could go to a special organ recital in a nearby church for entertainment. Paul relates stories of Virginia Courtauld's pet lemur whose cage featured two floors and who was partial to nipping guests' ankles.[259]

John Seely died in 1963 and was buried in the Cheke Chapel in Mottistone. In 1966, a fibreglass Edwin Russell statue of St Catherine was erected in a niche in St Catherine's chapel garden in Westminster Abbey as a memorial to John Paget. The inscription in Latin reads:

> John Mottistone. This is a sign of love and sadness. P.E.P. 1966 A.C.D.

P.E.P. refers to Paul Paget and A.C.D. to the then Dean of Westminster, Alan Campbell Don. Paget himself died in 1985.

John Seely left the Mottistone Estate to the National Trust. It is because of this that I can volunteer and take pleasure in the beautiful gardens, house and grounds of Mottistone Manor.

---

[259]Clive Aslet and Paul Paget. 'An Interview with the Late Paul Paget 1901-1985', *The Thirties Society Journal*, no. 6 (1987): 16-25, accessed October 30, 2020. http://www.jstor.org.arts.idm.oclc.org/stable/41859261.

JOE CARSTAIRS

Caroline Diamond

'The fastest woman on water'[260] – powerboat racer Joe Carstairs – is possibly the most high profile lesbian associated with the Isle of Wight. She is an example of someone whose story may have remained relatively unknown had it not been for the book telling her story *Queen of Whale Cay* and projects similar to ours like *Hidden Heroes*.[261] Joe was a fascinating, fierce, proud and brave woman, the UK's most successful female motorboat racer in the 1920s with numerous lovers said to have included Greta Garbo and Marlene Dietrich.[262]

There was a moment of serendipity in February 2018 when representatives from the National Lottery Heritage Fund came to the Island and gave a presentation to say that funding was available for our area and to explain the nature of the projects it supports. The venue was the East Cowes Classic Boat Museum and the evening was the launch night of an exhibition about Joe Carstairs. East Cowes is the mini industrial quarter of the Isle of Wight, home to boatyards and the GKN Aerospace factory and the museum, sandwiched in a dark, innocuous corner between the sea and the Red Funnel Ferry Terminal. Another notable, perhaps unexpected, landmark in East Cowes is Waitrose, sited to take advantage of second homeowners and Cowes Week sailing-types who can hop over from neighbouring Cowes on the floating bridge. At the time of writing, the floating bridge is best known on the Island for the amount of time it spends 'out of service', making a trip from East Cowes to Cowes instead of two to three minutes, a good 25-minute drive through the Island's capital Newport via traffic blackspot Coppins Bridge and along the Island's only dual carriageway.

I went to the event with Elaine Chambers, Island resident and author of *This Queer Angel* and East Cowes Councillor, Karl Love, the Island's first openly gay councillor. The talk from the National Lottery Heritage Fund was inspiring and the exhibition was excellent. We learned that Joe Carstairs

---

[260]Kate Summerscale. *The Queen of Whale Cay*. London: Bloomsbury, 2012, 86

[261]Isle of Wight Hidden Heroes, accessed February 10, 2020, http://www.iwhiddenheroes.org.uk/

[262]Kate Summerscale. *The Queen of Whale Cay*. London: Bloomsbury, 2012, 37

was born Marion Barbara Carstairs in 1900 but known as Joe. This wealthy lesbian sportswoman and entrepreneur died in 1993 and her god-daughter, Jane Harrison-Hall, wrote to the *Daily Telegraph* suggesting that Joe might be an interesting subject to feature in the newspaper's obituaries. Kate Summerscale, who is best known for her book *The Suspicions of Mr Whicher*, was the recipient of the obituary request as she was working for the *Daily Telegraph* at the time. Fascinated by the enigmatic, cross-dressing Carstairs, she decided to research her life and wrote the book *The Queen of Whale Cay* about her.

Joe was an heiress, independent both financially and personally, proud, headstrong and tough. Her childhood was unsettled and, as late as 1975 she claimed that 'To this day... I don't know my father's name'.[263] Joe's mother, Evelyn, was an American oil heiress who had numerous affairs. It is interesting to consider how Joe would identify if she were around nowadays. She said of herself: 'I was never a little girl. I came out of the womb queer'.[264] She had a difficult relationship with her mother, who enjoyed alcohol and heroin, and married for a second time and had two more children.

Joe Carstairs ʌ (*on the right*). *Courtesy of the Classic Boat Museum, East Cowes*

Joe's passion was for machines and boats. She enjoyed sailing her dinghy in the Solent but she proved too much of a free spirit and a bully for her parents who sent her by ocean liner to boarding school in America. In a one-page autobiography she compiled in her nineties, Joe simply wrote 'Left family aged eleven'.[265]

At fifteen, she met Roger de Perigny, her mother's third husband and a French Count. Joe loved the way he treated her like a son, offering her cigars and letting her drive his car. He even took her to a brothel. Her ambition was to be a doctor and at sixteen years old she moved to France to be an ambulance driver where she had her first sexual encounter with a woman. It was Oscar Wilde's niece, Dolly who was to make a great impression on seventeen-year-old Joe in Paris. Both enjoyed the lifestyle and the sexual diversity and Dolly had the same independent nature and appetite for mischief and misbehaviour. Joe was infatuated with Dolly, and found her 'almost mystical.'[266]

'"Yes you are a lesbian, I have heard all about it. All over Paris."' said Joe's mother after summoning her in 1918.[267] Evelyn threatened to disinherit Joe who, to secure her inheritance, then married her childhood friend Jacques de Pret, a spiteful move as Joe had thought Jacques and her mother were lovers. The marriage did not last and after working in Northern Ireland as a driver, Joe moved to Hampshire in the 1920s.

Joe became an accomplished yachtswoman and won many competitions in her yacht, Sonia. After a time when she was short of money, she became wealthy again, inheriting from both her mother and grandmother and using some money to buy a powerboat in 1925. Joe wanted a hydroplane, a fast and dangerous vessel, and turned to Sam Saunders, the head of an East Cowes boat-building firm who supervised the construction. Joe called the new boat Gwen after her former lover Gwen Farrar, a variety star. After the boat overturned on a test run she called it Newg, reversing the letters. Joe Carstairs struck up a devoted friendship with Joe Harris who was mechanic and chauffeur to Sam Saunders and worked with him for five years. She went on to win races in the UK and at Cannes and achieved the fastest time in the Duke of York's Trophy first round. Joe was always competing against men because no women's races existed.

Joe was rumoured to have had many girlfriends including her secretary Ruth Baldwin. In 1925 Ruth gave Joe a gift which she named Lord Tod Wadley, a leather doll a foot long made by Steiff toymakers. Although Joe Carstairs had no interest in having children, Lord Tod Wadley became a precious a possession to her, dressed like Joe in Savile Row suits and Italian leather shoes. His name was on a plaque alongside hers at the front door of Joe and Ruth's house. Joe asked Sam Saunders to build another boat for her and called it Leumas, his name in reverse.

---

[263]Kate Summerscale. *The Queen of Whale Cay*. London: Bloomsbury, 2012, 37

[264]Ibid.,14.

[265]Ibid., 17.

[266]Ibid., 28.

[267]Ibid., 33.

Although Joe Carstairs was strong and independent and raced successfully in Britain and America where she was often the only British contestant, she wasn't popular with the media and was viewed with suspicion. As Kate Summerscale writes in *The Queen of Whale Cay*:

> By the late 1920s the tide was turning against the likes of Joe Carstairs. Her vaunted pluck was beginning to be seen as a rebellion against nature. In the immediate aftermath of the war, masculine women were perceived – at worst – as contemporary curiosities but in 1928 the publication of Radclyffe Hall's 'The Well of Loneliness' irrevocably sexualised them. The heroine of Radclyffe Hall's novel was, like Joe Carstairs, a well-to-do woman who dressed in men's clothes. Like Carstairs, she had served as an ambulance driver in France, and like Carstairs she had a female lover. The book was banned.[268]

There are comparisons here with the suspicion with which trans people are sometimes treated today and the argument about trans women competing in sport. It shows how little progress we have made in terms of acceptance.

Joe's boat racing career was on the decline and after losing a race from Ryde to Le Havre she began to consider emigrating. She bought the island of Whale Cay in the Bahamas in 1934, spending little time in Britain from then on.

[268]Kate Summerscale. *The Queen of Whale Cay*. London: Bloomsbury, 2012, 89.

LORD LOUIS MOUNTBATTEN

Melissa Gilmore

Lord Louis Mountbatten's connection to the Isle of Wight comes via his appointment as Governor of the Island in 1965, as well as his later appointment as Lord Lieutenant in 1974. However, his legacy on the Island lasts to this day via the Mountbatten Hospice, named in his honour.

Mountbatten was born on 25 June 1900 to Prince Louis of Battenberg and his wife Princess Victoria of Hesse and by Rhine. The First World War led his father to change the family title, switching from the German Battenberg to the anglicised Mountbatten. The great-grandson of Queen Victoria, Mountbatten had somewhat of a royal childhood. His godparents included Queen Victoria and Nicholas II of Russia; during his childhood, he visited the Imperial Court of Russia in St Petersburg and he became quite close to the Russian Imperial Family.[269]

As an adult, Mountbatten had a long career in the British Armed Forces, becoming Supreme Allied Commander of the South East Asia Command during the Second World War. From 1954 to 1959, he held the title of First Sea Lord – the same position previously held by his father – and he served as chief of the Defence Staff from 1959 to 1965. Outside of the Armed Forces, in 1947 he became the last Viceroy of India and was the first governor-general of independent India from 1947 to 1948.

In July 1922, Mountbatten married Edwina Ashley, heir to the fortune of the British merchant banker Sir Ernest Cassel. Their marriage was not without its quirks, with Mountbatten admitting to his official biographer that: 'Edwina and I spent all our married lives getting into other people's beds.'[270] He notably had a years-long affair with Yola Letellier, whose life inspired Colette's novel *Gigi*.[271]

In his 2019 biography of Lord and Lady Mountbatten, Andrew Lownie devotes a whole section to the question of Mountbatten's sexuality. His

---

[269]Andrew Lownie. *Mountbattens: Their Lives And Loves*. Blink Publishing, 2019, 14.

[270]Philip Ziegler. *Mountbatten: The Official Biography*. London: Phoenix Press, 2001, 53.

[271]Pamela Hicks. *Daughter of Empire: Life as a Mountbatten*. New York: Weidenfeld & Nicolson, 2017, 24.

research finds that Mountbatten's bisexuality and his liaisons with men were well-known throughout the whisper network of the Armed Forces.[272] He references work by a number of other journalists and authors, including Charlotte Breese's *Hutch* where she writes:

> When he was Supreme Allied Commander in South East Asia, several officers boasted of their liaisons with him. A naval friend came across him on an island, when he was serving in Malta, nude in flagrante with another officer...[273]

Rumours about Lord Mountbatten's sexuality were in circulation both before and after his death, buoyed by his friendships with Noël Coward and Tom Driberg. Lownie points to a *Private Eye* story published just after Mountbatten's assassination in 1979, which claimed:

> Residents living close to his London home at 2 Kinnerton Street, SW1 have hair-raising stories to tell of the rollicking all-male frolics held there by the ageing matelot. Lord Louis, it seems, had a preference for young servicemen.[274]

Lownie was able to correspond with a number of first hand sources, including author Michael Thornton, who wrote:

> [I] utterly disbelieved his insistence that there was no evidence to suggest Mountbatten was bisexual. My own knowledge of Dickie over the years suggested the opposite conclusion and Noël Coward, whom I knew extremely well for the last thirteen years of his life, told me it was "beyond doubt" and to his certain knowledge that Dickie had had male as well as female lovers.[275]

---

[272] Andrew Lownie. *Mountbattens: Their Lives And Loves*. Blink Publishing, 2019, 318.

[273] Ibid.

[274] Ibid., 316.

[275] Ibid.

Ron Perks, who was assigned as Mountbatten's driver in Malta in 1948, told Lownie that:

> One day as we were driving along, Mountbatten asked if I knew the Red House. I said I did and he asked if I would take him there, which I did. [...] I didn't know what it was and only learnt after I came out of the service that it was an upmarket gay brothel used by senior naval officers. You're taught to keep out of trouble in the Navy and I've never said a word about the incident until now.[276]

Upon the release of Mountbatten's FBI files, Lownie found numerous reports of Mountbatten's relationships with men, along with reports of his wife's various affairs.[277] Parts of the report remain sealed.

In 1979, Mountbatten was assassinated while fishing in Ireland. An IRA bomb planted on his boat was detonated shortly after leaving shore, killing Mountbatten along with his two grandsons, Nicholas and Paul, and Dowager Lady Doreen Brabourne.

[276] Andrew Lownie. *Mountbattens: Their Lives And Loves*. Blink Publishing, 2019, 326.

[277] Ibid., 328.

KEITH BIDDLECOMBE

Franko Figueiredo-Stow

Keith Biddlecombe was born on the Isle of Wight in 1936 and grew up here with a Roman Catholic mother and father and an elder brother in the Royal Navy; Biddlecombe also enlisted in 1952. In an oral history interview recorded by the Queer in Brighton project, Biddlecombe tells the story of his arrest in Malta, his medical examination and the Military Police's questioning and attempts to find his sexual partners. He claimed that the police offered to reduce a potential five-year prison sentence to twelve months if he gave them names. Biddlecombe revealed the name of one officer who subsequently shot himself rather than face a trial.[278] Biddlecombe was only twenty years old when charged with buggery and gross indecency.

He spent his twenty-first birthday in Shepton Mallet Prison in Somerset[279] and was soon let out for good conduct. However the Royal Navy destroyed his references forcing him to start rebuilding his career from scratch. He worked for the metropolitan water board, coal mines, managed a warehouse for a ceramic company, worked on one of the counters of a department store and finally found that he was skilful in costume making and window dressing. His work includes iconic costumes of Elizabeth 1, Victoria, Queen Matilda and a millennium celebratory window based on Haley's comet, some which have been featured in Isle of Wight Carnival floats.

Years later, after leaving the Navy, Biddlecombe returned to his mother's house on the Island for a two-week holiday with his partner Bill. Although Biddlecombe's mother had, it seems, accepted her son's homosexuality, Bill was made to sleep downstairs. Touchingly, Biddlecombe says "when we left mother said goodbye to us and flabbergasted me by saying 'now, look after each other. That was quite a moment of acceptance.'"[280]

In 2017, Biddecombe was a recipient of an Attitude PRIDE Award, which celebrates the everyday, and sometimes unsung, heroes of the LGBTQ+ community: 'those who have worked tirelessly in the third sector, who have triumphed over tragedy, who have championed rights or challenged stigma in the face of adversity.'[281] He moved to Brighton in 2001.

NIKKI DORAKIS

Franko Figueiredo-Stow

Activist, psychiatric nurse, pagan priest and writer, Nikki Dorakis was born Enrico Cortesi in Ventnor on the Isle of Wight.

Nikki Dorakis ʌ (*born Enrico Cortesi*) *aged 20 in 1974. Courtesy of Mara Fraser.*

He was heavily involved in the gay rights movement and founded the Campaign For Homosexuality (CHE) group on the Isle of Wight in the 70s. Nikki says "being an 'out' gay male in a rural community certainly makes for an interesting life".[282] He's lived and worked abroad in Algeria, Saudi Arabia and the United States and spent over a year back-packing around the world with his then partner, Mike. Nikki finally settled back on the Island in the late 90s.

Disappointed by the lack of Gay fiction, specifically male gay fiction, he started writing novels, *The Lynx* being his first outing as a writer.[283]

[278]Keith Biddlecombe, interview by Queer in Brighton project, The Keep, East Sussex Archives.

[279]Patrick Strudwick, 'This Is What It Was Like To Go To Jail In England Just For Being Gay', BuzzFeed, accessed July 15, 2017), https://www.buzzfeed.com/patrickstrudwick/this-is-what-it-was-like-to-go-to-jail-in-england-just-for.

[280]Keith Biddlecombe, interview by Queer in Brighton project, The Keep, East Sussex Archives.

[281]The Winners of the Attitude Pride Awards 2017, in Association with United Airlines and Sleepeezee. *Attitude.* accessed July 18, 2019. https://attitude.co.uk/article/the-winners-of-the-attitude-pride-awards-2019-in-association-with-united-airlines-and-sleepeezee-1/21327/

[282]Nikki Dorakis, Amazon.co.uk: Nikki Dorakis, accessed February 15, 2021. https://www.amazon.co.uk/Nikki-Dorakis/e/B007O7AJ8A%3Fref=dbs_a_mng_rwt_scns_share.

[283]Ibid.

PATRICK GALE

Clifford Williams and Caroline Diamond

Patrick Gale is a successful gay author who frequently writes about gay experiences and appealing to a diverse, not just LGBTQ+, audience. He was born in 1962 on the Isle of Wight but now lives in Cornwall with his husband. Patrick's father was Prison Governor at HMP Camp Hill briefly overlapping with his grandfather, who was governing nearby HMP Parkhurst. Although the family left for the prison at Wandsworth when Patrick was still a baby, family holidays for the next few years were spent visiting his Island grandparents and swimming at Compton Bay. Patrick spent his childhood in Winchester and from the age of thirteen attended Winchester College Boarding School, a single-sex school, as a day student.

LGBTQ characters feature in many of Patrick's books from his first book published in 1985 *The Aerodynamics of Pork*, which features two intertwined love stories: a lesbian story about a policewoman in the 1980s, and the story of Seth, a gay schoolboy and a musical prodigy, on the eve of his sixteenth birthday. *Rough Music* published in 2000 is the story of one family at two defining points in time, 30 years apart. Will Pagett, a young boy, is gay and knows he is different; 32 years later he is having an affair with a married man and seeks solace on a beach holiday with his aging parents. *Take Nothing With You* is Patrick's sixteenth novel, published in 2018, and concerns Eustace, a cellist and gay widower who is HIV positive. The book looks back at his childhood in Weston Super Mare and his search for love, and is now being developed as a stage play.

Patrick ∧ *playing on a beach as a young person, circa 1966. Courtesy of Patrick Gale.*

The story of Patrick's father is interesting and a reflection of how life was for LGBTQ+ people in the years prior to 1967 when homosexuality was illegal for men. Patrick's mother found a stack of love letters in her husband's desk shortly after the end of the Second World War which she thought were from a girlfriend. They were from a male friend and she destroyed them for fear of them falling into the wrong hands. At that time, people assumed that gay men were paedophiles and Patrick's mother was mindful of this when Patrick was born, ensuring that Patrick wasn't left alone with his father. Patrick used this story as part of his television two-part drama for the BBC *Man In An Orange Shirt* (2017), which won an International Emmy and is now being developed as a musical.

Patrick Gale was one of the interviewees in the Y-Services Voices For Heritage young people's LGBT history project in Winchester.[284]

PHAEDRA KELLY

Franko Figueiredo-Stow

Bruce David Laker, aka Phaedra J. Kelly, was born in 1955 and saw themself 'stranded on the Isle of Wight' from 1972.[285] They lived in Freshwater and later in Ryde as Bruce and also Phaedra Kelly an artist, poet and activist. Their achievements for the trans community and appreciation of a non-binary world were not championed locally but, appropriately, Phaedra was featured in *Isle of Wight Hidden Heroes* exhibition in 2018–19.

Globally, Phaedra made significant strides for the trans community. It is fair to say that they were ahead of their time in terms of gender politics, developing the notion of gender transiency and coining the term, which was included in the *Oxford English Dictionary* in the 1990s, 'gender transient'.[286]

In 1989, Phaedra was rejected by the Beaumont Society. The society had no interest in the varieties of trans culture. Phaedra went on to find some like-minded folk and constituted themselves as the School of Transconscient Arts Movement. They exhibited at local exhibitions, including Island galleries and libraries, and published in local outlets.

---

[284]Y-Services is a youth service charity operating in the county of Hampshire. Since 2017 their four Young LGBT+ groups (based in Fareham, Gosport, Winchester and Havant) have engaged in a Heritage Lottery funded LGBT+ history project.

[285]'My Island - Phaedra Kelly', *Isle of Wight County Press*, June 3, 2016, 3.

[286]Roberts JoAnn, 'Lady Like Profile, Phaedra Kelly', *LadyLike* No. 3 - Digital Transgender Archive, accessed September 3, 2020, https://www.digitaltransgenderarchive.net/files/73666455b.

In 1983, Phaedra's wedding at the Isle of Wight Registry Office made national headlines. Phaedra met Vanda, a cis woman, and they married at the registry office with Vanda as the groom and Phaedra in traditional bridal attire. They then had a second shamanistic wedding of the male and female in Phaedra and the male and female of Vanda. Phaedra/Bruce explains

> It's about a discipline of duality with an open mind, without changing sex with hormones, with pills, with injections or surgery, living one's dualism as much as possible. If I am Phaedra, I allow elements of Bruce through, and there is no self-hating or loathing going on. If I am Bruce I allow elements of Phaedra – it's horses for courses, but like the transvestite, and to some degree the trans person living full time, I live with a separate identity. I have accepted my separate identity as well.[287]

There was a duality, not just in terms of gender. Locally, Phaedra was not always taken seriously as demonstrated in an interview by local columnist Charlotte Hofton, well known for her narrow views. Hofton visited Phaedra to discuss the Turner Prize and Grayson Perry, to whom she refers as a 'transvestite potter'. The article is pure vitriol and ends with Hofton's conclusion: 'That settles it. I bet the transvestite potter's not a genius. Boot him off the shortlist and replace him with Phaedra. A transgender genius in his skirt and stilettos riding a Bactrian camel — now, what could be more artistic than that?'[288]

When asked what Phaedra did not miss about the Isle of Wight when away, her response was 'being excluded and banned from everything.'[289]

A prolific contributor to the *Isle of Wight County Press* letters page, Phaedra often took part in the Island's annual carnival processions held in all the larger towns. In their later years, Phaedra could often be found performing poetry and music at open mic nights in local pubs like the King Lud in Ryde.

Throughout the 1980s, Phaedra attended drag balls, and corresponded with and supported transvestites and transsexuals from all over and eventually they founded International Gender Transient Affinity (IGTA), which aided Amnesty International in its first sexual minorities case. From 1990, Phaedra became a leading advocate and research assistant for the Transgender Archive at the University of Ulster, playing a major role in the establishment of the archive publications.[290] The archive was donated to Victoria Transgender Archives in 2013.[291]

From 1987 to 1990 Phaedra also published *CHRYSALIS* in Freshwater, the IGTA magazine for the gender non-conforming community. Phaedra also wrote for various local, national and international publications, authored several fictional novels and three poetry collections. *The Naked Transient* is one of their most notable books.

In recent years, Phaedra regularly performed with the Ecurbrekal Poetry Band, which was founded in 2009. Phaedra/Bruce passed away in March 2019.[292]

Phaedra Kelly ⋀ *representing/promoting IGTA's work at London Pride in the early 90s. Courtesy of Jez Laker.*

[287]Zagria, 'Phaedra Kelly (1955 – 2019) Activist', January 1, 1970, https://zagria.blogspot.com/2011/02/phaedra-kelly-1955-activist.html#.X1ZKpdNKjvU. accessed 3 Sep 20

[288]Charlotte Hofton, 'Phaedra One Day, Bruce the Next', *Isle of Wight County Press*, June 6, 2003, 19.

[289]'My Island - Phaedra Kelly', *Isle of Wight County Press*, June 3, 2016, 3.

[290]Richard Ekins, 'On the Classification and Framing of Trans-Gender Knowledge', GENDYS Conference 1990 - Building a Trans-Gender Archive, accessed September 3, 2020, http://www.gender.org.uk/conf/1990/90ekins.htm.

[291]Richard Ekins, 'Digital Transgender Archive', A Concise History of the University of Ulster, Trans-Gender Archive (1986-2010) - Digital Transgender Archive, accessed September 3, 2020, https://www.digitaltransgenderarchive.net/files/h989r326r.

[292]Nigelbrade, 'IWLF Programme 2015', Issuu (Isle of Wight Literary Festival 2015), accessed September 23, 2020, https://issuu.com/nigelbrade/docs/iwlf_programme_2015.

KENNETH KENDALL

Caroline Diamond

My memories of Kenneth Kendall are of a classic BBC Newsreader, well-liked and distinguished-looking with a clear, plummy, reassuring voice. A quintessential Englishman, he was born in India where his father worked as a mining engineer and was later brought up in Cornwall after moving to England aged ten. He was never championed as a gay icon, very few people were until recently, and was more likely to have been described as a 'national treasure'.

Kenneth studied modern languages at Corpus Christi College, Oxford University for a year before being called up to serve in the Army. He reached the rank of Lieutenant in the Coldstream Guards but returned to university to complete his degree.

In 1955, Kenneth was the first newsreader to be seen, as well as heard on television. Prior to this, newsreaders were usually radio broadcasters, so the visual newsreader was a new phenomenon. Obviously, radio presenters were known for their voices rather than their appearance and Kenneth was once president of the Queen's English Society. He was elegant, over six feet tall, an ambitious journalist who would research, write and read his own scripts.

Newsreaders were somewhat anonymous, did not have their names published and were far more stern-faced and businesslike than the newsreaders of today. Television producers did not want them to become celebrities, although many women contacted the BBC to ask for Kenneth's name.

The *Guardian's* obituary says: 'He became known for his elegant dress sense and received dozens of proposals of marriage from female viewers.'[293] Kenneth was one of a new group of television newsreaders which included Richard Baker and Robert Dougall. 'He was unflappable in the face of the possible disasters of live television. Even when a false tooth shot out in the middle of a news bulletin, and sat on the desk in front of him, he merely continued with his mouth almost closed, willing viewers to believe that nothing of the sort had happened.'[294]

After 26 years, Kenneth left the BBC, and appeared in films and episodes of *Dr Who* before co-hosting Channel 4's popular *Treasure Hunt* between 1982 and 1989 with Anneka Rice. He moved back to Cornwall and opened an art gallery with his partner Mark Fear. They had been together since 1989.

In 1992, they moved to Cowes and opened Kendall's Restaurant on Cowes Esplanade which they ran for a few years. Kenneth described it as 'the hardest work of his life'.[295] They converted the restaurant into another gallery, Kendall's Fine Art Gallery. They entered into a civil partnership in 2006. Mark Fear, a former vice-commodore of the Royal London Yacht Club, Cowes, was well known on the Island. Kenneth died in 2012 aged 88, overcome by grief, his partner committed suicide four months after. In his obituary, the *Independent* wrote:

> An enthusiastic campaigner for Aids [sic.] charities and other good causes, Kendall caused a stir during the 1992 Cowes Regatta by going out in a boat and handing the sailors free condoms and T-shirts advocating safe sex. At his 80th birthday party in 2004, organised by his partner in the gallery, he declared that the campaign was still relevant: 'dare say I would hand them out again were I to be asked.'[296]

KARL LOVE

Caroline Diamond

East Cowes Councillor Karl Love is one of the first openly gay local councillors on the Isle of Wight. He is from Yorkshire originally and is never afraid to speak out for the local LGBTQ+ community. He has been with his partner David for 30 years, first living on the Island from 1992 until 1998 when he worked as one of the Isle of Wight's first gay men's sexual health workers. Karl was involved in HIV prevention work, aiming to increase the numbers of people being tested. He distributed condoms as Captain

[293]'M Dennis Barker, 'Kenneth Kendall Obituary', *Guardian*, accessed December 14, 2020, https://www.theguardian.com/media/2012/dec/14/kenneth-kendall.

[294]Ibid.

[295]Ibid.

[296]Michael Leapman, 'Kenneth Kendall: Much-Loved Newsreader Who Became the First to Be Seen', *Independent* accessed December 16, 2020. https://www.independent.co.uk/news/obituaries/kenneth-kendall-much-loved-newsreader-who-became-first-be-seen-screen-8420896.html.

Condom out on the streets at events like Cowes Week Sailing Regatta and he visited secondary schools to give talks on sexual health. In 1994, he organised the Island's first Pink Picnic. Karl got a new job and moved to Kent before returning to East Cowes in 2010 and setting up the Isle of Wight Gay Men's Chorus, another first for the Island.

ANNA MURRAY

Caroline Diamond

Anna Murray worked in one of the few dedicated LGBTQ+ roles on the Island as Age UK's LGBTQ+ Domestic Abuse and Hate Crime Lead. She also helps to run the Island's only women's LGBTQ+ group with Caroline Diamond. Anna runs Time For T, the only trans support group on the Isle of Wight. The group worked with Boots to offer make-up sessions to LGBTQ+ people and this scheme was rolled out to Boots' shops on the mainland. In 1997, Anna was involved with probably the first and very discreet, Island Gay and Lesbian Youth Network (IGLYN) who organised social activities like film nights and ice skating. In an article she wrote for this project, Anna talks about the 'shared grief, the understanding of how hard it was for a lot of people to be out'. In 2016, Anna organised a vigil in Newport for the victims of the Orlando massacre and she worked with Hampshire Constabulary's Lesbian and Gay Liaison Officers (LAGLO). Anna arranged for the Pride flag to be flown outside the police station and at County Hall. It was at the vigil that discussions about an Isle of Wight Pride started.

TOM PRIESTLEY

Franko Figueiredo-Stow

Tom was born in 1932 and spent some years living in Brook Hill House in the 1950s with his father the writer J.B. Priestley and his stepmother, Isle of Wight-born Jaquetta Hawkes. The house is private but it is very visible on the top of the hill as you drive through Brook near the Military Road, South West Wight.

When J.B. Priestley's first biographer, wanted to know how the thrice-married Priestley responded to finding out that his only son was gay, Tom replied that he had no idea: 'It's not something we ever talked about.' He suggested the biographer should ask Priestley's widow, Jacquetta Hawkes. She told him that Jack had been "disappointed"; he found it "difficult to adjust to". Tom thought: "Well, so did I!"[297]

Tom is an award-winning film editor and has edited some iconic films such as Roman Polanski's *Tess* (1979) and Jack Clayton's *The Great Gatsby* (1974). In the past decade, he has twice returned to the Island to share memories of his life with his father in lectures held at Seely Hall in Brook.[298] *On The Wight* reported on an evening of 'interesting and funny anecdotes' followed by a film of Tom interviewing his father about his career and family life.[299]

The National Trust website reports that: 'The Priestleys' secluded and idyllic life at Brook Hill House came to an end in the 1960s largely because of their celebrity.'[300] Jacquetta was active in a number of campaigns including the reform of the law on homosexuality and family planning.

[297]Valerie Grove, 'Out of the Wilderness: How J B Priestley Is Enjoying a Revival', *New Statesman*, accessed September 15, 2020, https://www.newstatesman.com/culture/2014/09/out-wilderness-how-j-b-priestley-enjoying-revival.

[298]'Tom Priestley: An Interview (Podcast)', Isle of Wight News from *OnTheWight*, accessed October 9, 2020, https://onthewight.com/tom-priestley-an-interview-podcast/.

[299]Rachel Brooks, 'J B Priestley: A Talk', Isle of Wight News from *OnTheWight*, accessed October 11, 2020, https://onthewight.com/j-b-priestley-a-talk/.

[300]https://www.nationaltrust.org.uk/mottistone-estate/features/jacquetta-hawkes-mottistone-mystery-solver

WHAT THE FUTURE HOLDS

Franko Figueiredo-Stow

So, what does the future hold for our LGBTQ+ community on the Isle of Wight? Where do we go from here? The plight of the LGBTQ+ community is influenced by a country's politics and how that filters down to everyday people. History has shown us that, although things are better than they used to be, things don't constantly improve in terms of LGBTQ+ rights, it is a fluctuating picture and hard-won rights can quickly be taken away. We need to continue to share the reality of life for LGBTQ+ individuals and to encourage our allies to use their voices too.

Our research, together with the oral histories we have recorded, presented us with stories of persecution, struggle, inclusion, guilt, hope and some unique perspectives on our hidden history. As we hear the interviews and read written accounts, one thing is clear: the dynamic nature of language reflects the shifting societal, cultural, and social meanings of sexuality and gender in our society, and it is easy to be scared by this. If we don't have first-hand experience of LGBTQ+ folks' lives, it is easy to resort to stereotypes. However, once you know somebody, you know their history, you begin to know their personality and recognise them as someone just like you, a person who is different from other people only in one respect.

Our history brings us together, our stories connect us and as we share them we obliterate the fear that comes from ignorance. Education is key. In a recent article published in *The Economist* about the globalisation of gay rights, it was argued that 'as more gay people come out, tolerance will spread'.[301] So here we are, and in danger of sounding clichéd, welcoming a new beginning.

At the end of each interview we asked if there was anything the interviewees would like to leave on record, any dreams or hopes for the future. Here are some of the responses:

---

[301]'As More Gay People Come Out, Tolerance Will Spread,' *The Economist*, accessed August 8, 2020, https://www.economist.com/leaders/2020/08/08/as-more-gay-people-come-out-tolerance-will-spread?fbclid=IwAR0QqNlba OaR9EPGSM-hQw9DoCY21OL-TGYCaL0SP58CpZXRcmbNGopZLrQ

Melissa

I guess I want to talk about what I want people to take away from this project. I talked a lot about the feelings of isolation and the feelings of fear and discomfort that I feel existing the way that I do in the world but I also want to let people know that I love my identity. I love being queer. It is something that I take such delight in and I want people to know that they can feel that way, that that's something that they can have. I suppose it is a strange thing to find so wonderful, but being queer has given me such a sense of community and such a sense of support from my community. I don't know that I would have felt that if I'd been straight. I don't know if I would have been able to access that because it's something that we've formed for ourselves, we've built it for ourselves because we had to. It's something that is a part of our activism, it's part of how we relate to other people within our community. There's inter-community discussions and discourse, we don't agree on everything, but it is still something that I feel, I feel embraced by my community and I feel like I can go to my community and be supported and be educated and find such a sense of belonging and such a sense of joy. I didn't choose this but if I had been able to choose this I think I would have just because of how much joy I've found from my identity. That's something that I want people to know that they can have. That's something I want people to seek out and find for themselves; to know that they are not alone, not even on the Isle of Wight, there's people here for them. There's still a lot of work to be done, there's still a lot of work to be done in this country and in our own community, but that we can do that. We can do that together, we can really build something beautiful.

Robin

Well, I would like young folk to realise from where we came and how life wasn't… I am not saying that life is easy for young queer people now. I am sure it's not in many cases, but they ought to have tried it when it was punishable by two years hard labour, which it was. It was Roy Jenkins who brought the law through in '66, the '66 government, yeah, that's right '67. I can remember there was a lesbian called George actually, she ran a pub on the Island, the Tiger Tavern it was at Sandown, it no longer exists. She was in London at the time, she was, "oh, I can remember when the Act was passed all the queers came out and danced in the streets", I thought, "oh, how wonderful".

Karl S

We chose to stay on the Island, we could have gone off. We've made friendships here, we have put down roots and we do like it. We certainly like it more now than we did. I think it is a pity that there isn't more of a gay community or LGBTQ community on the Island. Hopefully that will come and I think it will. I think things have changed in the last few years, probably more in the last few years than in the previous ten. It is a slow process but I think things will improve and I think things generally are better for LGBTQ people than they were. That's all I have to say really.

Lucy

Go for it! People are more accepting than you think they are, that's been my experience. I think I have been particularly lucky; I've got a fantastic family, fantastic friends, live in a lovely area with... not everybody is so lucky. You do hear some horror stories but generally I would say that people are more accepting than you think they are and just go for it. I think people are just so understanding and accepting over here. Even as, say, coming down from Birmingham to the Island, people were accepting. Some places you go they don't like people moving over, some places are very insular, but I think the Isle of Wight has got a really open and accepting culture.

Jess

I just feel that people need to be a bit more accepting and I don't understand why people are so obsessed with wanting to know what people identify as or who they are in a relationship with or potentially who they are having sex with because it literally makes no difference to anybody's life. I just don't really understand why it is such an issue still. And I think people should take a little bit more time out to stand up for people who are having issues in the street and not be bystanders because that is a massive thing. Not one person ever stepped forward when I was having an issue with somebody or being assaulted in the street even as a fifteen-year-old child. Why are adults walking past that are allowing that to happen? I'm not sure, I think people need to take a bit more responsibility. That's probably it.

Lucy

Joanne

Just don't judge anyone. That is my biggest thing in life. Just live and let live, it amazes me that people are so focused and worried about what you'll do. That's what I think, live and let live. Just don't judge anyone and just be nice! It is, isn't it? That's what I say to Kian, 'be nice', so that's all. That's a real sort of old mammy thing to say isn't it? [Laughs]. You know, that is, I am not political, do you know what I mean? I'm not. I'm not going to jump up on a soap box but if someone upsets one of mine, I'll be the first to be up there. Um, just live and let live, that's what I think.

Caroline

I think the message is for people to be authentic and to have the courage to do that but also to stand up to homophobia as well because we all know it still exists and it does take courage and passion. I remember somebody once saying to me about coming out; you have to think about what you are prepared to lose. I didn't know what she meant and she said, "well, you could lose your friends, you could lose your family, you might lose your job", so when you come out this is what has got to cross your mind. I think now that is a fairly old-fashioned view because people are generally more tolerant but there are still occasions when people are homophobic. I think it's also about making heterosexuals, straight people, aware that life isn't easy and that it is not a choice, it is about human beings being their true selves and being able to live their lives the best way. I probably could think of more but I think that's the general thrust of it really. And for people to be more open-minded and tolerant of each other. But I think it's nice just for people to be able to be confident that they can be LGBT and not have to hide it. I mean, I know on the Island we don't see many same-sex couples holding hands but it would be great to get to a stage where you could see that and it wasn't, you know, people weren't looking and the same with trans people. It would be nice if they feel that they could be accepted into the community for themselves. But I think on the Island things are moving in the right direction, so yes, I think that's about it.

Callum

I think, in hindsight, probably growing up, and if I was able to tell my younger self not to worry I probably would. I spent way too much time telling myself that people around me who I had very close relationships with would, you know, that relationship would change because of who I was. I told myself that for a very long period of time, probably about ten years, and it wasn't until fairly recently that I came out. So I think, for me it was a huge learning experience in terms of going on this adventure and finding out who I was as an individual and now I am who I am and happy to be who I am now and things are good.

Sydney

I will give one piece of general advice which is that people can surprise you in either direction; if you are worried about how people are going to take your coming out then they might turn out to be your greatest allies but also people who you think might be cool might not be so just be aware of that. But hopefully more the former than latter. And also to any young trans people specifically, I would say that very, very, very few cis gender people think about being the opposite sex to the extent that you do and your desire to be a different gender is probably very, very strongly indicative of the fact that you are probably trans. If you think you are trans and you've been thinking about it for more than a month or two you probably are trans and you should probably, you'll want to get on with things sooner rather than later if you are in a safe place. So yeah, that's my advice.

Anonymous

A lot of people love the Island, that's fine, you can walk your dog and all that sort of stuff but for me, for nightlife, for events that are going on, I just felt, "it's not for me". It's a very family-orientated place and I just didn't feel like, I mean, that's the other thing, nowadays LGBT people can have families. I've got friends who have got children, so it is quite interesting, but yeah, there's nothing there for me. Those kinds of romantic aspects that come from old-fashioned movies are very much models for us, aren't they? For a lot of the gay community. I do think since then a lot of relationships are open now and I think it just keeps growing, the LGBT community, because you sort of think, "right, we've got protections at work, we've got marriage equality", but things just keep growing.

I always think it is quite hard for the LGBT community to flourish in such a small space and the Isle of Wight is quite small but it is good that it is growing there but I do think things just need to be continuous there. Now you have got Pride you have to continue it, if you end it in some sort of way then things are going to step backwards. I think Pride can be a kind of guard can't it? A kind of soldier against homophobia and transphobia. I think it can be quite powerful, Pride can. It is possibly one of the more powerful things to do because there are a number of you coming together and that's really important.

Karen

I think being gay on the Isle of Wight is alright. I personally haven't had any issues with homophobia – apart from that once. I find everybody on the Isle of Wight alright and I just don't make a big thing about being gay I just do my thing and that's nice. I don't have to try and be something I'm not.

I have always come back to the Isle of Wight because this is where I belong, this is where I live. It's nice to go up to London and do Soho or go to Brighton but I like the pace of life on the Isle of Wight.

I wouldn't have done anything different because it makes me the person I am and you learn from what has happened to you. So no, I wouldn't change anything, even the really, really, really bad times I wouldn't change.

Karl L

The Island's given us more than we've given to them. Now I am an Isle of Wight Councillor. I didn't set out to do that, I became an Isle of Wight Councillor because essentially I have always been a Community Development Worker but when I got cancer – I got stage IV cancer so it was very close to not being recoverable, but I recovered. At that point I said, "I am going to put something more back into the community", though I think I pretty much did quite a bit already. So I said I would either be a Justice of the Peace or I'll try to become a County Councillor. I want to make a difference, not just to LGBT but for the people of this Island. But when I went to the County Council everybody knew I was gay, we'd made a TV programme which had gone out so we were very out. We were a bit worried about making that TV programme in terms of being labelled and stereotyped and targeted but we never have been.

But I don't want to be known for my sexuality, I want to be known for what it is that I can try and contribute to society as a whole. So for me the values of equality and inclusion are absolutely fundamental but that is not just about … as soon as you say equality or diversity, inclusion, people think you are talking about LGBT. I am talking about everything; about women's rights, the inclusion of young people in making decisions, the inclusion of people in being part of local government and local democracy. I want that to be more inclusive.

Rosa

There was a book I read once, it wasn't a particularly good book, it was quite a boring book but what attracted me to it was the title. It was written by a lady called Susan Jeffers and the title of the book was *Feel the Fear and Do it Anyway*. I have always lived by that because I think it is a great thing to do, it is a great message. It is a very small message but it means a huge thing and I think, to my little self, to my young self, I would say that, "feel the fear but do it anyway".

APPENDIX 1: A GUIDE TO LGBTQ+ TERMINOLOGY

Jared Mustafa-Holzapfel

When recording oral histories, understanding the language being used by both interviewee and interviewer is vital to understanding and interpreting the story being told. This is especially important when recording the histories of underrepresented groups. Whilst the collection here does not involve translation between different languages, understanding language is not limited to the act of translation. The use of slang or community terminology specific to the LGBTQ+ community is often not known or fully understood outside of the community. Often such slang is designed to be used in public spaces without others knowing the speaker is LGBTQ+ as, especially in the past, being 'outed' in public was dangerous. Such terminology includes categorical terms, such as Gay and Lesbian and phrases used to describe a queer safe space without including lesbian or gay, such as Women's Disco instead of Lesbian Disco. This short article looks at the evolution of this terminology to provide context to the terminology used within this book.

It is a logical step to begin with the acronym LGBTQ+ itself. In 1970, shortly after the Stonewall Riots in New York, the Gay Liberation Front (GLF) was formed to co-ordinate the rising social and political movement on gay rights.[302] It was not until the 1980s that LGB – Lesbian, Gay and Bisexual – began to be used and the T was not added until the 90s.[303] LGBTQ – Lesbian, Gay, Bisexual, Transgender, and Queer – emerged later in the 1990s and has continued to evolve, with the '+' added to include these evolving identities. Some within the community use LGBTQIA+ which includes Intersex and Asexual as well.

As the bracket for identities has grown and the gay rights movement has made steps forwards, language has evolved away from secretive covert phrases to more overt 'we're here and we're queer' expressions – see *RuPaul's Drag Race*, for example. Prior to the LGBTQ+ acronym there was Polari, also known as 'the gay language'. 'Polari has roots in 1600s England and is a mixture of Molly slang (Regency England men who dressed in drag [...]), thieves cant [...], East London cockney slang, and Italian brought home by sailors in the Mediterranean.'[304] Through the use of slang, a Polari speaker is able to openly discuss queerness without explicitly naming it as such. A rather infamous example is 'tipping the velvet' which refers to oral sex between two women. This phrase had a resurgence in the early 2000s thanks to Sarah Waters' Victorian lesbian romance novel *Tipping the Velvet* and its BBC television adaption of the same name. Whilst Polari itself has fallen out of mainstream use, older generations of LGBTQ+ individuals still know and reference it, and it is still studied academically.[305] David Bowie included some Polari in his 2016 album *Blackstar*.[306]

Not all slang was linked to Polari however, such as referring to a homosexual or lesbian person as 'a friend of Dorothy'. 'A friend of Dorothy' in the 1950s referenced the 1939 film *The Wizard of Oz* starring Judy Garland and could be used for gossiping or finding out if another individual was also gay within a more public environment.

Whilst such language was used within the community, language outside of the community was rarely as forgiving or subtle. Some of the terms used over the centuries to label LGBTQ+ individuals include buggery, character defect, cross-dresser, deviant, female husband, immoral, invert, pervert, sapphism, sodomite, tribade, and many others. This language appears in legal

---

[302]Paul Baker, 'A Brief History of Polari: The Curious After-Life of the Dead Language for Gay Men', *The Conversation*, accessed June 26, 2020, https://theconversation.com/a-brief-history-of-polari-the-curious-after-life-of-the-dead-language-for-gay-men-72599.

[303]Maggie Baska et al., 'How Has the LGBT+ Acronym Evolved?', *PinkNews*, accessed June 26, 2020, https://www.pinknews.co.uk/2017/11/06/how-has-the-lgbt-acronym-evolved/.

[304]Chadwick Moore, 'Lavender Language, The Queer Way to Speak', *OUT*, accessed June 26, 2020, https://www.out.com/out-exclusives/2016/8/17/lavender-linguistics-queer-way-speak.

[305]Paul Baker, 'A Brief History of Polari: the Curious after-Life of the Dead Language for Gay Men', *The Conversation*, accessed June 26, 2020, https://theconversation.com/a-brief-history-of-polari-the-curious-after-life-of-the-dead-language-for-gay-men-72599.

[306]Chadwick Moore, 'Lavender Language, The Queer Way to Speak', *OUT*, accessed June 26, 2020, https://www.out.com/out-exclusives/2016/8/17/lavender-linguistics-queer-way-speak.

documentation, medical records and research, journalism, and other written records. Ultimately such language presented the LGBTQ+ individual as morally reprehensible or broken in some integral manner. Such a homophobic attitude is readily internalised by an LGBTQ+ person and is still present in homophobic discourse about same-sex desire and gender identities today.

As social attitudes towards LGBTQ+ individuals have changed over time – from homosexuality being illegal in the UK until 1967, the publicly vocal fight against Section 28 until 2003, to today – so too has the language used by, within, and around the community at large.[307] Many terms that were meant to be offensive, such as dyke, poof and queer, have been reclaimed – taken back by those who were meant to be hurt by them, and embraced.[308] As Ben Schnetzer's character Mark tells Bromley in the 2014 film *Pride* – 'there was a long and honourable tradition in the gay community and it has stood us in good stead for a very long time, when somebody calls you a name [...] you take it, and you own it'.[309] The act of owning such terms decreases their power as threatening to the individual.

Because of this long history, language is vigilantly monitored by the LGBTQ+ community today. For example, after push back from the trans community, gender reassignment surgery is now referred to as gender confirmation surgery to distance the individual from the negative connotation of medical terminology – the individual is no longer someone who needs treatment to be fixed, rather the individual's gender identity is being affirmed.[310] These kinds of linguistic changes can empower the individual in question by confirming the validity of their identity externally; in choosing 'confirmation' the title of the surgery supports the physical change that the surgery itself will enact. It is a small change, but for the individual having that surgery and for their loved ones, it can make a significant psychological difference.

In addition, whilst some language has moved towards a more progressive attitude, others have turned towards the comical. The term 'gal pals' has become common parlance online in reference to how heterosexual society is often blind to lesbian relationships. An example of this in use is when, in response to a lesbian couple's wedding photographs posted online, a heterosexual individual commented how lovely it is to get married the same day as your best friend and to ask what the husbands were wearing.[311] Screenshots of this exchange flew around social media and the LGBTQ+ community still draws humour from the ridiculous assumption today.

It is impossible to list the full history of queer language in a single short article. There is an abundance of detailed histories of language within the LGBTQ+ community including Paul Bakers' *Fabulosa! The Story of Polari, Britain's Secret Gay Language*,[312] William Leap's *Language Before Stonewall: Language, Sexuality, History*[313] and Lucy Jones' *Dyke/Girl: Language and Identities in a Lesbian Group*.[314] These texts, and others, explain in detail the evolution of language within the UK and there are even more studies on international language development.

Throughout the collections of histories within this book, the terminology used by interviewees will vary due to differences in age, class status, their LGBTQ+ identity, and ethnicity. So, whilst this short article is by no means exhaustive, the intent here is to provide some context and examples of how queer language has evolved over time.

[307]Steven Dryden, 'A Short History of LGBT Rights in the UK', The British Library, accessed June 26, 2020, https://www.bl.uk/lgbtq-histories/articles/a-short-history-of-lgbt-rights-in-the-uk.

[308]André Wheeler, 'Why I'm Reclaiming the Homophobic Slur I Used to Fear', *Guardian*, accessed March 9, 2020, https://www.theguardian.com/commentisfree/2020/mar/09/lgbt-gay-men-slur-homophobia.

[309]*Pride*, dir. Matthew Warchus(Twentieth Century Fox, 2014)

[310]The surgery undertaken by some transgender individuals as part of their physical transition, commonly referencing genital surgery.

[311]Ryan Broderick, 'Someone Commented "BFF Goals" On This Photo Of A Lesbian Wedding And Everyone Lost Their Shit', *BuzzFeed News*, accessed June 26, 2020, https://www.buzzfeednews.com/article/ryanhatesthis/someone-commented-bff-goals-on-this-photo-of-a-lesbian.

[312]Paul Baker, *Fabulosa!: The Story of Polari, Britain's Secret Gay Language*. London: Reaktion Books, 2019.

[313]William L. Leap, *Language Before Stonewall: Language, Sexuality, History*. Basingstoke: Palgrave Macmillan, 2019.

[314]Lucy Jones. *Dyke/Girl: Language and Identities in a Lesbian Group*. Basingstoke: Palgrave Macmillan, 2012.

APPENDIX 2 : CARELESS WORDS AND WAYS FORWARD

Here, Laura Franco Henao includes some of the questions she has been asked when telling people that she was dating a woman. Would a straight person get asked these questions, even from people he/she is not close to?

Who is the man in your relationship?	Nobody. That is kind of the point.
Do you like men as well? /Have you been with men before?	I especially get this question from men. Why is it so important whether I have been with men or not before being with a woman? Are they implying that I am wasting my life with a woman, when I could be with a man?
When did you know?	Does it matter?
I have a lesbian friend/ cousin/neighbour…	Really?
You do not look like one.	Sorry I left my LGBTQ+ costume at home today.
Ah, so you are a lesbian?	Because I like one woman, it does not mean that I ONLY like women. Do not assume my sexuality.
So, do you feel attracted to your female friends?	Just because I like some women does not mean I like ALL women.
You are too pretty to be gay.	You are too stupid to be a person. Then, they defend themselves saying that "how can you get like this when I told you that you are pretty?". Oh sorry, I have to be grateful you said only 'ugly' women should like women so you can have the 'pretty' ones.

But who do you like more? Women or men?	Why do I have to choose? They are not mutually exclusive.
How do you have sex?	This person is usually crossing a privacy line, but also I understand that you do not know because the porn industry has portrayed for decades two women together as something that could not be further away from reality and as a product for male pleasure.

What can we do to help?

Whether you are part of the LGTBQ+ community or not, there are things as a society that we can do to be allies of the movement and help.

Listen to people's stories and do not assume you know everything. Try to stay away from uncomfortable questions. You will find out what makes people uncomfortable by really listening to them.

Raise awareness. The most important thing is to be safe but try not to stay silent if you see anybody disrespecting another person because of their sexual/romantic orientation, gender identity or expression.

Do not force people to come out. Respect their own terms and pace.

Action

Join the movement, campaigns, support your peers. Help us build safe spaces for LGTBQ+ people and bring LGBTQ+ real stories to life so it becomes part of children's education and part of the normality at work and at home. We need real visibility on TV, social media and in public spaces. Also, LGBTQ+ people are not just the rich cisgender white gay men.

APPENDIX 3: HOW TO BE A TRANS ALLY

Sydney Cardew

It's a sad fact that transphobia is still rife within British culture and society. It is found in our press, in our institutions, and in our communities. It is even present within the LGBTQ+ community; and, as the project has evidenced, there is transphobia on the Isle of Wight. Many recognise transphobia as an injustice, but don't know what to do when they witness it,so how does one act as an ally for the trans community, and how can you take some of the pressure off trans people? I can't pretend to speak for all trans people, but I can offer my own personal observations and ideas. I'll break it down into simple points. Starting off, and most importantly:

Educate yourself

With the emphasis being explicitly on the word 'yourself'. Don't expect every trans person to be your teacher. Some of us love answering questions about gender identity, dysphoria, medical transition and so on; many of us don't. The impulse to listen to trans people about their experiences is understandable, but there are plenty of trans people who have put their stories and experiences out there online, in books and other resources. Don't trust just one voice – there are strong differences of opinion among different trans people, and there is not one overarching trans experience, intersecting with all other sorts of experience. Be discerning and explore widely. Try and understand the issues and causes that are of particular importance to the trans community, and understand why they are important. Trans-positive charities like Stonewall, Mermaids and Gendered Intelligence, and activists they follow and repost on social media, are a great place to start. Once you've got that essential grounding, though language and terminology around gender and identity are often changing, you can confidently:

Challenge transphobia and ignorance

Bigotry, both active and passive, thrives when it goes unchecked. If someone makes a transphobic joke or remark, speak up and tell them why that's not okay. If someone repeats a myth about trans people, counter it! This sort of thing is very difficult to do; it makes you unpopular at parties and might get you some sighs or rolled eyes; online it might get you nasty comments, you'll probably get called a snowflake. Imagine how much worse it is for trans people to have to do this sort of thing! We are already vulnerable, and we make ourselves more vulnerable when we speak out in our own defence. On the other hand, I have often been buoyed up by seeing a person stand up and take a decent position. You are doing us all a service. But while you're at it, make sure you:

Don't get sucked into debates about our existence

Trans people are real; not only in the sense that we are real people made of flesh and blood (something which people who like to endlessly debate and challenge our existence and our rights often seem to ignore), but also in the sense that we really are who we say we are and who we strive to be. Trans women are women, trans men are men, non-binary people are non-binary. Doctors, historians, anthropologists and sociologists all agree with our own lived experiences of being transgender. These are the fundamental things that most trans people would want their allies to be absolutely certain of. It is important to realise that those who wish to debate these points, no matter what ideological position they are coming from, never wish to do so from a position of genuine intellectual curiosity. Their goal is to delegitimise and erase trans people, to reduce us to curiosities and freaks. You may feel the need to enter into these debates if something particularly egregious is said, but all the time you do so, please try and bear in mind what a trans person witnessing the discussion might think.

Now with those basic points dealt with, we can be a bit more specific with regards to the 'other letters' of the LGBTQ+ community, and their interaction with the T. Of course, there are unfortunately some people within the community who are virulently, openly transphobic, to the point of calling for the T (and often the +) to be ejected; I doubt any of those people will have picked up this book and read this far. If they have, then all I can say to them is that I sincerely hope they come to look back on their past attitudes with regret. Here are some more general points for those who do not consciously hold negative attitudes towards trans people. First:

Stop making the discussion about you

One of the most common topics of discussion about trans people that I have personally seen among cis LGB+ folks is the thorny question of which of us they'd be ok having sex with, and in what circumstances. Often conditions are discussed; how long must we have been on hormones? How should our genitals be configured? Not only is this sort of discussion deeply rude, objectifying and normally totally irrelevant, it's also frankly rather presumptuous. If someone holds my womanhood to be conditional in any way, then it is not they who are going to be deciding if they get to have sex with me, no matter what their thoughts on the matter. Which brings us to a broader point:

Just stop talking about our genitals

Every time a trans person has a conversation about being trans, they dread the looming question "Have you had ... The Surgery?". There are very few times when it is actually appropriate to ask this question, especially to someone you've just met; it reduces trans people to sexual objects, and it's just rather rude. Would you walk up to a cis woman you'd met at a party and ask her what her vulva looked like? I generally wouldn't, and I've been to some pretty wild parties! This principle really extends to all questions about the medical side of transition. Though this side of things is very important to many people's transitions, few people ultimately want to have their gender identity discussed as if they were being treated for piles or migraines. If a trans person is interested in having that sort of conversation with you, then let them initiate it. There are surely some of us ready and eager to talk on the topic, often at great length, but it's safest to assume that it's something that any individual trans person is thoroughly sick of. We tend to have very complex relationships with our bodies, and it can be very painful for some trans people to be forced to dwell on certain topics. On top of this, questions like "are you on hormones?", as well as having the potential to be read as a veiled barb about someone's appearance, carry an unfortunate implication. Many people view trans people who are taking hormones as more 'legitimate' or 'valid' in some way than those who are not. This is not the case and remember that acquiring hormones can be a long, gruelling and tortuous process in the UK.

Stop demanding we prove ourselves

Do not indulge in the temptation to judge trans people on how 'well' they are transitioning, on what steps they have taken, on whether they live 'full time' in their preferred gender, on their appearance, or in any other way. Do not make your understanding of someone contingent upon your perception, when that conflicts with their inner truth. If you find it difficult to see someone as what they tell you they are, then if you consider yourself to be an ally, the burden is on your shoulders to do the hard work. Presenting can be exhausting for many trans people for various reasons; some trans women find shaving their faces difficult or painful, some trans men have trouble wearing binders. Sometimes people just want a break, or sometimes perhaps they are making a deliberate statement. Perhaps most importantly, in an LGBTQ+ context, allow trans people to express their gender (or lack of it) however they wish. Remember perhaps how you yourself have felt being forced into certain behaviours and roles that do not fit you. Let trans women be butch, let trans men be camp and let non-binary people be whatever they understand themselves to be. Above all:

Believe us
And please
Be kind to us
As you would be with anyone. And remember:

We're all in this together

The phrase 'trans rights are human rights' is more than just a slogan. When cultural prejudice is stirred up against trans people, or even worse, laws are formulated which discriminate against us, it is not only trans people who suffer. In the United States, gender non-conforming women (many of them lesbians) have found themselves attacked by vigilantes or dragged by security from toilet facilities in the wake of 'bathroom panics'. It goes more broadly though; behind much of the anti-trans sentiment circulating today lurks the influence of extremist religious groups, who see trans people as the first step in their fight back against the rights of LGBTQ+ people, and ultimately women. The political struggle of trans people, after all, is at its core a struggle for self-determination and bodily autonomy, a struggle which affects an awful lot of cisgender people as well.

CONTRIBUTORS

This book is a reflection of the generosity and enthusiasm of many contributors who produced research articles, interviews, stories and poems.

We are crediting all those who were happy to be named. Not all contributions have been credited, as some were made on the condition that the authors remained anonymous. We are indebted to all.

David E. Bennett

A gay and genderqueer librarian working at the University of Portsmouth Library with a passion for social justice, celebrating the diverse exuberance of life, challenging harmful myths and encouraging others to embrace the world just beyond their comfort zone. When not promoting library services, diversity and inclusion at work, David enjoys writing professional magazine articles and is working to complete a Senior Leaders' Degree Apprenticeship. He maintains the website for the CLAUD (Consortium that supports university libraries) to make their services more inclusive and accessible, chairs #uklibchat debates among librarians on Twitter, and blogs (very) occasionally on topics of professional interest. In his spare time, he seeks out interesting local LGBTQ+ charities to support, plays occasional tabletop roleplay games, is learning to play the piano, and struggles to keep fit by practising martial arts.

John Brownscombe

John is a gay man born on the Isle of Wight in the late 1960s, leaving for University in the late 1980s where he met his partner, now husband. They worked in London until the mid 1990s then moved to the Island. Having never really been into the 'scene', living on the Isle of Wight never felt limiting. In his early career there was an assumption that John was straight, only close friends and family knew otherwise. As society's attitudes and progressive legislation led to greater equality, John found it easier to be authentic without fear of rejection or prejudice.

Changes in 2016 internationally and nationally indicated a shift back to a society of less tolerance and increasing levels of prejudice and hate. John was determined to be more visible and active and became one of the founding members of Isle of Wight Pride and recently Trustee for the Isle of Wight Pride charity. As an Island lad, John forever remembers the honour of leading the IW Pride 2018 parade, the cheering, waving crowds in the packed Union Street, Ryde. It was a momentous and deeply moving occasion, one that as a young boy on this rural island, John would never in his wildest dreams have imagined possible.

Sydney Cardew

Sydney was born in 1987 and grew up in the small village of Rookley on the Isle of Wight, before moving to the nearby town of Newport at the age of twelve. She has lived on the Island most of her life, apart from a stint in Bournemouth to attend university, where she studied Fine Art. She met the love of her life while she was back on the Island finishing her master's degree, and they were subsequently married in 2016. Though assigned male at birth, Sydney wrestled with her gender identity for much of her life, and finally came out and began living openly as a woman in 2019, grateful for the support of her friends and family. She is proud to be trans and identifies as a lesbian.

She tries to make ends meet through working in part-time jobs whilst pursuing her passions as a freelance illustrator, poet and game designer. Her interests include amateur theatre, live action roleplay, board games, running, coffee and morris dancing.

Elaine Chambers

Elaine joined the Army in 1982, aged 21, as a student nurse. After qualifying as a staff nurse, she obtained a commission, becoming a junior sister in the rank of lieutenant. Her ordeal began in 1987, after rumours about her sexuality reached the military police. After being forced to resign, she met Robert Ely, who had been discharged from the Parachute Regiment after nearly 20 years' service, and they founded Rank Outsiders, a campaign and support group, in 1991.

Since leaving the Army, Elaine initially struggled to find work that could rival the prospects and camaraderie of her Army career – she has had nearly 20 different jobs, mostly in nursing but also including stints at Eurostar, as a security guard at the Tower of London and briefly as a tree climbing instructor. She is now working as a medical administrator for a GP practice, following a momentous decision to take her name off the nursing register after her parents suffered serious ill health. She lives on the Isle of Wight.

Wendy Cooper

Wendy is a deep thinker, an explorer of the mind. She loves people and socialising as much as she loves spending time alone, by the river or high up on the Tennyson Trail. She was drawn to the project because of her conviction that history should reflect the views of the everyday person. "I found the training in oral history enlightening and inspirational." Wendy has lived on the Island since her teenage years and is a Ventnor person at heart. Interests include permaculture, writing and music. "It has been a joy to meet all the participants in the project and to be a small part of what is clearly a missing record of the lives of LGBTQ+ people on the Island." Wendy brought up two sons, and now lives in Shanklin.

Caroline Diamond

Caroline has lived on the Isle of Wight for 21 years. She is a lesbian who came out in 2012. She was born in Manchester and her childhood was spent travelling all over the world in Bahrain, Hong Kong and Germany, and across the UK, moving every two and a half years due to her father's Army career. Caroline has three grown-up children and dedicated much of the 1990s to bringing them up. She is curious about people and local life and she worked for the *Isle of Wight County Press* as a correspondent for ten years and as a freelance writer for publications including the *Beacon* and *Island Life*. Recently Caroline has been keen to support LGBTQI+ people, working as a Youth Work Assistant for BreakOut Youth, and she is always looking for opportunities to make the Isle of Wight a diverse and inclusive place to be.

Alan Figueiredo-Stow

Alan lives in Shanklin with his husband and works full time for the Isle of Wight council. Prior to this, he worked with autistic children and also taught English as a foreign language. This inspired him to start exploring the use of language, which then led him to try out different writing styles and genres, where he is currently enjoying this pastime, and has been known to lend advice with proofreading when called upon.

These days also enjoying any free time with Pudsey, their rescue dog, who has introduced a wonderful sense of fun with walking, playing and watching this pup's antics. Alan also has a grown-up daughter, who grew up on the island but now lives on the mainland working as a veterinary nurse; they get to see each other wherever possible and have been known to take the opportunity to go off camping to enjoy our beautiful island further. Some of his other interests when not working include gardening and growing his own vegetables and herbs, and generally being out amongst nature. Baking is also a favourite pastime for Alan, and since lockdown he has attempted to master the art of 'growing' a decent sourdough starter to make bread, having some success, but not always succeeding in this endeavour though. Alan is a passionate advocate for LGBTQ+ equality, in fact equality full stop.

Franko Figueiredo-Stow

Franko is a gay and genderqueer artist living with his husband on the Isle of Wight. Franko is the co-founder and artistic director of StoneCrabs Theatre Company and started his career as an actor and writer. He has trained as an actor in Brazil and the UK, and has a Masters in Theatre Practices from Rose Bruford College. Franko has worked as an actor and stage director at Gamboa, Vila Velha and Castro Alves Theatre in Brazil (Bahia) and the Gate Theatre, Royal Court and Young Vic in the UK (London). At the age of seventeen, he won the Raimundo Correia award for poetry which saw his poems being professionally published. He has written and translated plays, has contributed articles to the *Guardian* and used to be a regular contributor to the *Brasil Observer* newspaper.

Robin Ford

Robin was born on the Isle of Wight in 1942, and identifies himself as a queer person. At sixteen years old he joined the Young Conservatives on the Island only to be chucked out for having joined the CND campaign. Later he became a councillor, a Mayor and a high school teacher in Cowes. Robin started writing in his mid-fifties after a long period of mental illness which, once settled, seemed to 'unfreeze' the part of his mind inclined to poetry. Robin is immensely influenced by the countryside of the Isle of Wight.

Melissa Gilmore

Melissa is a non-binary person from the Isle of Wight who identifies as queer and bisexual. Born in Scotland to an English mother and an American father, they moved to Ascot in 1992 before moving to the Island in 1998. They stayed on the Island until 2008 when they left for the University of Bath, where they studied English Literature and Creative Writing. After graduation, they returned to the Island for a few years ahead of relocating to London in 2014, where they worked as an Operations Executive and Content Copywriter.

Returning to the Isle of Wight in 2018, they began volunteering with Out On An Island in June 2019 and have contributed content to both this book and the project's social media channels. They carried out a number of oral history interviews, as well as being interviewed for the project themselves. Melissa now works as an admin assistant for StoneCrabs Theatre. In their spare time, they enjoy reading, amateur knitting and watching ice hockey. Their party trick is telling obscure animal facts and over the years they have also volunteered at Quarr Abbey, the Isle of Wight Bat Hospital and Battersea Dogs and Cats Home.

Bronwyn Hamilton-Brown

Following a career in music, noted as 'the Rock Goddess', famed for throwing guitars from high-rise buildings and debauched shenanigans with licentious young babes, Bronwyn has now retired, exhausted. But seriously, having worked in education for many years Bronwyn now lives a life of (mostly) leisure on the beautiful island. However, as a relentless traveller, Bronwyn is often to be seen on different continents discovering the delights of beaches and cities.

Prior to finishing her working life, Bronwyn was a teacher, a headteacher, and an inspector and advisor, steering schools to better performance and outcomes. Interests include reading, particularly LGBTQ literature, poetry, history and art. Visiting art galleries around the world has been, and continues to be, an activity that excites and exhilarates. Lately, she's often covered in mud, digging for England at her new allotment!

Laura Franco Henao

Laura has been living on the Isle of Wight since September 2018. In her written work you will find out how Laura became comfortable to have the confidence to write and share her story and why she did it. Laura comes from Spain and is an economist. She is passionate about social and environmental issues, especially inequality, discrimination, climate change, and human rights. She is interested in understanding how our economic system and mindset have led us to dramatically overshoot our planet's environmental boundaries and to accumulate wealth in the hands of a few while millions of people cannot still meet their basic needs. She hopes to contribute to a different way of thinking that will lead us to build a just, thriving and inclusive world for future generations.

Margaret Montgomerie

Margaret is a LOL (late onset lesbian), not finding Sapphic love until she moved to the (then) Sheffield Dyke enclave of Meersbrook in her late thirties. There really was something in the water, Margaret and two of her friends had their heads turned, not by each other, but by other women loving women. After that she embraced the wholemeal world of lesbian politics (Sheffield Women's Cultural Club) and the intoxicating world of LGBTQ club, dance and performance nights. However a lasting relationship developed following the most unlikely circumstances – a restructuring meeting at work. Early in her relationship with Anne the pair made the decision to take redundancy and explore a future together.

Nineteen years later the pair are still on their adventure. The latest stage of which has seen them gradually move south, from Sheffield to Leicester and now to the Isle of Wight, Anne starting a new job at Portsmouth University and Margaret taking early retirement. Margaret spends her time trying to grow a gorgeous garden at home and volunteering for the National Trust in the truly beautiful garden of Mottistone Manor.

Jared M.D. Mustafa-Holzapfel

Jared is a PhD candidate at the University of Southampton, working towards his English Literature thesis in 'Queerness in Anglophone Arab Literature of the Twenty-First Century'. He completed his Bachelors in English (2013) and Masters in Twenty-First Century Literature (2017) at the University of Southampton. Born and raised on the Isle of Wight, he left the Island in 2010 to begin his studies. Jared identifies as a queer transgender man, and lives on the mainland with his husband, dog, house rabbit, and other critters.

Anne-Kathrin Reck

A mainlander who started out living in big cities which she describes as essential for survival at that stage in her life, Anne-Kathrin is originally from Germany. She studied and spent seven years in Leipzig then moved to the UK thirty years ago to yet another big city, Manchester.

Why England? Because she grew up behind the Iron Curtain and got bored with her PhD, spotted a job advert near the lift in the high-rise she worked in et voilà! In hindsight Anne-Kathrin feels she spent slightly too much time in the East Midlands, but she thanks Derby and Leicester, as there was enough there to entertain at that time, not least in footballing terms and finding historic traces under a car park, before she moved south back to her wife's roots.

Anne-Kathrin's compromise was always to move to a place with more than two platforms at its main station. Now she embraces Island life and says: 'Yes, life can be gay here, a growing gay community waving flags, celebrating life, dancing, performing, book discussing, interested in other people's history.' Anne-Kathrin likes it here and she says she has found a new home.

Charlotte Reynolds

Charlotte was born on the Island and grew up here. After a gap year teaching in Vietnam, and travelling in South-East Asia, she studied Geography at University, becoming interested in cultural and historical geography, and how places change over time. Following a year teaching English in Japan, she undertook a Masters in Cities and Cultures, before commencing a career in Town Planning. After further studies, in Historic Building Conservation, she worked as a Conservation Officer in local authorities, including the New

Town of Milton Keynes, and the historic city of Oxford. She then joined the Heritage at Risk team at Historic England, encouraging the repair of historic buildings across the East Midlands.

In 2017 Charlotte returned home to the Island, experiencing another side of the heritage world by volunteering at Carisbrooke Castle Museum, and volunteering and then working for the National Trust at Newtown Old Town Hall. There she became fascinated by the story of the Ferguson's Gang, shared as part of this project.

She enjoys Morris dancing, and since being back by the coast, has become a keen year-round sea swimmer. She has also found renewed enthusiasm for making art, enjoying painting and pottery.

Maureen Sullivan

Maureen Sullivan moved to the Island twenty years ago with her husband and three children, one of whom is trans, and all of whom are now adults living happily on the mainland. After a career in teaching she is semi-retired and enjoying life, involving herself in amateur theatre and music. She volunteered to be part of the Out On An Island project because she is very interested in history, stories and people, and believes that social history should chronicle the lives of everyone alive at the time. She has thoroughly enjoyed learning more about the history of this lovely island and the people on it.

Charlotte X

Charlotte identifies as a gay woman. She was born on the Island then left at eighteen to go to university to study Psychology. She returned to the Island when she was 32, to be closer to her family as she was expecting her first child. Charlotte says she is married in the eyes of The Lord but not law, as same sex marriage was not legal and she was the first in Dorset to have her Civil Partnership in a Church. Charlotte has a job she loves in health care. She describes herself as "a Mummy to two wonderful children" and has one amazing lady who she says "totally gets her".

Dr Clifford Williams

Clifford Williams grew up as a gay teenager in south London in the 1970s. He attended what was the first officially registered gay youth group in the country. He has recently completed a history of that group, in a book called *Courage To Be: Organised Gay Youth In England 1970-1990*. Williams is currently working on a book examining the policing of gay and bisexual men 1950–2010. His previous books include *A History of Women Policing Hampshire and the Isle of Wight 1915–2016* and *111 Years of Policing Winchester*. Although not an islander, Williams has family roots in Cowes. He studied Social Anthropology and History at SOAS, Criminology at Cambridge and completed a PhD at the University of Bradford. From 2017–19, Williams was a volunteer with a young persons' LGBT+ history project which examined Hampshire's queer history. He produced a booklet on the county's LGBT history as a result, *A Queer A-Z of Hampshire*. The second edition of this booklet is now out of print. Although identifying as a bisexual man, Williams has never been keen on labels and stereotypes.

Mark Woolford

Mark grew up in the town of Godalming in Surrey. A gay member of the LGBTQ+ community, he identifies as male. At the age of 23 he moved to Brighton where he was delighted to finally meet other gay men and be honest with himself and others about who he is. Whilst in Brighton he became involved with volunteering for Allsorts Youth Project that ran a drop-in for LBGTQ+ youth in the area, that he enjoyed being part of. Mark moved to the Isle of Wight in 2017 and recently became a member of the Out On An Island team as he was interested in the work that they carry out and he also thought it would be a good way of meeting other members of the community.

He said he was "delighted to be asked to write a chapter for this book documenting the history of the Island's LGBTQ+ community and found researching and writing up the subject to be a fascinating and rewarding exercise".

BIBLIOGRAPHY

Preface

Ballard, Esme and John Medland. The Isle of Wight History Centre, online resource for news and links to the Island's past, from prehistory to recent times 2013. https://www.iwhistory.org.uk/heritageorganisations/ accessed 18 January 2021.

Isle of Wight Council, Equality & Diversity Fact Sheet Jan 2019.

Pagnuco, Tanja. *Biafra to England*. London: StoneCrabs Theatre Co., 2011.

Out On An Island

Pepper Creative, 'Safeguarding the Future of the Island's Finest Landscapes', accessed July 10, 2020, https://www.wightaonb.org.uk/

JSNA – Demographics and Population, 'JSNA – Demographics and Population – Census 2011', accessed July 10, 2020, https://www.iow.gov.uk/Council/transparency/Our-Community1/JSNA-Demographics-and-population/Census-2011.

LGBTQ+ Role Models, where are we now?

Bartlett, M., 'Outsized Role Models Take a Queer Turn', *Metro*: media & education magazine. v 172 (2012).

Bird, Jason D.P., Lisa Kuhns, and Robert Garofalo. 'The Impact of Role Models on Health Outcomes for Lesbian, Gay, Bisexual, and Transgender Youth', *Journal of Adolescent Health* 50, no. 4 (2012): 353–57. https://doi.org/10.1016/j.jadohealth.2011.08.006.

Bradley, K., 'Gay History Teaching Generates Debate', *Evening Standard*, October 28.

Butchart-Kelly, T. 'Gay Sportsmen Are Good Role Models', *Evening Standard*, August 18, 2015.

Cook, Jennifer R., Sharon S. Rostosky, and Ellen D. Riggle, 'Gender Role Models in Fictional Novels for Emerging Adult Lesbians', *Journal of Lesbian*

Studies 17, no. 2 (2013): 150–66. https://doi.org/10.1080/10894160.2012.691416.

Goldthorp, Jacqueline D. 'Can Scottish Public Library Services Claim They Are Socially Inclusive of All Minority Groups When Lesbian Fiction Is Still so Inaccessible?' *Journal of Librarianship and Information Science* 39, no. 4 (2007): 234–48. https://doi.org/10.1177/0961000607083215.

Gomez, Gabriel, Gerri Spinella, Victor Salvo, and Owen Keehnen. 'The Legacy Project: Connecting Museum Advocacy to Gay, Lesbian, Bisexual, and Transgender (GLBT) Role Models', *Journal of Museum Education* 38, no. 2 (2013): 193–206. https://doi.org/10.1080/10598650.2013.11510770.

Gomillion, Sarah C., and Traci A. Giuliano. 'The Influence of Media Role Models on Gay, Lesbian, and Bisexual Identity', *Journal of Homosexuality* 58, no. 3 (2011): 330–54. https://doi.org/10.1080/00918369.2011.546729.

Hudson, David. 'The Gay Man Who Bombed a Building and Deserves to Be Celebrated as a Hero', *Gay Star News*, September 24, 2018, https://www.gaystarnews.com/article/gay-willem-arondeus-building/.

Hymowitz, C., J. Kaplan, C. Giammona and T. Giles. 'Apple's CEO Comes Out, Could Fill Role Model Void for LGBT Workers', *HR Focus*, 91(12), 2014:12-13.

Kramer, L. 'Yesterday, Today and Tomorrow', *Advocate*, March 30, 1999. 782.

'LGBT Travel Leaders Urged to Become "Role Models"', *Travel Trade Gazette UK & Ireland*, 3119. October 16, 2014, 4.

Matsuno, Emmie, and Tania Israel. 'Psychological Interventions Promoting Resilience Among Transgender Individuals: Transgender Resilience Intervention Model (TRIM)', *The Counseling Psychologist* 46, no. 5 (2018): 632–55. https://doi.org/10.1177/0011000018787261.

Moss, Stephen. '"He Was a Gay Guy Who Won": Why I Wrote a Play about Ice-Skating Genius John Curry', *Guardian*, Guardian News and Media, August 21, 2017. https://www.theguardian.com/stage/2017/aug/21/looking-for-john-curry-olympics-tony-timberlake-assembly-hall-edinburgh-festival.

Nguyen, Jimmy. 'Why We Need More LGBT Minority Role Models', *The Root*, January 12, 2017. https://www.theroot.com/why-we-need-more-lgbt-minority-role-models-1790894443.

Riddle, D. I. 'Relating to Children: Gays as Role Models', *Journal of Social Issues* 34, no. 3 (1978): pp. 38-58, https://doi.org/10.1111/j.1540-4560.1978.tb02613.x.

Sadowski, Michael, Stephen Chow, and Constance P. Scanlon. 'Meeting the Needs of LGBTQ Youth: A "Relational Assets" Approach', *Journal of LGBT Youth* 6, no. 2-3 (2009): 174–98. https://doi.org/10.1080/19361650903013493.

Spitko, E. G. E., 'A Reform Agenda Premised Upon the Reciprocal Relationship Between Anti-lgbt Bias in Role Model Occupations and the Bullying of LGBT Youth', *Connecticut Law Review,* 48(1), (2015): 71-117.

Health

Bachman, Chaka L., and Becca Gooch. 'LGBT in Britain – Health', Stonewall, April 17, 2019. https://www.stonewall.org.uk/lgbt-britain-health.

Battle, Daniels, Pastrana, Turner, and Espinoza. 'Never Too Old To Feel Good: Happiness and Health among a National Sample of Older Black Gay Men', *Spectrum: A Journal on Black Men 2*, no. 1 (2013): 1. https://doi.org/10.2979/spectrum.2.1.1.

'Callers Keep Gay Switchboard Busy', *Isle of Wight County Press*, May 10, 1996, 44.

'Campaign to Halt Spread of Aids', *Isle of Wight County Press*, November 26, 1993, sec. Healthwatch, 56.

The Letters of Oscar Wilde, edited by Rupert Hart-Davis. Pp. Xxv, 958. London: Rupert Hart-Davis. 1962. 84s.

Irish Historical Studies 13, no. 51 (1963): 282–84. https://doi.org/10.1017/s0021121400008786.

Equalities Office, Government. 'National LGBT Survey Research Report', www.gov.uk, July 23, 2017. https://www.gov.uk/government/consultations/national-lgbt-survey.

Felman, Adam. 'What Is Health?: Defining and Preserving Good Health', *Medical News Today*, MediLexicon International. Accessed March 3, 2021. https://www.medicalnewstoday.com/articles/150999#what_is_health.

Garretson, Jeremiah J. *The Path to Gay Rights: How Activism and Coming Out Changed Public Opinion*. New York: NYU Press, 2018. 69-95.

Gay Guide, Isle of Wight, 'www.iowgayguide.org.uk – Redirection Service Provided by Easyspace'. www.iowgayguide.org.uk – redirection service provided by Easyspace, accessed September 20, 2020, https://web.archive.org/web/20050307053351/http://www.iowgayguide.org.uk/.

'Helpline for Gay Gets Health Authority Cash', *Isle of Wight County Press*, November 13, 1992, 16.

Leon, Alexander. 'LGBT People Are Prone to Mental Illness. It's a Truth We Shouldn't Shy Away From', *Guardian*. Guardian News and Media, May 12, 2017. https://www.theguardian.com/commentisfree/2017/may/12/lgbt-mental-health-sexuality-gender-identity.

Marriott, Kay. *Speaking Out, Gay Men and Lesbians on the Isle of Wight Write About their Lives and Early Experiences*. Isle of Wight: Delta Press,1997, 5.

Metcalf, Hilary, and Nathan Hudson-Sharp, 'Inequality among Lesbian, Gay Bisexual and Transgender Groups in the UK: a Review of Evidence', National Institute of Economic and Social Research, May 12, 2017. https://www.niesr.ac.uk/publications/inequality-among-lesbian-gay-bisexual-and-transgender-groups-uk-review-evidence.

National Archives. 'The Passing of the 1967 Sexual Offences Act'. The National Archives blog. The National Archives, July 24, 2017. https://blog.nationalarchives.gov.uk/sexual-offences-act/.

Partridge, Ralph. *Broadmoor: A History of Criminal Lunacy and Its Problems*. London: Chatton & Windus, 1953. Pp. 272.

Journal of Mental Science 100, no. 418 (1954): 271–72. https://doi.org/10.1192/bjp.100.418.271-c.

Wilde, Oscar. *The Letters of Oscar Wilde*, edited by Rupert Hart-Davis. London: Rupert Hart Davis, 1962.

Suicide

Downs, Alan. *The Velvet Rage: Overcoming the Pain of Growing up Gay in a Straight Man's World*. Cambridge, MA: Da Capo Life Long, 2012.

'Former Newsreader's Partner Took Own Life', *Isle of Wight County Press*, November 1, 2013, sec. News, 11.

Gunness, Chris, *The Art of Change with Stephen Fry – Episode 1*. Barbican, accessed September 22, 2020. https://www.barbican.org.uk/read-watch-listen/the-art-of-change-with-stephen-fry-episode-1.

Hunte, Ben. 'Lockdown: Suicide Fears Soar in LGBT Community', *BBC News* (BBC, July 2, 2020), https://www.bbc.co.uk/news/health-53223765.

Mitchell, Ben. 'Man Leapt Overboard from Ferry', *Isle of Wight County Press*, February 1, 2019, 40.

Molyneux, Peter. *NHS Choices*. NHS, accessed March 3, 2021. https://www.england.nhs.uk/blog/why-identity-matters/.

Todd, Matthew. *Straight Jacket: Overcoming Society's Legacy of Gay Shame*. London: Black Swan, 2018.

LGBTQ+ People in the County Press

Wight, Rev. Hugh, 'Acts of perversion world away from homosexuality', *Isle of Wight County Press*, February 4, 1994, 8

Coming Out

Ackroyd, Peter. *Queer City: Gay London from the Romans to the Present Day*. New York: Abrams Press, 2018, 196.

Akuson, Richard. 'Opinion: "This Is Quite Gay!"', *New York Times*, July 6, 2019. https://www.nytimes.com/2019/07/06/opinion/sunday/social-media-homophobia.html.

Beachy, Robert. *Gay Berlin: Birthplace of a Modern Identity*. New York: Alfred A. Knopf, 2014, 51.

Bérubé, Allan. *Coming Out Under Fire: The History of Gay Men and Women in World War II*. Chapel Hill: UNC Press, 2010, 98.

Brabaw, Kasandra. 'What We Mean When We Talk About Coming Out (Of The Closet)', *Refinery29*. Vice Media Group, October 12, 2018. https://www.refinery29.com/en-ca/2018/10/213864/coming-out-meaning-history-origin.

Braidwood, Ella. '"Gay plague": The vile, horrific and inhumane way the media reported the AIDS crisis', *PinkNews*, November 30, 2018. https://www.pinknews.co.uk/2018/11/30/world-aids-day-1980s-headlines-tabloids/.

Burns, Christine. *Trans Britain: Our Journey from the Shadows.* London: Unbound, 2018, 30.

Carr, Sarah and Helen Spandler. 'Hidden from History? A Brief Modern History of the Psychiatric "Treatment" of Lesbian and Bisexual Women in England'. Lancet Psychiatry, *Insight* 6, no. 4 (2019). 289-290.

Chauncey, George. *Gay New York: Gender, Urban Culture, And The Making Of The Gay Male World, 1890-1940.* New York: Basic Books, 1994, 7.

Collins, Jason. 'Why NBA Center Jason Collins Is Coming out Now', *Sports Illustrated*, April 29, 2013. https://www.si.com/more-sports/2013/04/29/jason-collins-gay-nba-player.

CPS. 'Hate crime'. https://www.cps.gov.uk/crime-info/hate-crime.

David, Hugh. *On Queer Street: A Social History of British Homosexuality 1895-1995.* London: HarperCollins, 1997, 130.

Demir, Ezgi. '"Love is Love": Queerness and Respectability Politics.' *The Goose Quill,* May 1, 2019. https://medium.com/the-goose-quill/love-is-love-queerness-and-respectability-politics-e57f8777f2

Doder, Dusko. 'Of Moles and Men', *The Nation,* June 29, 2015. https://www.thenation.com/article/archive/moles-and-men/.

'Dr. Hart Explains Change to Male Attire', *Albany Daily Democrat* (No. 259). 26 March 1918. 1.

Jennings, Rebecca. 'The Most Uninhibited Party They'd Ever Been To: The Postwar Encounter between Psychiatry and the British Lesbian, 1945–1971', *Journal of British Studies* 47, no. 4 (2008). 894.

Kennedy, Hubert. *Karl Heinrich Ulrichs: Pioneer of the Modern Gay Movement.* Concord, CA: Peremptory Publications, 2012, 70.

Licata, Salvatore and Petersen, Robert P. *The Gay Past: A Collection of Historical Essays.* New York: Routledge. 106–107.

Milk, Harvey. 'That's What America Is'. Speech, San Francisco Gay Freedom Day Parade, San Francisco, June 25, 1978.

Shilts, Randy. *And The Band Played On: 20th Anniversary Edition.* New York: St. Martin's Griffin, 2007.

Sigusch, Volkmar and Karl Heinrich Ulrichs. *Der erste Schwule der Weltgeschichte.* Hamburg: Männerschwarm, 2000.

Stack, Liam. 'Overlooked No More: Karl Heinrich Ulrichs, Pioneering Gay Activist', *New York Times*, July 1, 2020. https://www.nytimes.com/2020/07/01/obituaries/karl-heinrich-ulrichs-overlooked.html.

Stewart, Philippa H. 'UK LGBT Hate Crimes Stats Make Shocking Reading', *Human Rights Watch*, October 23, 2019. https://www.hrw.org/news/2019/10/23/uk-lgbt-hate-crimes-stats-make-shocking-reading.

Stonewall. 'Key Dates for Lesbian, Gay, Bi and Trans Equality'. Stonewall, August 25, 2020. https://www.stonewall.org.uk/about-us/key-dates-lesbian-gay-bi-and-trans-equality/.

Summerskill, Clare. *Gateway to Heaven: Fifty Years of Lesbian and Gay Oral History.* London: Tollington Press, 2013, 114-115.

Ulrichs, Karl Heinrich. *Araxes: A Call to Free the Nature of the Urning from Penal Law*, trans. Michael Lombardi-Nash. New York: Urania Manuscripts, 2019, 11-14.

Marching with Pride

Hofton, Charlotte."Pride Parade - Do a Deal?," *Isle of Wight County Press*, December 9, 2016.

Peck, Tom. 'Tory MP Standing down after Telling Students Homosexuality is "Dangerous to Society"', *Independent.* Independent Digital News and Media, April 28, 2017. https://www.independent.co.uk/news/uk/politics/andrew-turner-tory-mp-stand-down-calling-homosexuality-danger-society-a7708671.html.

Going Out. How or where would you meet other LGBTQ+ people on the Isle of Wight?

Ross, Alice. 'Out in the Country – Rural Hotspots Found as Gay Population Mapped', *Guardian* (Guardian News and Media, April 19, 2017), https://www.theguardian.com/world/2017/apr/19/out-in-the-country-rural-hotspots-found-as-gay-population-mapped.

WightOUT 'Easter Bonnets at the Plough'. *WightOUT News*, May 2003, 2.

WightOUT Helpline, 'Welcome to the Beautiful Isle of Wight', www.iowgayguide.org.uk via Internet Archive Wayback Machine, accessed July

15, 2020, https://web.archive.org/web/20050307053351/http://www.iowgayguide.org.uk/.

Overcoming Criminalisation

Richard Davenport-Hines, Sex, Death and Punishment. Attitudes to Sex and Sexuality in Britain since the Renaissance, London, Collins 1990, XV + 439. *Nuncius* 5, no. 2 (1990): 377–79. https://doi.org/10.1163/182539190x00589.

Bachman, Chaka L., and Becca Gooch. 'LGBT in Britain – Health', Stonewall, April 17, 2019. https://www.stonewall.org.uk/lgbt-britain-health.

BBC. 'UK Military Gay Ban Illegal', *BBC News*, September 27, 1999. http://news.bbc.co.uk/1/hi/uk/458625.stm.

British Newspaper Archives, 'The Obscenity Trial of Miss Radclyffe Hall's novel, "The Well of Loneliness"', 16 November 1928 in Headlines from History, 2013. https://blog.britishnewspaperarchive.co.uk/2013/11/15/the-obscenity-trial-of-miss-radclyffe-halls-novel-the-well-of-loneliness-16-november-1928/?ds_kid=39700045269534934&gclid=Cj0KCQjw6uT4BRD5ARIsADwJQ1--vw-hwcuz2SQFOccos1mS4qgp6x9KxhREzI5Hqu_poP8xvYFjUn8aAolSEALw_wcB&gclsrc=aw.ds accessed 23 July 2020

Chambers, Elaine. *This Queer Angel*. London: Unbound, 2019.

Davenport-Hines R. *Sex, Death and Punishment. Attitudes to Sex and Sexuality in Britain since the Renaissance.* London: Collins, 1990.

Department for Constitutional Affairs Online Archives. Transsexual people in People's rights. https://web.archive.org/web/20080511211217/http://www.dca.gov.uk/constitution/transsex/policy.htm accessed 23 July 2020.

Eskridge, William N. *Gaylaw: Challenging the Apartheid of the Closet.* Cambridge, MA: Harvard University Press, 1999, 161

Fone, Byrne R. S. *Homophobia: A History.* New York: Picador, 2001.

Great Britain. UK Government. John Frederick Wolfenden Wolfenden of Westcott, introduction by Karl A. Menninger. 'The Wolfenden Report: Report of the Committee on Homosexual Offences and Prostitution'. New York: Stein and Day, 1963.

Hopkins, Timothy, 'I Was Surprised', *The Isle of Wight County Press*, August 28, 1976, sec. Letters to the editor.

Iglikowski-Broad, Vicky. 'The Passing of the 1967 Sexual Offences Act', *The National Archives blog.* July 24, 2017. https://blog.nationalarchives.gov.uk/sexual-offences-act/.

Isle of Wight County Press, 'Big Costs for Ex-Officer in Gay Test Case', June 9, 1995.

Isle of Wight County Press. 'Compensation Order over Attack', February 1, 2008, sec. Local News.

Isle of Wight County Press, 'Andrew Turner Steps down as Isle of Wight MP after Outcry over Alleged Homosexuality Comments', March 22, 2018. https://www.countypress.co.uk/news/16107600.andrew-turner-steps-down-as-isle-of-wight-mp-after-outcry-over-alleged-homosexuality-comments/.

Isle of Wight County Press, 'Ryde Waiter Might Be Jailed for Attack on Gay Man', October 20, 2000, sec. Local News.

Internet History Sourcebooks. Accessed July 23, 2020. https://sourcebooks.fordham.edu/ancient/1075assyriancode.asp.

Katz, Steven T. *The Holocaust in Historical Context.* New York: Oxford University Press, 1994.

Levack, Brian P. *The Witch-Hunt in Early Modern Europe.* London: Routledge, 2016.

The National Archives. Gender Recognition Act 2004. https://www.legislation.gov.uk/ukpga/2004/7/contents accessed 23 July 2020.

Norton-Taylor, Richard. 'Forces Ban on Gays Is Lifted', *Guardian,* Guardian News and Media, January 13, 2000. https://www.theguardian.com/uk/2000/jan/13/richardnortontaylor.

Samek, Alyssa A. 2016. 'Violence and Identity Politics: 1970s Lesbian-Feminist Discourse and Robin Morgan's 1973 West Coast Lesbian Conference Keynote Address', *Communication and Critical/Cultural Studies,* 13:3, 232-249. https://doi.org/10.1080/14791420.2015.1127400.

Shipman, Tim. 'Boris Johnson Scraps Plan to Make Gender Change Easier', News, *Sunday Times,* June 14, 2020. https://www.thetimes.co.uk/article/boris-johnson-scraps-plan-to-make-gender-change-easier-zs6lqfls0.

Tatchell, Peter. 'Beyond Equality: Why Equal Rights Are Not Enough'. Peter Tatchell Foundation, January 9, 2018. https://www.

petertatchellfoundation.org/beyond-equality-why-equal-rights-are-not-enough/.

Troman, Kristen, 'Two Decades plus of Safer LGBT+ Communities in Hampshire and the Isle of Wight', *Fyne Times,* May 20, 2019. https://www.fyne.co.uk/two-decades-plus-of-safer-lgbt-communities-in-hampshire-and-the-isle-of-wight/.

Weeks, Jeffrey. *Coming Out: Homosexual Politics in Britain from the Nineteenth Century to the Present.* London: Quartet Books, 1991.

White, Yve, 'Passionate Speeches at Protest for Trans and Non-Binary Rights', Isle of Wight News from *OnTheWight,* July 16, 2020. https://onthewight.com/passionate-speeches-at-protest-for-trans-and-non-binary-rights/.

Wilde, Oscar. *De Profundis.* Amsterdam: Meulenhoff, 1971.

Morality, Media Hypocrisy and Public Sex on the Isle of Wight

Attitude, 'Why Do so Many Gay Men Still Go Cruising and Cottaging?'. October 5, 2018, https://www.attitude.co.uk/article/why-do-so-many-gay-men-still-go-cruising-and-cottaging/15681/.

Button, Simon. 'Why Do so Many Gay Men Still Go Cruising and Cottaging?' *Attitude,* October 5, 2018. https://www.attitude.co.uk/article/why-do-so-many-gay-men-still-go-cruising-and-cottaging/15681/

Galloway, Bruce. *Prejudice and Pride: Discrimination Against Gay People in Modern Britain.* London: Routledge,1983, 43

Gay News issue 47, 1974

Gay News issue 50, 1974.

Gay News issue 54, 1974.

Houlbrook, Matt. *Queer London: Perils and Pleasures in the Sexual Metropolis, 1918-1957.* Chicago: University of Chicago Press, 2020, 62.

Isle of Wight County Press, 'Freshwater Man Found Passing Sex Notes Under Door in Toilets', February 28, 1992, 9.

Isle of Wight County Press, 'Head Found Guilty of Importuning in Toilets', September 11,1992, 1.

Isle of Wight County Press, '9 Fined for Acts of Gross Indecency', December 10, 1993, 3.

Jarman, Derek, and Michael Christie. *At Your Own Risk: A Saint's Testament.* Woodstock, NY: Overlook Press, 1994.

Johnson, Gareth. 'What Are the Laws about Cruising for Sex?', *Means Happy,* January 21, 2021, https://meanshappy.com/what-are-the-laws-about-cruising-for-sex-in-the-uk/.

Johnson, Gareth. 'A Modern Guy's Guide to Cruising', *GMFA,* accessed June 10, 2020. https://www.gmfa.org.uk/fs148-a-modern-guys-guide-to-cruising.

Kirby, Graham. 'Cottaging: How Having Gay Sex in Public Toilets Changed My Life', *Vice,* accessed June 16, 2020, https://www.vice.com/en_uk/article/av9zjg/gay-britain-uk-cottaging-sex-in-public-toilets-696.

Myers, Justin/The Guyliner. 'You've Probably Had Chemsex and You Didn't Even Know It', *British GQ,* July 2, 2019. https://www.gq-magazine.co.uk/article/chemsex-cruising-bareback.

Norton, R. *Mother Clap's Molly House: The Gay Subculture in England 1700–1830.* London: GMP Publishers, 1992, 66.

Perry, Simon, 'Cllr David Whittaker Found Guilty Of Sex Charge', Isle of Wight News from *OnTheWight,* January 11, 2011, https://onthewight.com/cllr-david-whittaker-found-guilty-of-sex-charge/.

Rea, Samantha, 'Straight Men Share Why They Love Having Sex in Public Loos', *Metro,* Metro.co.uk, December 12, 2019. https://metro.co.uk/2018/04/10/straight-men-share-love-sex-public-toilets-7454131/.

Sexual Offences Act 2003, https://www.legislation.gov.uk/ukpga/2003/42/contents, accessed July 20, 2020

Strudwick, Patrick, 'This Is Why Men Meet For Sex In Public Toilets', *BuzzFeed,* August 12, 2017. https://www.buzzfeed.com/patrickstrudwick/men-are-still-meeting-for-sex-in-public-toilets-and-the.

Swinford, Steven, 'Tory MP stands down after allegedly telling students that homosexuality is "wrong and dangerous to society"'. *Daily Telegraph,* April 28, 2017

Trevelyan, Lucy, 'The Legal Status of "Cottaging" in the UK', InBrief.co.uk, March 21, 2017, https://www.inbrief.co.uk/offences/cottaging/.

Section 28: politics, intent, spin, impact and aftermath.

Booth, Janine . 'The Story of Section 28', *Workers' Liberty,* January 2004, https://www.workersliberty.org/node/1531.

Chapman, Elizabeth L. 'No More Controversial than a Gardening Display? Provision of LGBT-Related Fiction to Children and Young People in U.K. Public Libraries', *Library Trends* 61, no. 3 (2013): 549, 553, https://doi.org/10.1353/lib.2013.0010.

Clark, M., M. Gosnell, and D. Witherspoon, 'AIDS - Special Report', *Newsweek*, August 12, 1985, 20-27.

Goldthorp, Jacqueline D., 'Can Scottish Public Library Services Claim They Are Socially Inclusive of All Minority Groups When Lesbian Fiction Is Still so Inaccessible?', *Journal of Librarianship and Information Science* 39, no. 4 (2007): 240, https://doi.org/10.1177/0961000607083215.

Knitting Circle. *Knitting Circle: Law; 1989 Section 28 Gleanings*, accessed February 22, 2021, https://web.archive.org/web/20070818063344/http://www.knittingcircle.org.uk/gleanings2889.html.

Local Government Act 1986 (Amendment) Bill [H.L.], *Hansard*, 18 December 1986, 310. accessed February 22, 2021, https://api.parliament.uk/historic-hansard/lords/1986/dec/18/local-government-act-1986-amendment-bill#column_.

Local Government Bill, *Hansard*, 2 February 1988), accessed February 22, 2021, https://api.parliament.uk/historic-hansard/lords/1988/feb/02/local-government-bill#column_999.

Local Government Bill, *Hansard*, 11 January 1988, accessed February 22, 2021, https://api.parliament.uk/historic-hansard/lords/1988/jan/11/local-government-bill#column_965.

Local Government Bill [H.L.], *Hansard*, 6 December 1999, accessed February 22, 2021, https://api.parliament.uk/historic-hansard/lords/1999/dec/06/local-government-bill-hl-1#column_1102.

Park , Alison, and Rebecca Rhead. 'Homosexuality ', NatCen, accessed February 22, 2021. https://www.bsa.natcen.ac.uk/latest-report/british-social-attitudes-30/personal-relationships/homosexuality.aspx.

'Prohibition On Promoting Homoxexuality by Teaching of by Publishing Material', *Hansard*, 15 December 1987) accessed February 22, 2021,

https://api.parliament.uk/historic-hansard/commons/1987/dec/15/
prohibition-on-promoting-homosexuality#S6CV0124P0_19871215_
HOC_423.

Sanders, Sue and Gill Spraggs, 'Section 28 and Education', schools-out.org.
uk, 1989, 11 http://www.schools-out. org.uk/wp-content/uploads/2013/11/
Section-28-and-Education-Sue-Sanders-Gillian-Spragg-1989.pdf.

Vincent, John, 'Why Do We Need to Bother?: Public Library Services
for LGBTQI People', *Library Trends* 64, no. 2 (2015): 288, https://doi.
org/10.1353/lib.2015.0050.

Walker, Janine and Jo Bates, 'Developments in LGBTQ Provision in
Secondary School Library Services since the Abolition of Section 28',
Journal of Librarianship and Information Science 48, no. 3 (October 2016): pp.
269-283, https://doi.org/10.1177/0961000614566340.

Historical LGBTQ+ figures on the Isle of Wight
Oscar Wilde & Lord Alfred Douglas

Dibb, Geoff. *Oscar Wilde a Vagabond with a Mission – the Story of Oscar Wilde's
Lecture Tours of Britain and Ireland.* London: The Oscar Wilde Society, 2013

Ellmann, Richard. *Oscar Wilde.* London: Penguin, 1997.

Isle of Wight Observer, 'The Dress of the period', October 11, 1884. 5

Letter to Lord Alfred Douglas from Grosvenor Crescent, London SW1, no
date. Magdalen College Oxford Archives Ref MC.P204/1/13c/20.

Murray, Douglas. *Bosie: a Biography of Lord Alfred Douglas* (New York:
Hyperion, 2000), 266-269.

Novak, Daniel, 'A Wilde Ryde: Oscar Wilde in the Isle of Wight', *The
Wildean*, January 12, 1998

Alfred, Lord Tennyson

Kolb, Jack. 'Hallam, Tennyson, Homosexuality and the Critics'. The
Free Library, accessed March 2, 2021. https://www.thefreelibrary.com/
Hallam%2c+Tennyson%2c+homosexuality+and+the+critics.
-a084841799

Plummer, Douglas. *Queer People: The Truth about Homosexuals.* New York: The Citadel Press, 1965.

Tennyson, Alfred Tennyson. *In Memoriam.* London: Macmillan, 1904.

Robert Nichols

'Ancestry: Genealogy, Family Trees and Family History Records', accessed August 20, 2020, https://www.ancestry.co.uk/.

Blunden, Edmund, and Sayoni Basu. 'Nichols, Robert Malise Bowyer (1893– 1944), poet and playwright'. *Oxford Dictionary of National Biography.* May 25, 2006. Oxford University Press. accessed August, 13, 2020, https://www.oxforddnb.com/view/10.1093/ref:odnb/9780198614128.001.0001/odnb-9780198614128-e-35223/version/1.

Charlton, Anne, and William Charlton. *Putting Poetry First: a Life of Robert Nichols, 1893-1944.* Wilby, Norwich: Russell, 2003.

Coote, Stephen. *The Penguin Book of Homosexual Verse.* Harmondsworth, London: Penguin Books, 1986, 46, 305.

Exploring Surrey's Past, 'Homosexuality and the First World War', accessed February 18, 2021, https://www.exploringsurreyspast.org.uk/themes/subjects/diversity/lgbt-history/fwwhomosexuality/.

Marsh, Edward. *Georgian Poetry.* London: Poetry Bookshop, 1918.

'Nichols, Robert Malise Bowyer (1893–1944), Poet and Playwright'. *Oxford Dictionary of National Biography,* accessed August 13, 2020, https://www.oxforddnb.com/view/10.1093/ref:odnb/9780198614128.001.0001/odnb-9780198614128-e-35223.

Shanklin and District History Society [S&DHS], 'East Mount and the Nichols' in 'The Story of The Shanklin Hotel', *S&DHS Newsletter,* No 37, January 2019. 3.

Siegfried Sassoon Diaries [1915–25], ed. R. Hart-Davis, 3 vols., 1983–5

Siegfried Sassoon Letters, 1917-30, Oxford University: Bodleian Library, Special Collection

Thomas, Helen. Secretary, Shanklin & District History Society, email message to author, August 15, 2020.

Thompson, Jonathan, 'New Diaries Reveal the "Dark Secrets" of Siegfried Sassoon's Swooning', *Independent.* Independent Digital News and Media, July 18, 2013, https://www.independent.co.uk/news/uk/this-britain/new-diaries-reveal-the-dark-secrets-of-siegfried-sassoon-s-swooning-affair-321646.html.

Algernon Charles Swinburne

Buchanan, Robert Williams, and Thomas Bird Mosher. *The Fleshly School of Poetry, and Other Phenomena of the Day.* London: Strahan, 1872

Conliffe, Ciaran. 'Algernon Swinburne, Dissolute Poet'. Headstuff.org, December 19, 2016. https://www.headstuff.org/culture/history/terrible-people-from-history/algernon-swinburne-dissolute-poet/.

Everett, Glenn. 'A. C. Swinburne: Biography'. Victorianweb.org accessed October 20, 2020. http://www.victorianweb.org/authors/swinburne/acsbio1.html.

Moore, T. V. 'A Study In Sadism: The Life Of Algernon Charles Swinburne'. *Journal of Personality* 6, no. 1 (1937): 1–15. https://doi.org/10.1111/j.1467-6494.1937.tb02235.x.

Virginia Woolf

Blamires, Harry. *A Guide to Twentieth Century Literature in English.* London: Methuen, 1983.

Usui, Masami. 'Julia Margaret Cameron as a Feminist Precursor of Virginia Woolf', 2007. Doshisha.repo.nii.ac.jp. info:doi/10.14988/pa.2017.0000011068

Woolf, Virginia. *The Complete Works.* Musaicum Press, 2017.

Woolf, Virginia. *A Room of One's Own.* Orlando: Harcourt, 1991

Ferguson's Gang

Bagnall, Polly, and Sally Beck. *Ferguson's Gang.* London: National Trust, 2015.

John Seely and Paul Paget

Aslet, Clive, and Paul Paget. 'An Interview with the Late Paul Paget 1901-1985'. *The Thirties Society Journal*, no. 6 (1987): 16-25. Accessed October 30, 2020. http://www.jstor.org.arts.idm.oclc.org/stable/41859261.

Joe Carstairs

Isle of Wight Hidden Heroes, accessed February 10, 2020, http://www.iwhiddenheroes.org.uk/.

Summerscale, Kate. *The Queen of Whale Cay*. London: Bloomsbury, 2012.

Lord Louis Mountbatten

Hicks, Pamela. *Daughter of Empire: Life as a Mountbatten*. New York: Weidenfeld and Nicolson, 2017.

Lownie, Andrew. *Mountbattens: Their Lives And Loves*. Blink Publishing, 2019.

Ziegler, Philip. M*ountbatten: the Official Biography*. London: Phoenix Press, 2001.

Keith Biddlecombe

Attitude Pride, 'The Winners of the Attitude Pride Awards 2017', in Association with United Airlines and Sleepeezee. *Attitude*, July 18, 2017. https://attitude.co.uk/article/the-winners-of-the-attitude-pride-awards-2019-in-association-with-united-airlines-and-sleepeezee-1/21327/

Biddlecombe, Keith. Interview by Queer in Brighton project, The Keep, East Sussex Archives.

Strudwick, Patrick, 'This Is What It Was Like To Go To Jail In England Just For Being Gay'. *BuzzFeed*, July 15, 2017, https://www.buzzfeed.com/patrickstrudwick/this-is-what-it-was-like-to-go-to-jail-in-england-just-for.

Phaedra Kelly

Ekins, Richard, 'On the Classification and Framing of Trans-Gender Knowledge', GENDYS Conference 1990 - Building a Trans-Gender Archive, accessed September 3, 2020, http://www.gender.org.uk/conf/1990/90ekins.htm.

Ekins, Richard, 'Digital Transgender Archive', A Concise History of the University of Ulster, Trans-Gender Archive (1986-2010), accessed September 3, 2020, https://www.digitaltransgenderarchive.net/files/h989r326r.

Hofton, Charlotte, 'Phaedra One Day, Bruce the Next'. *Isle of Wight County Press*, June 6, 2003, 19.

Nigelbrade, 'IWLF Programme 2015', Issuu (Isle of Wight Literary Festival 2015), accessed September 23, 2020, https://issuu.com/nigelbrade/docs/iwlf_programme_2015.

'Phaedra J. Kelly, 'My Island', *Isle of Wight County Press*, June 3, 2016.

Roberts, JoAnn, 'Lady Like Profile, Phaedra Kelly'. *LadyLike* No. 3 - Digital Transgender Archive, accessed September 3, 2020, https://www.digitaltransgenderarchive.net/files/73666455b.

Zagria, 'Phaedra Kelly (1955 – 2019) Activist', January 1, 1970, https://zagria.blogspot.com/2011/02/phaedra-kelly-1955-activist.html#.X1ZKpdNKjvU.

Kenneth Kendall

Barker, Dennis. 'Kenneth Kendall Obituary', *Guardian*. Guardian News and Media, December 14, 2012, https://www.theguardian.com/media/2012/dec/14/kenneth-kendall

Leapman, Michael, 'Kenneth Kendall: Much-Loved Newsreader Who Became the First to Be Seen', *Independent*, accessed December 16, 2020. https://www.independent.co.uk/news/obituaries/kenneth-kendall-much-loved-newsreader-who-became-first-be-seen-screen-8420896.html.

Tom Priestley

Brooks, Rachel, 'J. B. Priestley: A Talk', Isle of Wight News from

On The Wight, October 11, 2009, https://onthewight.com/j-b-priestley-a-talk/.

Grove, Valerie, 'Out of the Wilderness: How J. B. Priestley Is Enjoying a Revival', *New Statesman*, September 15, 2014, https://www.newstatesman.com/culture/2014/09/out-wilderness-how-j-b-priestley-enjoying-revival.

Perry, Sally, 'Tom Priestley: An Interview (Podcast)', Isle of Wight News from *On The Wight*, May 9, 2010, https://onthewight.com/tom-priestley-an-interview-podcast/.

https://www.nationaltrust.org.uk/mottistone-estate/features/jacquetta-hawkes-mottistone-mystery-solver

What the future holds

'As More Gay People Come out, Tolerance Will Spread', *The Economist*. The Economist Newspaper, accessed August 8, 2020, https://www.economist.com/leaders/2020/08/08/as-more-gay-people-come-out-tolerance-will-spread?fbclid=IwAR0QqNlbaOaR9EPGSM-hQw9DoCY21OL-TGYCaL0SP58CpZXRcmbNGopZLrQ.

Evolution of Queer Language

Baker, Paul, 'A Brief History of Polari: the Curious after-Life of the Dead Language for Gay Men', *The Conversation*, accessed June 26, 2020, https://theconversation.com/a-brief-history-of-polari-the-curious-after-life-of-the-dead-language-for-gay-men-72599.

Baker, Paul. *Fabulosa!: The Story of Polari, Britain's Secret Gay Language.* London: Reaktion Books, 2019

Baska, Maggie, et al., 'How Has the LGBT+ Acronym Evolved?', *PinkNews*, accessed June 26, 2020, https:// www.pinknews.co.uk/2017/11/06/how-has-the-lgbt-acronym-evolved/.

Broderick, Ryan, 'Someone Commented "BFF Goals" On This Photo Of A Lesbian Wedding And Everyone Lost Their Shit', *BuzzFeed News*, accessed June 26, 2020, https://www.buzzfeednews.com/article/ryanhatesthis/ someone-commented-bff-goals-on-this-photo-of-a-lesbian.

Dryden, Steven. 'A Short History of LGBT Rights in the UK', *The British*

Library, accessed June 26, 2020, https://www.bl.uk/lgbtq-histories/articles/a-short-history-of-lgbt-rights-in-the-uk.

Jones, Lucy. *Dyke/Girl: Language and Identities in a Lesbian Group.* Basingstoke: Palgrave Macmillan, 2012

Leap, William L. *Language Before Stonewall: Language, Sexuality, History* Basingstoke: Palgrave Macmillan, 2019.

Moore, Chadwick, 'Lavender Language, The Queer Way to Speak', *OUT*, accessed June 26, 2020, https://www. out.com/out-exclusives/2016/8/17/lavender-linguistics-queer-way-speak.

Pride, dir. by Matthew Warchus (Twentieth Century Fox, 2014).

Waters, Sarah. *Tipping the Velvet.* London: Virago, 1998

Wheeler, André, 'Why I'm Reclaiming the Homophobic Slur I Used to Fear', *Guardian*, accessed March 9, 2020, https://www.theguardian.com/commentisfree/2020/mar/09/lgbt-gay-men-slur-homophobia.